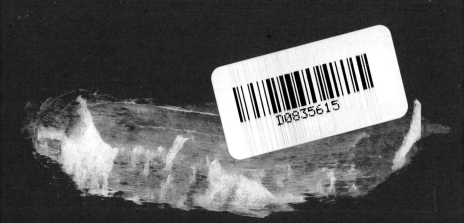

FI/INI MA

Development Policy and Administration

Readings in Indian Government and Politics-1

Development Policy and Administration

Readings in Indian Government and Politics–1

Edited by

Kuldeep Mathur

Sage Publications
New Delhi/Thousand Oaks/London

Copyright © Kuldeep Mathur, 1996

First published in 1996 by

Sage Publications India Pvt Ltd
M-32 Greater Kailash Market-I
New Delhi 110 048

Sage Publications Inc
2455 Teller Road
Thousand Oaks, California 91320

Sage Publications Ltd
6 Bonhill Street
London EC2A 4PU

Published by Tejeshwar Singh for Sage Publications India Pvt Ltd, phototypeset by Pagewell Photosetters, Pondicherry, and printed at Chaman Enterprises, Delhi.

Library of Congress Cataloging-in-Publication Data

Development policy and administration / edited by Kuldeep Mathur.
     p.   cm.—(Readings in Indian government and politics)
    Includes bibliographical references (p.).
    1. India—Economic policy—1980–   2. India—Economic condi-
tions—1947–   I. Mathur, Kuldeep.   II. Series.
    HC435.2.D475   1996   338.954—dc20

ISBN: 81–7036–579–1 (India-hb)   0–8039–9340–4 (US-hb)
        81–7036–580–5 (India-pb)   0–8039–9341–2 (US-pb)

Sage Production Editor: Sona Sabharwal

Contents

List of Tables

Sage Readings in Indian Government and Politics

Preface

This series focuses on significant themes in contemporary Indian government and politics. Each volume explores a wide range of problems and issues in specific areas of Indian politics and locates them within wider debates on politics, society, economy and culture.

The series focuses on the interface of social forces, political institutions and processes in an attempt to understand the changing grammar of Indian politics. A variety of approaches have been deployed by political scientists and social scientists to understand the relationships between state and society, democracy and development, state and classes controlling its power, formation of public policy and its implementation, and between issues of cultural recognition and distribution, as also between different segments and regions, religion, caste, languages and culture. The analysis of some of these themes and issues from different perspectives and approaches constitutes the principal endeavour of this series. The review of issues of theoretical and substantive importance both within institutional structures and outside them can illuminate the complex interplay of socio-political forces and political processes and the dynamics of social formation and political transformation in modern India. The aim is to strike a balance between empirical observation and theoretical analysis of political processes.

Each volume in the series consists of a detailed Introduction and a selection of essays essential for the understanding of the theme. Using this pattern, each volume will critically appraise the state of research in the theme, re-examine old problems and open up new issues for inquiry.

The series will be of interest to anyone concerned with the study of Indian government and politics. However, it will be of special interest to students of political science, sociology and contemporary history and to policy makers, bureaucrats, journalists and social activists.

Ghanshyam Shah
Zoya Hasan
Kuldeep Mathur

Acknowledgements

This volume brings together a collection of papers that combine policy perspectives with analyses of implementation of some development programmes. Individually these papers, published in different books and journals, are a contribution to their own substantive areas, but read together, they provide an outline of the emerging concerns in the studies of Indian public administration. The volume is meant for graduate students and scholars embarking on their programmes of study and research in Indian universities and institutions of research.

In preparing this volume I have received tremendous support at NIEPA and I must especially thank Sushma Asija, Sudhir Dagar, Padam Singh Bisht and Deepak Makol and Najma Rizivi from the library. Special gratitude must be expressed to Harsh Sethi of Sage, who was of great help and readily provided comments and advice whenever I turned to him.

I should also like to thank the following publishers for permission to include papers originally published by them in this volume: Oxford University Press, New Delhi; Christopher Hurst and Co., London; Basil Blackwell Publishers, Oxford; and Manchester University Press, Manchester.

The papers, with their complete citations, that have been included in this volume are:

Mozoomdar, Ajit, 1994   'The Rise and Decline of Development Planning in India', in T.J. Byres (ed.) *The Rise and Decline of Development Planning in India*, New Delhi, Oxford University Press.

Dayal, Ishwar, 1982   'Organization for Policy Formulation', in K.D. Madan (ed.) *Policy Making in Government of India*,

	New Delhi, Government of India Publications (considerably revised and enlarged version included).
Mathur, Kuldeep and James W. Bjorkman, 1994	'Institutional Framework for Policy Advice: The Cabinet Secretariat and the Prime Minister's Office' in *Top Policy Makers in India*, New Delhi, Concept.
Potter, David, 1994	'The Prime Minister and the Bureaucracy', in James Maner (ed.) *Nehru to the Nineties: The Changing Office of the Prime Minister of India*, New Delhi, Viking Penguin Christopher Hurst and Co.
Mathur, Kuldeep, 1994	'Designing Poverty Alleviation Programmes: International Agencies and Indian Politics', in G.K. Chaddha (ed.) *Policy Perspective in Economic Development: Essays in Honour of Prof. G.S. Bhalla*, New Delhi, Har-Anand Publication.
Mukarji, Nirmal, 1989	'Decentralization Below the State Level: Need for a New System of Governance', *Economic and Political Weekly*, Vol. 24, No. 9.
Mathew, George, 1994	'Panchayati Raj in India', in George Mathew (ed.) *Status of Panchayati Raj in the State of India*, New Delhi, Concept.
Webster, Neil, 1992	'Panchayati Raj in West Bengal: Popular Participation for the People or the Party?', *Development and Change*, Vol. 23, No. 4, Basil Blackwell Publishers.
Shah, Tushaar, 1993	'Agricultural and Rural Development in the 1990s and Beyond', *Economic and Political Weekly*.

Sheth, D.L. and
Harsh Sethi, 1991

'The NGO Sector in India: Historical Context and Current Discourse', *Voluntas*, Vol. 2, No. 2, Manchester University Press.

1

Introduction: The Emerging Concerns in Public Administration

KULDEEP MATHUR

When talking about the failure of the planned strategy of development, particularly in the achievements· of the various five year plans, the discussion usually veers around the impediments created by the inherited bureaucratic and administrative system of the British colonial days. The planners were quite conscious of the need for a different system to implement the planned objectives of development and wrote so in chapters of several plan documents. The government responded to this concern by appointing several committees to suggest changes in the system. International experts also participated in this endeavour, and the report of Paul Appleby, a Syracuse University professor brought in as a consultant by the Ford Foundation on the request of the Government of India, did much to raise expectations about administrative reform. More reports and committees followed and national concerns culminated in the appointment of a high powered Administrative Reforms Commission in 1966. Scores of recommendations·spread in innumerable reports were presented. It is a matter of debate whether this effort at reform spread over the first two decades of India's Independence made any substantive impact on the practice of public administration in India. Reports on improving the implementation of Poverty Alleviation Programmes during the 1970s and 1980s continued to chant the same litany of complaints against an ineffective administration and offer as many suggestions to reform it.

In this expression of concern for administrative reform, public administration emerged as an academic discipline and found a place in many universities and institutions of research in India during the 1960s and 1970s. The scholarly response in the initial years was to describe and analyze the administration and to attempt to show whether it had any capability to fulfil the developmental needs. Much of this work was inspired by the comments of American scholars like Paul Appleby (1953) or La Palambra (1963), who expressed the view that bureaucratic dispositions and development needs did not match each other and that this mismatch resulted in poor plan performance. A separate field of study, development administration, was already emerging as an important dimension of American aid efforts and was soon to become a major intellectual export to the developing countries. The Ford Foundation alone spent US$ 360,000 in grants and US$ 76,000 in providing funds to specialists and consultants to improve public administration in India during 1951–62 (Braibanti, 1966: 148). This American thrust came soon to dominate the concern of Indian public administration.

A vast amount of literature, largely based on field studies, was generated (see Pai Panandiker, 1973; Mathur, 1986). Most studies were by and large embedded in the behavioural science paradigm that swept the social sciences after the Second World War and were concerned with at least two major dimensions in their thrust (see for a review Mathur, 1996). One was that of professionalization of the administration, emphasizing management orientation in implementing development programmes and the other was of bringing about behavioural and attitudinal change among administrators. These studies emphasizing skills and techniques—behavioural and otherwise—laid the basis of much of teaching and training activities in public administration. But according to many, public administration suffered as a social science discipline. Scholars began questioning their own work. Many described it as 'a discipline in bondage' (Bhattacharya, 1987: 48), while others preferred to talk of an engulfing 'identity crisis' in the discipline. A recent volume bringing together assessment of the research and teaching in public administration was titled Public Administration Quest for Identity (1996).

Dissatisfaction with the intellectual concerns of the discipline in the last decade or so arose from several factors. Of course, a major source of the disappointment was the feeling of inadequacy that emanated from the fact that scholarly contributions were not very helpful in making reform activity productive. Increased knowledge did not lead to improved practice. What began to be questioned, then, was the nature of this knowledge and the framework used to generate it. The emphasis on profession and extensive use of teaching to help build it into one induced public administration to become inward looking. The consequences of the socio-political context in which it was embedded were not fully taken into account in examinations of its functioning. Great store was set by techniques and skills and it was assumed that the existing structure would be able to absorb them and transform itself in the process. Experience showed that this was not a tenable assumption. Then the concept of development administration began to lose attraction as the field experience began to present contrary data. The division of administration into development and regulatory wings appeared to be arbitrary and unrealistic. Effective law and order machinery was as much necessary as development administration. The process of development was also a process of displacement of established groups or of the rise of new ones and therefore generated social conflicts.

What this means is that administration needs to be seen as part of the political process itself. Social and political forces have to be included as determinants of administrative performance. Economic constraints and social pressures cannot be relegated to the background. When administration is involved in the implementation of redistributive policies, the operational process cannot be free of conflicts and of the nature of policy design. The way conflicts are resolved also influences the fortunes of the administrators who seek to resolve them. Their interests are also at stake and they come as interested parties in the political arena itself. In this sense, it is difficult to regard administration as insulated from politics. The bureaucracy uses its power and plays a key role in influencing policy outputs. The political context of administration thus becomes quite significant in understanding what the administrators will do or can do at any particular period.

One way to reorient the studies in public administration is to explore alternative ways of analyzing it. It could be seen as the implementation strategy of public policy. This would help establish linkages between the political forces that help determine a policy and those that establish an implementation design and work for its fulfilment or non-fulfilment. These political forces are not merely represented by the political leaders like the ministers or members of legislative bodies but more importantly by those groups who would like to see a particular policy be made so that they could stand to gain either directly by diverting public resources to themselves or indirectly by getting state patronage to do what would be most advantageous to them. Variations in industrial licensing policy or getting a land reform bill without actual teeth are examples of the way such groups work. The administrative organization chosen or designed to implement these laws in turn will reflect the 'real' goals of these laws and not the stated ones alone. Poor performance of administrative organizations is therefore directly linked with the characteristics of policy determination. Thus, investigating reasons of poor performance only at administrative level cannot provide sufficiently coherent answers.

Looking at administration as the implementation strategy of public policy means that the effort at dichotomizing policy and administration has to be given up. The changed outlook also means that while administration owns a problem only after it has come out of the policy-formulation pipeline, implementation is treated as a continuous decision-making activity in which conscious linkages between choice of policies and strategies of implementation are made. Policy goals, programme choices and implementation strategies are linked in producing policy outputs. To assume that only one component is a determinant of output leads to creation of artificial autonomy not warranted by the implementation process.

Implementation embodies the social and political processes that influence the course of administrative action. It places administration in the larger network of power capabilities of groups and individuals interacting within the political system in order to determine the direction of the flow of public goods.

The story of uneven spatial development or differential treatment of the poor in the special programmes to alleviate rural poverty is too well known to be repeated here (see Rath, 1985). The ability of the organized sector in the economy to divert public resources for their immediate consumption and not for investment is another but similar story (Bardhan, 1985). All these diversions take place through political processes and mediations of amenable political leadership. Either the policy is so explicitly made or the implementation so designed that public resources are directed towards those who have the ability to assert their power in the political system. As Gupta (1981) has argued '. . . design suggests who can potentially gain control of benefits. Implementation merely manifests it.' Unless the traditional assumptions of organization design and monitoring performance are questioned, implementation of programmes of equity will continue to be either mere rhetoric or help the unintended target groups.

The recognition of such a perspective can help us understand variations in policy performance because they are dependent on the bargains struck at the political level. In addition, administration in India is the arena where most political battles are fought. The policy of distributing resources to the poor is accepted at the national level, but when it comes to its implementation at the local level, 'leakages' occur. 'Administrative discretion' is used to help the privileged and at other times 'political interference' is manipulated to achieve the same results. In keeping these concerns out of the purview of research focus, most researchers in public administration tend to lose touch with reality.

Thus, one possible reason why most attempts at administrative reform have not succeeded in our country is due to our weakness on the conceptual front. Adherence to the Weberian model and Taylorian norms of work has considerably constrained the generation of alternatives. Overwhelming academic response to administrative problems was through analyses of structural attributes that caused bottlenecks in coordination or communication, or of the behavioural irritants that led to friction in either a team of bureaucrats only or one of bureaucrats and politicians. The prescription was already decided and not questioned, and therefore when the problems persisted, the solution was to increase the dosage of further division of labour, increased specialization or tighter controls through improved lines of communication and authority.

The problem was that the empirical insights did not reflect the dominant concerns in the discipline where Weberian influences held the attention of most scholars who explained variations in administrative performance by examining issues of neutrality, training and professionalism, structure of hierarchies and processes of work and behavioural orientations. The mismatch between theoretical concerns and empirical reality led to the anxiety reflected in expressions like 'discipline in crisis'.

As the intellectual concerns in public administration prepare to face the challenges from the experience of the past three decades, the story of administration as an impediment to development has taken a drastic turn. If the 1950s saw an effort to strengthen state intervention as a recipe for triggering development, the 1980s ended with disastrous accounts of the failures of regulatory and interventionist states and an effort to dismantle the state machinery and its roles. Neo-liberal economic theory tended to build its case on how rulers extract resources and invest them. It argued that rulers in interventionist states tend to use resources for their own benefit to the detriment of the development of their societies. The argument of state failure is based on how monopoly rents are created through the imposition of regulation and control of the economy. Political pressures dominate economic policy formulation and execution, leading to misallocation of resources. Corruption and favouritism surround bureaucratic allocations of investment licences, import licenses and the award of government contracts. A consequence of this system is that government machinery is used for personal interests. The policy recommendation that follows from this diagnosis is to minimize state intervention and to rely increasingly on markets for resource use and allocation.

Within this perspective, India has embarked upon an ambitious programme of economic reform. Policies dismantling the regulatory mechanism and introducing greater private initiative in the economy have been introduced since 1991. This paradigmatic shift now introduces a fresh challenge to public administration. It tends to reduce the scope of intervention, but at the same time expects a change in the quality of intervention in chosen sectors. The implication is that bureaucratic machinery is not the only instrument of policy implementation; there are alternatives in the civil society in which cooperative endeavours or community based organizations can develop their own capability of resource management and use. The role of the state is to provide an environment in which such institutions can grow and to help them to sustain themselves. The withdrawal of the state makes way for the voluntary sector. Indeed, the Eighth Plan makes a plea for a greater role of the voluntary sector as well as the market forces. In this new dispensation, then, the buzz words are bureaucratic accountability, decentralization, participation, and community-based organizations or NGOs.

The neo-liberal agenda in India, then, provides an important opportunity for administrative reform that has been tardy up to now. Administrative institutions are open to market scrutiny and if they do not change they cannot survive. It also provides an opportunity of seeking alternatives in implementation of public goals by looking at diverse ways of linking individual/community to local resources.

Public administration in India is embedded in the wider context of society, state and public policy and the papers brought together in this volume help delineate the various dimensions of this context. The expression of concern for administrative reform in the post-Independence period helped an academic discipline to grow and contribute towards an understanding of how public administration actually functioned. But this understanding rarely led to improved explanation of why it functioned the way it did and therefore adequate strategies of learning about reform did not follow. Much had to do with the possible reason that most research studies either did not have rigorous theoretical underpinnings or were heavily influenced by a paradigm that was inward looking and perceived bureaucracy as a more or less autonomous instrument of implementing the objectives of development policies and programmes. Administrative performance was not placed in the wider social and economic context and an insufficient analysis was done of what the policy really intended to do and whether this was feasible or desirable. This restricted the understanding of administrative phenomena and, in spite of an array of empirical studies, made little significant impact on improving the understanding of administration in action. Alternative paradigms should be explored by strengthening linkages with other social science disciplines, for administrative functioning is closely tied to policy parameters and political commitment to achieve the concerned policy goals. The design of this volume and the arguments in many of the papers show how these parameters can be delineated and political dynamics explored in order to improve the understanding of the implementation process.

Keeping this perspective in mind, Chapter 2 includes extracts from the Second and Eighth Five Year Plans, which set the broad scope of policy making in India. The Second Plan identified a strong state presence in the sphere of socio-economic development and offered a vision of a socialist pattern of society emphasizing that 'the task before an underdeveloped country is not merely to get better results within the existing framework of economic and social institutions, but to mould and refashion these so that they contribute effectively to the realization of wider and deeper values'. It then went on to argue that the state has to undertake heavy responsibilities and play a dominant role in bringing about social and economic changes in society. Subsequent Plan documents continued to emphasize the effectiveness of administration in achieving plan objectives. The Eighth Plan, coming after thirty-five years of the Second Plan, asked for a re-examination of the role of the state and that of the public sector. Guided by global developments in which more and more economies were getting integrated under a common philosophy of growth, market forces and liberal policies, the plan emphasized autonomy and efficiency induced by competition. It sought to reverse the entire strategy of development in which the state and its administration played a significant role.

Chapters 3 and 4 analyze the failures of the state, which are the reasons that have led to the shift in its role. Mozoomdar examines the processes of development planning and argues that the system was not flexible enough to deal with sharp economic fluctuations. While acknowledging that considerable expertise has developed over the years, he suggests that the crisis of planning is linked to the loss of consensus on planning objectives and priorities. The conflict has to be resolved in political terms, and the centrality of development planning can be restored only if a political consensus is established for more equitable and sustainable development. Shah emphasizes that the state will continue to be a major actor even in the national ambience of deregulation and liberalization, but its role will have to be sharper and qualitatively different. New institutions of development will have to be nurtured, and rather than direct action, the state may focus on creating and using strategic organizations as instruments of change. He gives considerable attention to the design of interventions, which entails a rethinking about relations between the state and society.

Chapters 5 and 6 turn to the processes and organizations of policy making in India. Dayal examines the strengths and weaknesses of policy formulation and suggests that integrative structures for policy making have not emerged. While sectoral policy making is important, inter-ministerial linkages need to be established. He also suggests that within the vast consultative machinery that has developed over the years, the role of specialist groups has weakened.

The processes of policy formulation influence the kinds of policy objectives that emerge. A clear policy that minimizes conflicts with other sectors and lays down goals that are achievable and not in conflict with one another has a greater chance of success. It also helps in creating effective implementation structures. Mathur and Bjorkman focus their attention on the civil servants as policy advisers and the institutional framework for such advice. They examine the role of the prime minister's office (PMO) and that of the cabinet secretariat and argue that power politics notwithstanding, the PMO offers a prime minister an opportunity to obtain professional advice elsewhere than the government service only. It also offers a forum for interaction of opposing expert advice.

Much has been written about the Indian bureaucracy and the distinctive features of its structure and tradition. In Chapter 7, Potter delineates the relationship between the prime minister and the civil services. In analyzing this relationship he describes those social forces which were too strong to allow administrative reform to take place. It is significant that Jawaharlal Nehru mellowed over the years and changed his early insistence to do away with the Indian Civil Services. The other prime ministers were not committed to change in any way. Mathur's essay in Chapter 8 carries forward the analysis of political and social forces and shows how they weakened the efforts to achieve the goals of alleviating poverty in India. The policy was not formulated in a way that expressed clear commitment to achieve specific goals and the institutional arrangements merely reflected this half-hearted agenda.

Decentralization has been high on the agenda of Indian political leadership since Independence. A number of committees have recommended ways of decentralizing planning and administrative functions. The story of Panchayati Raj, introduced in 1959, is documented in Chapter 9 by Mathew, who identifies the reasons why this experiment failed to take off and cautiously welcomes the new dispensation under the Seventy-Third Amendment of the Constitution. Webster, in Chapter 10, examines the functioning of Panchayati Raj in a district in West Bengal during the period before the new act came into force. In the past few years the CPM in West Bengal has been widely commended for the effort at decentralization of planning. Elections have been held regularly and panchayats have been given increased significance in local planning and implementation of development programmes. This political commitment is analyzed to examine the actual performance of these institutions with regard to mobilizing popular participation and its impact. In Chapter 11, Mukarji proposes decentralization of governance at the district level and considers decentralizing some functions—like planning—as inadequate. He forcefully makes a plea for extending the two-tiered federal system to a three-tiered one in which the district will have powers granted by the Constitution. This would demand entirely different structural arrangements at the district level including a reformulation of panchayat institutions.

With reference to decentralized governance, the role of NGOs has received considerable attention in the last two decades. As Sheth and Sethi point out in Chapter 12, NGOs have mushroomed over the years and have been widely accepted as instruments of implementing development programmes. They think that this is not an adequate role and that NGOs have the potential to establish self-governing institutions which can fill the political and administrative space that liberalization and decentralization offer.

It is yet to be seen how the system of governance in the country responds to the policies of economic liberalization that are being adopted since 1991. The centralized bureaucratic system will have to change drastically. The legal system entailing new concepts of property rights will bring in different kinds of demands of enforcement of contracts, etc. The way the functioning of the federal system has unfolded itself, it is doubtful whether the traditions and structures of a centralized governance can sustain themselves for long. As the articles in this volume show, the issue of administrative reforms needs to become a critical issue in political decision making if developmental challenges have to be met. Researchers need to delineate the relationships that administration forges with other social sectors so that a more realistic perspective of the feasibility of implementing policy goals can be created.

References

Appleby, Paul 1953. *Public Administration in India: Report of a Survey*, Delhi, Government of India.

Bardhan, Pranab 1985. *Political Economy of India's Development* New Delhi, Oxford University Press.

Braibanti, Ralph (ed.) 1966. Transnational Inducement of Administrative Reform, in W.J. Siffin (ed.), *Approaches to Development, Politics and Change*, New York, McGraw-Hill Inc.

Gupta, Anil 1985. Organizing Equity: Are Solutions the Real Problem, *Journal of Social and Economic Studies*, 2(4).

La Palombara, J. (ed.) 1963. *Bureaucracy and Political Development* Princeton, Princeton University Press.

Mathur, Kuldeep (ed.) 1986. *Second Survey of Research in Public Administration*, Delhi, ICSSR/Concept Publishers.

———— 1996. Research in Public Administration: An Overview, in A.K. Sharma and V. Bhaskar Rao (eds) *Public Administration: Quest for Identity* Delhi, Vikas.

Pai Panandiker, V.A. (ed.) 1973. *A Survey of Research in Public Administration* Delhi, ICSSR/Allied Publishers.

2

Plan Objectives and Role of the State: Excerpts from the Second and Eighth Five Year Plans

I

Second Five Year Plan

Objectives and Techniques

Significant as the achievements of the First Plan have been, it is apparent that they have to be regarded as no more than a beginning. The task is not merely one of reaching any fixed or static point such as doubling of living standards, but of generating a dynamism in the economy which will lift it to continually higher levels of material well-being and of intellectual and cultural achievements. The current standards of living in India are very low. Production is insufficient for satisfying even the minimum essential needs of the population, and a large leeway has to be given before the services and amenities required for healthy living can be brought within the reach of a significant proportion of the population. There are large areas or regions of the country that are underdeveloped even in relation to the rest of the country, and there are classes of the population that are almost untouched by modern progressive ideas and techniques. It is necessary to proceed faster with development, and this, it must be emphasized, is possible only to the extent that a larger measure of effort, both financial and organizational, is forthcoming. For several plan periods to come, it is on the mobilization of this effort rather than on the gains and returns arising from it that attention has to be concentrated. These gains and returns are important, but more important, perhaps, is the satisfaction that a community gets from attempting a worthwhile task which gives it a chance to channelize its energies to productive and socially useful purposes. The costs of development, viewed in this light, are in themselves a reward. There is no doubt that given the right approach to problems of development, including social policy and institutional change, a community can draw upon the latent energies within itself to an extent which ensures development at rates much larger than nice calculations of costs and returns, or inputs and outputs, may sometimes suggest.

The Socialist Pattern of Society

A rising standard of living, or material welfare as it is sometimes called, is of course not an end in itself. Essentially it is a means to a better intellectual and cultural life. A society which has to devote the bulk of its working force or working hours to the production of the bare wherewithals of life is to that extent limited in its pursuit of higher ends. Economic development is intended to expand the community's productive power and to provide the environment in which there is scope for the expression and application of diverse faculties and urges. It follows that the pattern of development and the lines along which economic activity is to be directed must from the start be related to the basic objectives that the society has in view. The task before an underdeveloped country is not merely to get better results within the existing framework of economic and social institutions, but to mould and refashion these so that they contribute effectively to the realization of wider and deeper social values.

These values or basic objectives have recently been summed up in the phrase 'socialist pattern of society'. Essentially this means that the basic criterion for determining the lines of advancement must not be private profit but social gain, and that the pattern of development and the structure of socio-economic relations should be so planned that they result not only in appreciable increases in national income and employment but also in greater equality in incomes and wealth. Major decisions regarding production, distribution, consumption and investment—and in fact all significant socio-economic relationships—must be made by agencies informed by a social purpose. The benefits of economic development must accrue more and more to the relatively less privileged classes of society and there should be a progressive reduction of the concentration of incomes, wealth and economic power. The problem is to create a milieu in which the socially and economically less privileged man, who has so far had little opportunity of perceiving and participating in the immense possibilities of growth through organized effort, is enabled to put in his best in the interests of a higher standard of life for himself and increased prosperity for the country. In the process, he rises in economic and social status. Vertical mobility of labour is no less important than horizontal mobility, for nothing is more destructive of hope and inhibitive of effort than a feeling that the accident of birth or a poor start in life has resulted in poor economic and social status. For creating the appropriate conditions, the state has to take on heavy responsibilities as the principal agency speaking for and acting on behalf of the community as a whole. The public sector has to expand rapidly. It has not only to initiate developments which the private sector is either unwilling or unable to undertake, but also to play the dominant role in shaping the entire pattern of investments in the economy, whether investments are made directly by the state or by the private sector. The private sector has to play its part within the framework of a comprehensive plan accepted by the community. The resources available for investment are thrown up in the last analysis by social processes. Private enterprise, free pricing and private management are all devices to further what are truly social ends; they can only be justified in terms of social results.

The use of modern technology requires large-scale production and a unified control and allocation of resources in certain major lines of activity. These include exploitation of minerals and basic and capital-goods industries, which are major determinants of the rate of growth of the economy. The responsibility for new developments in these fields must be undertaken in the main by the state, and the existing units have also to fall in line with the emerging pattern. Public ownership, partial or complete, and public control or participation in management are especially required in those fields where technological considerations tend towards a concentration of economic power and wealth. In several fields private enterprise can, under present-day conditions, make little headway without assistance and support from the government and in these cases, the public or semi-public character of the resources drawn upon has to be recognized. In the rest of the economy, conditions have to be created in which there is full scope for private initiative and enterprise either on an individual or on a cooperative basis. In a growing economy that gets increasingly diversified, there is scope for both the public and the private sectors to expand simultaneously. However, if development is to proceed at the pace envisaged and to contribute effectively to the attainment of the larger social ends in view, it is inevitable that the public sector must grow not only absolutely but also in relation to the private sector.

The socialist pattern of society is not to be regarded as some fixed or rigid pattern. It is not rooted in any doctrine or dogma. Each country has to develop according to its own genius and traditions. Economic and social policy has to be shaped from time to time in the light of historical circumstances. It is neither necessary nor desirable for the economy to become a monolithic type of organization offering little play for experimentation either of forms or of modes of functioning. Nor should the expansion of public sector mean the centralization of decision making and exercising of authority. In fact, the aim should be to secure an appropriate devolution of functions and to ensure that public enterprises have full freedom to operate within a framework of broad directives or rules of the game. The organization and management of public enterprises is a field in which considerable experimentation will be necessary and this, in fact, holds for the entire socialist regard for certain basic values and a readiness to adapt institutions and organizations and their rules of conduct in the light of experience. The accent of the socialist pattern is on the attainment of positive goals, the raising of living standards, the enlargement of opportunities for all, the promoting of enterprise among the disadvantaged classes and the creation of a sense of partnership among all sections of the community. These positive goals provide the criteria for basic decisions. The Directive Principles of State Policy in the Constitution had indicated the approach in broad terms; the socialist pattern of society is a more concretized expression of this approach.

Economic policy and institutional changes have to be planned in a manner that would secure economic advancement along democratic and egalitarian lines. Democracy, it has been said, is a way of life rather than a particular set of institutional arrangements. The same could well be said of the socialist pattern.

II

Re-examination and Orientation of the Role of the State and Planning for Development—The Eighth Five Year Plan (1992–97)

Objectives and Orientation

The launching of the First Five Year Plan in April 1951 initiated a process of development aimed not only at raising the standard of living of the people but also opening out to them new opportunities for a richer and more varied life. This was sought to be achieved by planning for growth, modernization, self-reliance and social justice. We have come a long way over the past forty years. The largely agrarian feudal economy of the time of Independence has been transformed into one based on a well-developed and a highly diversified infrastructure with immense potential for industrialization: income and consumption levels have risen significantly; the consumption basket has diversified; the incidence of poverty has visibly declined; the average life expectancy has gone up; death and birth rates have declined; literacy has improved; and the educational base has widened.

We now have a robust and resilient agricultural economy with near self-sufficiency in food production. Moreover, we have built a diversified industrial and service structure and have a large pool of skilled manpower and ample entrepreneurial capabilities. The growth performance of at least a decade preceding the Eighth Plan has thus been impressive. We also have the wherewithal for further progress. Hence, the task before the Eighth Plan is to use these advantages for further growth and to lay strong foundations for an even higher growth in the future.

The economy has passed through difficult circumstances during the last couple of years. The growing fiscal gap and the sudden depletion of foreign exchange resources created a situation which put severe strains on the economic system leading to drastic import curbs, a high rate of inflation, and recession in industry. This in turn has led to the projection of very low growth in 1991–92, which happens to be the base year of the Eighth Plan. Corrective measures have already been initiated by way of planned fiscal reforms and policy changes. The Eighth Plan will have to reorient some of the development programmes since its objective is to lay a sound foundation for a higher growth and to achieve the most significant goals, namely, an improvement in the standards of living, health and education of the people, full employment, elimination of poverty and a planned growth in population.

The public sector was assigned a place of commanding height in the Indian economic scene. It was expected to create the basic infrastructure for development, to be a pace-setter in taking risk and nurturing entrepreneurship, to take care of social needs, to help the poor and the weak, and to create an environment of equal opportunities and social justice. The public sector has expanded considerably and its expanse and influence may be measured not just by the size of its contribution to the GDP or its share in investment, but by the fact that it touches every aspect of life. In the process, people have begun to take the public sector for granted, regardless of certain crucial factors like efficiency, productivity and competitive ability. This has eroded the public sector's own sense of responsibility and initiative. Many public sector enterprises have turned into slow-moving, inefficient giants. A certain amount of complacency has set in which is not conducive to growth. While there are several social and infrastructural sectors where only the public sector can deliver the goods, it has to be made efficient and surplus-generating. It must also give up activities that are not essential to its role. The Eighth Plan has to undertake this task of reorientation.

The Eighth Plan will have to undertake re-examination and re-orientation of the role of the government as well as the process of planning. It will have to work out the ways and means of involving people in the task of development and social evolution. It will have to strengthen the people's participatory institutions. In keeping with these objectives, the process of planning will have to be reoriented so as to make planning largely indicative. This, in turn, will imply a somewhat changed role for the Planning Commission. The Planning Commission will have to concentrate on anticipating future trends and to evolve integrated strategies for achieving the highest possible level of development of the country in keeping with the international competitive standards. In place of the resource-allocation role, which very largely characterized the working of the Planning Commission in the past, it will have to concentrate on optimal utilization of the limited resources available. This will call for the creation of a culture of high productivity and cost efficiency in the government both at the central and state levels, and the Planning Commission will have to play the role of a change agent. At the same time, it must provide the broad blue-print for achieving the essential social and economic objectives and indicate the directions in which the economy and the various subsectors should be moving. It should pinpoint areas in which advance action should be taken to avoid serious bottlenecks. Planning must therefore proceed from a vision of the society to be created, and through an appropriate mix of policy instruments, influence the decisions of the various economic agencies to achieve the desired goals. In this sense, indicative planning is a more different exercise.

The Eighth Plan is being launched at a time that marks a turning point in both the international and domestic economic environment. All over the world, centralized economies are disintegrating. On the other hand, economies of several regions are getting integrated under a common philosophy of growth guided by market forces and liberal policies. The emphasis is on autonomy and efficiency induced by competition. We cannot remain untouched by these trends. We have to draw lessons from the development experiences of other nations during the last four decades. Development economics was largely theoretical when India started its planning in 1951. It has now acquired considerable empirical knowledge based on the rich applied experience of many nations among which there are both success stories as well as failures. Indian planning needs to draw on some of these lessons. It also needs to be guided by its own experience of the last four decades. If planning has to retain its relevance, it must be willing to make appropriate mid-course corrections and adjustments. In this process, it may be necessary to shed some of the practices and precepts of the past which have outlived their utility and to adopt new practices and precepts in the light of the experience gained by us and by other nations.

Imperative for Change

Starting with a poor base and getting further pressurized in the process of growth, the Indian economy was beset with a scarcity of resources and materials from the very beginning. The scarcity situation was sought to be tackled through a regulatory framework. Licences for production and imports, control of distribution and a regime of administered prices and subsidies were its main features. This regulatory mechanism did manage to save the economy from extreme difficulties like debt-trap and the social unrest that arises from the breakdown of supplies of basic consumption goods. The economy could sustain itself through the wars, the droughts and the oil shocks. Yet those who got the allocation of resources through the regulatory regime benefited more than the others. Vested interests got established. The regulatory framework was expected to protect the consumer against those who obtained the resources for production through the same mechanism. However, the latter often gained through the system at the cost of the consumer and the common man.

The equity objective was sought to be pursued through the redistribution of assets, but land reforms could not be implemented effectively. The problem of poverty could not be tackled through growth, which itself was slow for a long period of time. Hence, direct intervention through poverty alleviation programmes became necessary. Self-employment and wage-employment programmes were taken up in the government component of the public sector plan, but the constraints of government resources permit only a limited role for such programmes. Moreover, the orientation of these programmes has shifted from building assets of durable nature to providing relief jobs, and the programmes are beset with substantial leakages.

A sustained high growth rate has pushed the Indian population to unsupportable numbers. The 1991 Census revealed a population of 844 million. Such a dizzying rate of population growth negates whatever gains the nation has been able to achieve in the agricultural, industrial and service sectors. If this trend is not checked, it will never be possible to render social and economic justice to our masses. The current rate of population growth is simply not sustainable.

Growing unemployment has been a major problem of the eighties and is going to be even worse in the nineties. The provision of employment to all job seekers is going to be a major challenge for the planners of this decade.

The entire population does not have access to all the basic necessities, particularly drinking water and health facilities. Infant mortality is still high and literacy levels, particularly among the women, are low. The social infrastructure has to be attended to with a degree of urgency in the next phase of development.

There has been a marked acceleration in urbanization over the past two decades. If the present trends continue, urban population may account for about one-third of the total population by the turn of the century. Urban infrastructure for this size of population, even at a minimum level, will need considerable resources.

Although in the eighties, some signs of improvement in certain less advanced states have been observed, regional disparities continue to exist. Development institutions and organizational capabilities in the backward regions of the country and the delivery system for development programmes would need to be strengthened to deal effectively with the problems of development and redistributive justice.

Technological change in agriculture has led to increases in cropping intensities. However, in areas of developed agriculture, further absorption of labour is declining and there is need for greater economic diversification. In the face of the shrinking size of the average holding, the special needs of inputs, capital, processing and marketing for small landholdings should be paid attention.

From the point of view of long-range sustainability, the need for greater efficiency in the management of natural resources—land, water, minerals, etc.—has become urgent. A vigorous effort has to be made for recovering the wastelands and extending the green cover. A package of incentives to promote efficiency in the use of nature-based resources needs to be devised as a matter of priority. Efficiency in the use of energy and energy conservation need particular attention in view of the expanding needs and shrinking sources of fossil fuel.

On an overall stock taking, we find that at the threshold of the Eighth Plan, there is a considerable backlog in the provision of social consumption needs of the people, particularly the rural people and the poor. There is a reduced, but still unacceptably high level of poverty and hunger in the country, with a high concentration in some regions. Illiteracy, particularly among women, is very high. There is a high incidence of infant mortality. Decadent social practices like scavenging still prevail in large parts of the country. The widening gap between the growth of labour force and that of employment is assuming serious proportions.

The imperatives of growth in the face of these challenges require an innovative approach to development which is based on a re-examination and reorientation of the role of the government, the harnessing of the latent energies of the people through their involvement in the process of nation building, and the creation of an environment which encourages and builds up people's initiative rather than their dependence on the government, and which sets free the forces of growth and modernization. The state has to play a more facilitating role and concentrate on protecting the interests of the poor and the underprivileged.

The need to restructure the systems of economic management becomes unavoidable if India is to emerge as a vibrant and internationally competitive economy in the nineties. Systems of control and regulation developed for good reasons in the past have outlived their utility and some positively stand in the way of further progress. Such dysfunctional systems have to be overhauled in the light of emerging realities.

The industrial regulatory environment of the past has led to certain unintended results, which in turn have contributed to the weaknesses in our industry. Domestic competition has often been restricted, leading to a lack of quality- and cost-consciousness in segments of industry. The level of protection offered to Indian industry by way of quantitative import restrictions and tariffs has been too high, leading to a high cost of production and an inadequate technological dynamism. These weaknesses have to be removed in the context of the scarcity of resources, which puts a premium on efficiency, and also in the context of global economic trends which require a high degree of competitiveness. Indian industry is now ready to face the full pressure of domestic competition and the measures already taken in the sphere of industrial policy should help to achieve this objective. Indian industry must also be prepared to face international competition in a phased manner.

Steps have already been taken to reduce the degree of quantitative licensing in trade and industrial policy and it has been proposed to do away with quantitative restrictions altogether within a period of about three years. We have also made a start reducing tariff levels which must be reduced in a phased manner so that they become comparable with those in other industrializing developing countries within a few years. This is essential to make Indian industry internationally competitive. The Eighth Plan has to meet these challenges in the various sectors against the background of certain critical imbalances which have emerged recently, rather sharply. These are:

1. increasing fiscal and budgetary deficits, mounting public debt and severe constraints on the resources of the government and the public sector to undertake essential developmental activities;
2. a critical situation in the balance of payments; and
3. a high rate of inflation.

Thus, the Eighth Plan, while providing a new orientation to planning consistent with the new thrusts in economic policy, has to ensure that the public sector investment rests on a sound resource base and that the current account deficit is limited to a level sustainable by normal capital flows.

The Public Sector

The public sector has numerous achievements to its credit. The development of our crucial infrastructure sector has been pioneered by public sector units (PSUs). Many other vital segments of the industrial sector have also been built up by public enterprises. The public sector has contributed richly to the widening and diversification of our industrial structure and will continue to perform a key role in the coming years. However, certain critical weaknesses that are now apparent will have to be addressed. The public sector as envisaged by Jawaharlal Nehru was to contribute to the growth and development of the nation by providing surplus reinvestable resources. This has not happened as it should have. Many PSUs make substantial losses and have become a continuing drain on the exchequer, absorbing resources which are withdrawn from sectors where they are desperately needed for achieving other developmental goals. Apart from the fact that the present fiscal situation does not permit any more accumulation of unsustainable losses, there is also the fact that many loss-making PSUs do not serve the goal for which they were set up.

It is clear that a strong and vibrant public sector cannot be one with financially weak foundations. For the public sector to perform the role expected of it in the 1990s, the issue of loss-making public sector enterprises will have to be squarely addressed. The policy of the government meeting the cash losses of so many enterprises for all time to come is just not sustainable. This prevents scarce resources from being used in high-priority social sectors or in economic activities that promise a return. Efforts must be made to restructure and revitalize PSUs that are potentially viable through the infusion of new technology, rationalization of labour and even infusion of resources for diversification or modernization. Equally, patently unviable PSUs may have to be closed down with suitable social safety-net mechanisms including retrenching and redeployment, which are devised to protect the interest of workers. It should be recognized that in many cases the very rationale of the public sector entering certain industrial areas needs to be re-examined. There have been very good reasons in the past for the public sector to take the initiative in industrial areas where the private sector would ordinarily either not enter or would hesitate to do so. This may not be the case today and the restructuring of the public sector would essentially entail vacating such areas for private sector initiatives in the coming years. Recent government policies have already vacated large areas for private sector initiatives and this process of restructuring and reform would need to be carried further.

Building up People's Institutions

Our experience of development planning has shown that developmental activities undertaken with the people's active participation have a greater chance of success and can also be more cost-effective as compared to those undertaken by the government where people become passive observers. The non-involvement of people has also led them to develop an attitude of total dependence on the government for everything, so that there has been a lack of effort from and lack of accountability to the people in the system of administering development schemes.

In the Eighth Five Year Plan, it is necessary to make development a people's movement. People's initiative and participation must become the key element in the whole process of development. A lot in the areas of education (especially literacy), health, family planning, land improvement, efficient land use, minor irrigation, watershed management, recovery of wastelands, afforestation, animal husbandry, dairy, fisheries, sericulture, etc., can be achieved by creating people's institutions that are accountable to the community. Therefore the focus of attention will be on developing multiple institutional options for improving the delivery systems by exploiting the vast potential of the voluntary sector.

The importance of decentralized local-level planning and people's participation has been recognized. Yet the results achieved so far have not been very impressive. In this plan, therefore, a new direction is being given to achieve these objectives. So far the approach to people's participation consisted of programme-based strategies. In addition to such programmes, the Planning Commission has now worked out institutional strategies which will mean creating or strengthening various people's institutions at the district, block and village levels. This will enable them to synthesize the purpose of investment envisaged in the Plan with optimization of benefits at the grass-roots level by relating these programmes to the needs of people. This can only be achieved through the collective wisdom of the community, combined with the latest know-how available. This work has to be undertaken primarily by NGOs with the support of the government.

Various models of people's institutions have been functioning successfully in the country. Studies show that effective institutions have the following essential ingredients:

1. They are owned and managed by the users/stake holders, producers or beneficiaries themselves.
2. They are accountable to the community.
3. They have the capacity to become self-reliant over a period of time.
4. They have the capacity to diagnose the needs of the areas, interact with the governmental agencies in order to draw need-based local level plans and to implement these plans in close cooperation with the administration.

5. They tend to bring about the integration of various segments of the society for the achievement of common goals of development.

The role of the government should be to facilitate the process of people's involvement in development activities by creating the right type of institutional infrastructure, particularly in rural areas. These institutions are very weak, particularly in those states where they are needed the most for bringing about an improvement in the socio-demographic indicators. Encouraging voluntary agencies as well as schools, colleges and universities to get involved in social tasks and social mobilization; strengthening Panchayati Raj insti- tutions; reorienting and integrating all village-level programmes under the charge of Panchayati Raj institutions; and helping the cooperatives to come up in the organization and support of local economic activities for example, are some of the steps which the government must earnestly initiate. A genuine push towards decentralization and people's participation has become necessary.

Role of Planning

Given the background of our experience of planning for develop- ment of the last forty years and the strong imperatives for change that have emerged now, it is quite pertinent to ask the question: What will be the role of planning in the future? In order to answer this, one has to review the nature of planning in India and what is expected from it in future.

When the term 'planning' was officially defined for the first time in the First Five Year Plan document, the term used was 'democratic planning' as distinct from a 'plan based on regimentation'. The centralized planning of the type practised in socialist economies did not exist in India ever. In practice, the market has determined allocations in a major segment of the economy. The public sector, of course, has expanded with a wide-ranging influence over the economic life of the nation. Its lack of cost-consciousness, increasing ineffectiveness in achieving targets, and depletion of resources that cripple it from carrying on its activities without high-cost borrowing have compelled us to define and limit its role and to lay down the objective principles of its operations. It has also been discussed in the foregoing that the process of planning and the pattern of government activities hitherto followed have dampened the people's initiatives and their sense of responsibility towards building the nation. The process of planning needs to be corrected in this respect.

As a corollary to this, the role of the Planning Commission needs to be redefined. It has to play an integrative role in developing a holistic approach to the policy formulation in critical and inter-sectoral areas of human and economic development. In the social sector, schemes have to be subjected to coordinated policy-formulation. The existing multiplicity of agencies is not only wasteful but also counter-productive because of the long and repetitive procedures and the diffusion of authority involved. An integrated approach can lead to better results at much lower costs.

So far, resource allocation has been the predominant role of the Planning Commission. This has to change. Instead of looking for mere increases in the plan outlays, we should look for increases in the efficiency of utilization of the allocations being made and the prospects of a return on the investments. The Planning Commission has to play a mediatory and facilitating role among states, and sometimes central ministries, to usher in the change smoothly and to create a culture of high productivity, cost efficiency and sound financial discipline in the government. Through clear identification of goals and prioritization of schemes, efforts will be made to reduce bottlenecks, thereby making higher rates of growth possible. If each sector can plainly see what is expected of it, then it can gear itself up to meet the set targets.

Planning still has a large role to play in our country. It is needed for creating social infrastructure and for human development. We need to build schools, hospitals, institutions of excellence and scientific research. We have to plan and structure the system of education to cultivate the necessary calibre, skills and value systems. Private sector participation in these efforts, within the framework of nationally desirable objectives and goals, will be welcome. But the private sector is not capable of taking care of the needs of the entire society, particularly of the poor and the weak in remote and the rural areas, as yet. Market mechanism may be able to bring about an equilibrium between 'demand' backed by purchasing power and supply even in this sphere, but it will not be able to bring about a balance between the 'need' and the supply. Therefore, planning in this area will remain important.

Planning is necessary to take care of the poor and the down-trodden, who have little asset endowments to benefit from the natural growth of economic activities. Poverty alleviation programmes have definitely helped in reducing poverty and generating employment. A vision about the structure and the pattern of future growth is also important for its implications for the rate at which employment can be generated in the future.

The removal of large disparities in development between regions requires the flow of resources across regions. Experience has shown that market forces have not achieved this in adequate measure. The planning process has to manage the flow of resources across regions for accelerated removal of regional disparities. At present, the plan does provide for special area programmes such as the Hill Area Plan, Tribal Areas Plan and other schemes for backward areas. While these programmes aim at creating a basic infrastructure, the backlog of development is large and considerable efforts have to be made for the integration of such regions into the mainstream of economic activity in the country.

Planning, and more particularly public sector investment, will have a major role to play in strengthening the physical infrastructure, including energy, transport, communication and irrigation, in order to support the growth process on a sustainable basis.

Obviously there are areas in which markets cannot play an allocative role. Market mechanism is never adequate for protecting the environment, forests and ecology. Nor is it adequately equipped to give guidance about the use of scarce resources like rare minerals, land and water. A long-term perspective, and hence planning, is needed in these areas.

Planning and market mechanism should be so dovetailed that one is complementary to the other. Market mechanism must serve as an 'efficiency promoting device', while planning will be the larger guiding force keeping the long-term social goals in perspective.

So long as public sector investment constitutes a significant proportion of the total investment, planning, in so far as it relates to the public sector, has to be detailed, setting forth not only the objectives, but also examining the alternatives and identifying specific projects in the various sectors. Besides, the plan of the centre will have to be appropriately linked with the state plans, since both the centre and the states have responsibilities in almost all areas. All this is analogous to corporate planning. For the rest of the system, however, the plan will be indicative, outlining the broad directions in which the economy should be growing. The plan will, therefore, consist of: providing a vision of the future; constructing medium-term economic projection for the entire economy; evolving a system of information pooling and dissemination; identifying areas of development where the country is strong and where it needs to build up its strength; evolving appropriate policy measures to achieve the desired goals; and ensuring a degree of consensus in the system through meaningful dialogue with the 'social partners' of the government, namely the farmers, the trade unions, the business groups, etc. In a more deregulated environment, policy formulation and coordination will assume greater importance.

3

The Rise and Decline of Development Planning in India

Ajit Mozoomdar

In tracing the evolution of our planning system and trying to assess its strengths and weaknesses, it would be fair to begin by recalling India's pioneering role in development planning. In 1950 there was no body of relevant theory, contemporary experience or organizational model to draw upon. So the planning processes, first improvized and then improved upon, and the institutional mechanisms developed within the country's political and administrative framework, were in themselves notable achievements. The extensive literature on planning methods and problems since the fifties has drawn heavily on the Indian experience. Promoted by UN agencies, the Indian planning system has been transplanted to other developing countries with predictably mixed results. It is also necessary to emphasize that, at least in the early years of Indian planning, it was clearly recognized that development meant social as well as economic transformation, and hence planning would involve more than the implementation of a set of investment programmes to enlarge the size and scope of the country's economy.

Any attempt to review the experience of nearly forty years of planning effort critically must necessarily be highly selective in its approach. This survey begins with an introductory section recapitulating ideas concerning development planning shared by the country's political and intellectual leaders in the 1950s. These formed the basis for the extraordinary national consensus which prevailed for over thirty years but has been weakening ever since. The main problems thrown up in the course of development planning are then outlined as they unfolded in successive plans.

In the next section we consider the relation of development planning to the political process in India, the impact of dominant political ideas and the effects of changes in the political structure. The composition of the Planning Commission, the manner of its functioning and its relationship with the central government are then examined along with other parts of the structure of India's central planning machinery. The internal structure of the Planning Commission, as it has evolved, is briefly explained. Poor capability for policy analysis is identified as the most serious deficiency in India's planning machinery.

We then review what has been achieved in the technical areas of investment planning. The use of economy-wide models, perspective planning and the formulation of Five Year Plans are considered. Though these processes are well established, they are implicated in certain limitations which are discussed. After this we examine the capacities that have been developed for sectoral planning, project formulation, selection and appraisal, monitoring, and ex-post evaluation. This is followed by a section which deals critically with the policy instruments that are applied to Indian development planning.

The next section considers the implications of India's federal structure for development planning. The need for multilevel planning, the way it has evolved so far, and changes in the political environment are reviewed. Further adaptation of India's planning system to the requirements of a federal polity is seen as a critical issue. This brings us to the problems of decentralized planning and programme implementation below the state level. The social, political and administrative factors that need to be considered are at the heart of the development process if it is to mean the raising of incomes, removing destitution and improving living conditions in rural India.

In the concluding section, we try to evaluate the present status of planning in India. The diminishing national consensus on planning objectives and priorities and the crisis facing the Indian fiscal system are referred to. There is inadequate public understanding of the underlying issues as yet, but the conflict has to be resolved in political terms. If the eventual outcome is to reestablish a consensus for a more equitable and sustainable pattern of development, it may still be possible to restore the centrality of development planning in India's economic decision making. In that event, the effectiveness of the planning process could be improved in certain ways indicated at the end of the paper.

The Development Perspective

Looking back at the emergence of early ideas about development planning in India from the time of the Report of the National Planning Committee under Nehru to that of the formulation of the first two Five Year Plans, the main themes are easy to discern. Though poor and technologically backward compared to the countries of Europe and North America, India was seen as possessing natural resources and human skills capable of ensuring that within a space of approximately twenty-five to thirty years (Government of India, 1952), it could develop and diversify its economic structure in the same way as the West had done since the mid-nineteenth century. Since the main barrier to be overcome was the lack of capital stock, both in quantity and quality, it was soon realized that the development process would require the generation of adequate savings for rapid growth of investment. It was also realized that these investable resources would have to be shelled out mainly from growing incomes as the average consumption level was abysmally low. The driving force behind this process of forced savings and accelerated growth had to be the newly independent Indian state, through the instrument of a freely elected government representing the interests of all citizens. The central objective of development was clearly seen as raising the standards of living of the large number of poor people, which might entail limiting the growth of consumption of the relatively well-off sections. Agriculture had to be modernized and food production substantially increased. At the core of the development process, however, was rapid industrialization and it was hoped that eventually, a significant proportion of the population currently dependent on agriculture would shift to non-agricultural occupations.

India's development strategies were framed against the background of its recent history. Despite an early start in industrialization and significant investment in infrastructure under colonial rule, the only industries that were really developed at the time of Independence were cotton and jute textiles, tea, and food processing. Much of this was controlled by a few large firms. Foreign capital dominated industry and external trade. The growth of food production was slow and the country was prone to famine. The economy had been stagnant over the period 1900 to 1950. Four-fifths of the population existed in conditions of extreme poverty, and malnutrition and illiteracy were widespread. There was no reason to suppose that political independence would in itself unleash forces which would lead to agricultural and industrial growth.

It was argued that the motivating force behind industrialization should be direct investment by the state in setting up new enterprises for three main reasons. First, the large amounts of capital needed to establish the industrial base required for sustained and diversified growth could only be mobilized by the state. Second, public investment would achieve the desired industrial structure more easily without having to rely on high levels of corporate profit, which would further increase income disparities. Third, reliance on public rather than private enterprises to foster the growth of metal, minerals, machine-building and chemical industries, as well as fuel, power and transport would mean that economic power—which might also be used for political purposes—will not become concentrated in the hands of a few large industrial houses.

The role of private domestic capital was envisaged essentially as being the supplier of consumer goods and intermediate products, namely, textiles, vehicles, light machinery, cement, drugs and pharmaceuticals, processed foods and beverages. But even in these areas the state might be required to step in to fill the gaps left by the private sector.

Since external capital had been associated with foreign political dominance, disinvestment by foreign companies was to be encouraged, and new private foreign investment would not be permitted other than in the few cases where essential technology could not be imported without being associated with such investment. And in all such cases, the preferred organizational form would be joint ventures controlled by the domestic partner.

This set of ideas was accepted across the political spectrum excluding only small groups at the extreme left and right who accepted neither the possibility nor the advisability of the state playing an effective role in development. The history of economic planning in India over the last forty years, however its outcome may be judged, displays a remarkable continuity in the pursuit of the goals just outlined.

The vision of a readily achievable future through feasible processes of guided economy-wide growth proved over-optimistic. Hindsight provides us with several reasons that explain why the path of development has proved to be more arduous and protracted than was foreseen either by the Indian planners or any of the foreign economists who thronged to Delhi to help with the planning process in the exciting days of the fifties and early sixties.

Basically the idea that an economy as large as India's could be effectively industrialized and its agriculture modernized within a space of thirty years or so, raising average living standards from abject poverty to tolerable levels, had taken little account of the time it would take to create the necessary infrastructure of irrigation works, power plants, mines, factories, transport and communications across an entire subcontinent, or of the learning time involved in constructing and efficiently operating modern industrial enterprises. The rate of increase of the population also proved to be much higher than assumed in the First Plan, doubling the total number within thirty years. Moreover, the early plans had not taken note of the great regional variations in the ratio of population to resources, productivity, incomes, and education and health levels. Further, though economic dualism was a feature of the Second and subsequent plans, its full implications had hardly been understood. The imbalance between low agricultural growth and a relatively more rapid increase in non-agricultural incomes was one outcome. Another was the increasing claims on investable resources to support not only the consumption needs of the growing upper and middle classes, but also the requirements of a modernizing polity and of security in an unfavourable external environment. Also, it proved more difficult than had been foreseen to ensure the development of the private sector of industry consistently with plan objectives while at the same time preventing a widening of income disparities.

The difficulties in the way of expanding and structuring the Indian economy according to a preconceived design unfolded themselves as the plans proceeded. The first shock to the planners was the rapid increase in the demand for imports in the Second Plan, which indicated that capital inflows on concessional terms would be critical for sustaining the industrialization effort. Thirty years of reliance on foreign aid have followed with no end yet in sight. The extent to which the growth and diversification of the economy could be constrained by insufficiency of food supplies became apparent in the Third Plan, the lesson having been driven home by the droughts that occurred between 1964 and 1966. The mid-sixties were marked by other inter-sectoral imbalances as well, and the inflationary and balance of payments crises led to the suspension of medium-term planning for three years. Problems of detailed investment planning loomed large at this stage. Inadequacies in project design and choice, unrealistic phasing of investments over time, implementation delays and the lack of well-articulated programmes in some sectors were highlighted. These were gradually overcome. Meanwhile, planners' tasks were eased by the success of the new wheat-production technology in the north, which removed the food supply constraint by the mid-seventies, and the location of significant sources of oil offshore in the west. Investment priorities were substantially recorded in the Fourth Plan, with an emphasis on input-intensive agriculture, fuel, power and fertilizers.

Meanwhile, the results of the 1971 population census revived concern about the effect of demographic trends on the growth of per capita income and the reduction of underemployment. Indian economists initiated the world-wide debate on the extent and persistence of poverty. Redistribution of incomes, employment-creation strategies and the basic-needs approach became part of the vocabulary of international discourse and among Indian planners. This was reflected in the Fifth Plan (1974–79) and the Draft of the 1978–83 Plan.

Fortunately, the Indian economy was able to recover quickly from the inflationary crisis of 1973–75 and the effects of the first OPEC boost to international oil prices. The Indian economy also coped well with the second oil price increase, international inflation and recession in the period 1979–82, without significantly increasing its international indebtedness. These developments tended to confirm the planners' confidence in the correctness of the basic thrusts of Indian investment planning.

Among the main issues facing the planners in the eighties were that the number of people below the poverty line remained at an unacceptably high level; the growth of agriculture, especially food-grains output, was apparently levelling off; and sections of Indian industry established in the sixties were facing technological obsol-escence. In addition, the view long espoused by the World Bank, that the controls over industry were a critical factor constraining the growth of this sector, and that a higher overall growth rate was attainable through policy changes, gained influential adherents in the government. These concerns have been the major determinants of the priorities reflected in the Sixth and Seventh Plans.

Politics and Planning

Some of the failures of foresight or understanding were inevitable. But more than these, the gap between promise and performance is explained by the failure of the planners to take any account of the political and social constraints with which their strategies and programmes had to contend. For example, in the area of rural development, behind the rhetoric of social transformation, there has been no apparent awareness of the problems of large inequalities in asset distribution, caste domination, illiteracy, and the absence of effective local organizations. Again, there has been no considered policy about the tribal populations or migrant workers. It was assumed that the system of local administration could be expanded and motivated by training to serve as an agent of promoting both economic development and social change. Every plan spoke of participation and public cooperation, but no effort was made to scrutinize the actual relationship between the administration and the rural population. In industrial planning, the planners had unjustifiable faith in their ability to restrain the concentration of economic power and reduce regional disparities through a mixed system of regulation and incentives. The implicit assumption that given 'political will', the planners could achieve the desired distri-bution of productive assets between the private and public sector was never abandoned. However, a few structural changes in the economy which might affect the interests of the dominant classes have actually been proposed by the planners. The only conceptual changes and policy reforms which can be traced to the Planning Commission in recent years relate to the poverty alleviation and basic-needs approach of the Fifth Plan and the attempt to increase the employment intensity of development in the first version of the

Sixth Plan. The main elements of the policy consensus that have supported the Indian planning system since its inception could be related to the Directive Principles of the Indian Constitution. In early plan documents care was taken not to identify the plans' priorities and policies with the programmes and manifestos of the ruling party. The draft plans were discussed with all the political parties before their presentation in the National Development Council for formal acceptance by the state chief ministers on behalf of their constituents. Thereafter, the plan would be placed before the Parliament for ratification.

Discussions in the National Development Council confirmed the existence of a very wide area of agreement on plan objectives and strategies, despite disclaimers for the record by any communist chief ministers about the infeasibility of true development under a capitalist system. The Chief Ministers' contributions to the planning debate were confined to the claims of their respective states for larger shares in the public investment programme. When agrarian reform was undertaken in stages in successive plans, the states differed on details of legislation but raised no objection in principle. Subsequently, their performance in matters of tenurial reform and redistribution of surplus land has of course varied considerably. There were no dissenting voices in the states when the commercial banks or the coal industry were nationalized.

Whether the process, even if carried over a period of time, could be seen as establishing 'socialism' in any accepted sense of the term was always open to doubt. The alternative formulation—'a socialistic pattern of society'—was intended to reduce emphasis on the public ownership of productive assets but implied as much or more by way of removal of income and wealth disparities. In the later plan documents, however, both public ownership and greater equality were virtually abandoned as objectives by stating that plans were aimed at 'growth with social justice'. The explicit introduction of poverty reduction and alleviation criteria in the Fifth Plan confirms this shift in perceptions.

The public-ownership objective was essentially based on the understanding that political power within a state was closely linked to economic power and that the latter arose from ownership and control over 'basic industries' such as coal, steel and oil and the financial system. These 'commanding heights of the economy' should, therefore, be in the hands of the state.

The extension of the rhetoric of socialism to cover state owner-ship over some parts of the consumer-goods sector was a later development and was never incorporated into the objectives of planning. The argument that goods of mass consumption could be more cheaply produced and distributed by the public sector or that farmers' incomes could be increased by nationalizing the wholesale trade in foodgrains was never accepted by the Planning Commission. What needs to be noted, though, is that these issues have never been adequately discussed in the planning documents. The plan-ners have avoided sharp definitions of policy objectives, partly because these would require formulation in political terms.

An important instance of lack of definition relates to the stated objective of 'self-reliance'. Beyond stating that this did not mean autarky, the concept has never been clarified. There is a general sense that a country of India's subcontinental dimensions and resource endowments should, when developed, be an economy which is not unduly reliant on continuing imports of capital and technology, possess modern communications and financial services and should be capable of producing a wide range of capital goods, intermediates and consumer goods for its large domestic market. The moot point, however, has been the extent to which the inflow of foreign capital and technology was necessary till the state of development was determined. The dominant view has been that the ultimate objective might well be endangered by the liberal imports of capital and technology on the route to development. Hence the curbs on private foreign investment and imported tech-nology. As for capital available on concessional terms from inter-national institutions or bilaterally on a government-to-government basis, there were fewer inhibitions. However, in the Third and Fourth Plans, there were attempts to define a path of development which would lead to reduced reliance on aid (the target of 'zero net aid'). This objective was subsequently dropped quietly by the planners and the present policy appears to be to welcome all aid inflows and some private commercial borrowings to supplement these flows, limited only by the need to maintain the debt service ratio at a tolerable level.

Until the mid-seventies, the planning process was never identified with purely political ends. The aims of planned development being formulated in very general terms, a broad national agreement could prevail both in objectives and overall strategy. This consensus survived the establishment of communist-led governments in Kerala, the rise of the Dravidian movement in Tamil Nadu and the period of non-Congress coalition governments in the Hindi-speaking states in the late sixties. When the 'socialism' of Indira Gandhi's second government was grafted on accepted planning priorities in the early seventies, however, it was put forward as a party programme, though the Constitution's Directive Principles were still used as a referent. Then followed the attempt to present the Emergency of 1975–77 as being necessary for accelerated development; the 20 and 25 point programmes were the immediate outcome. The Janata government (1977–79) chose unfortunately to emphasize its political break with the recent past by terminating the Fifth Plan a year early, and the draft of the plan for 1978–83 was overtly linked to the party's programme. On her return to power in 1980, Mrs. Gandhi also insisted on a new Sixth Plan. There was not much change of substance, but the principle that a five year plan was also a party manifesto was confirmed. This development could have serious implications for national planning in the future although the Sixth and Seventh Plans have generally been accepted by opposition-ruled states albeit with some reservations in the case of West Bengal.

At the state level, the planning process was affected by the electoral process in only two ways till the seventies. There was a positive infiuence in that the ruling parties or factions tried to persuade the electorate that they would enlarge investment programmes and improve distribution of benefits to deprived groups and backward regions. Negatively, parties have tended to compete in offering greater benefits to particular groups by direct and indirect subsidies such as lower water and power rates and loan remission, thereby reducing the amount of net resources available for new investment.

In the mid-seventies, for the first time three states embarked on schemes devised by them to assist the deprived sections of their populations. These were outside the scope of the nation-wide poverty alleviation schemes recommended by the Planning Commission, and were put forward specifically as party programmes. The Rural Employment Guarantee Scheme of the Congress government in Maharashtra was eventually incorporated in a new national programme. The Free Mid-Day Meals scheme of the AIADMK Government in Tamil Nadu for school children, and the scheme for distributing rice at Re. 1 (later Rs. 2) per kg devised by the Telugu Desam in Andhra Pradesh have so far remained 'non-Plan schemes' so far as the Planning Commission is concerned, but there have been recent indications that the ruling party may adopt a part of these programmes causing a shift in national resource allocations.

The Machinery of Planning: The Planning System

India's political and intellectual leadership of the fifties understood that if planning was to be an instrument for comprehensively restructuring and developing India's economy and society, the task could not be compartmentalized. Development objectives had to inform all government policies and actions, and the machinery of government as a whole had to be involved in the development process.

The Planning Commission, which was to be at the apex of the planning system, was devised as a body of experts capable of charting the path of development (see, for an account of its compositions, etc. Paranjape, 1964; Planning Commission, 1988). It was to enjoy a degree of autonomy from the central government but not to conflict with it. Thus the professional full-time members of the Commission were not to be ministers, though they would enjoy parity of esteem with them. The deputy chairman attends meetings of the Cabinet, and may sometimes be a member of it. The staff is part of a planning ministry, which is not different from any other ministry. The Commission is an advisory body in form, so that it may only recommend policies, investment priorities or programmes to the central and state governments which in theory may or may not accept them. These require formal acceptance by the central and state cabinets before they become operative. In practice, however, this means that the Planning Commission has substantial executive authority in determining public sector investment programmes, both of the centre and the states. Further, in the case of the states, it has the final say in allocating plan assistance, which for most states provides the bulk of the resources needed to implement their investment programmes.

Unlike many other developing countries, planning and budgeting are completely separated in the Indian system, and the budget for both current and investment expenditure is the responsibility of the Ministry of Finance which also has complete control over all resources including external assistance. Thus the system needs close cooperation between the Commission and the Finance Ministry, any differences being resolved by discussion between the deputy chairman and the finance minister or by reference to the Cabinet.

The system makes the Planning Commission responsible for the longer-term goals of development and medium-level investment planning; the Finance Ministry for raising the resources for investment and current expenditure, fiscal policy and expenditure control; and the Reserve Bank of India for monetary policy. The coordination of these approaches is obviously not without its difficulties, and some countries prefer to bring the medium-term and short-term economic management together under the Ministry of Finance (sometimes called Ministry of Finance and Planning). This seems to be especially apt at the time of an economic crisis, when the interest of short-term management assumes overwhelming importance. But precisely because there is a necessary conflict at all times between the needs of long-term development and short-term stabilization, the Indian system of entrusting these concerns to two different agencies and resolving any differences at the cabinet level is to be preferred.

The responsibilities for sectoral planning, policy formation and project selection are shared by the Commission with the planning divisions of the sectoral ministries. Project formulation in the major sectors of industry such as steel, petroleum, fertilizers and engineering has been largely devolved to public sector corporations operating in these areas. Detailed planning for the states is their own responsibility, but major irrigation and power projects are subject to scrutiny by specialized agencies of the central government.

The technical and economic appraisal of major elements of the public investment programmes of the centre and the states was plainly inadequate in the earlier plans. Both formulation and appraisal were significantly improved in the early seventies with the establishment of the Project Appraisal Division of the Planning Commission and the Public Investment Board, which is a joint agency of the Planning Commission and the Ministry of Finance.

When planning was first undertaken in India, the decision to have the prime minister as the chairman of the Planning Commission had both a personal and an institutional significance. Jawaharlal Nehru was clear in his perception that development must be the primary goal of national policy after Independence and that planning was the key to development. He lent his whole weight to this endeavour. Institutionally, his chairmanship implied that the Commission had a status equal to the Cabinet. This was also reflected in the standing of the early members of the Commission, and Cabinet ministers served side by side with the full-time professionals who were to be responsible for the actual preparation of the plans. The Commission continued to enjoy Nehru's full support during his lifetime even when his personal involvement in the planning process declined in the later years of his premiership. Thereafter, concern with planning objectives, the importance of the planning process, and the Commission's influence within the government system tended to decline. The esteem in which the Commission was held by the public diminished, in part because of some visible failures of planning, but also because Nehru's successors were less concerned with the planning system. Lal Bahadur Shastri was faced with too many political and national security issues in his brief tenure. Indira Gandhi was inclined to judge the usefulness of the planning process in overtly political terms. For a brief period after securing her political position she did look to the Planning Commission to provide a dynamic for economic change. In later years her concern with the planning system clearly declined, and she sought economic advice mainly outside the Commission. Morarji Desai's perception of planning was limited. As a former finance minister he saw the system as inflexible and aiming at infeasible objectives. For Rajiv Gandhi the Planning Commission was simply another ministry. He appeared to regard the planning system as unduly restrictive, and would have liked planners to focus on development only in a long-term perspective.

From the Fourth Plan onwards, with younger professionals being appointed as full-time members of the Planning Commission, they have been equated with ministers of state. Only the deputy chairman retains the standing of a cabinet minister. Attendance of ministers, including the finance minister, in the Commission's meetings is infrequent, their involvement in the planning process minimal, and their personal contributions negligible.

The composition of the Planning Commission and its internal organization have been adapted to changes in perceived planning priorities without any radical changes over the years. Excluding the deputy chairman, the Commission has usually had five or six full-time members with functional responsibilities. Members have been chosen from among economists, retired officials with sectoral experience of planning and plan implementation, educationists, scientists and technologists. Sometimes a member with management experience in the private or public sector has been included, as also politicians with some experience of rural development. A background in the social sciences other than economics, or in medicine or engineering has apparently not been found relevant to development planning. Members are selected by the prime minister, usually though not always, in consultation with the deputy chairman. When—more often than not—the deputy chairman has had the necessary stature and personality, the Commission has been able to develop a collegiate approach to planning issues despite differences among the members regarding background, perceptions and political convictions.

The organizational structure of the Planning Commission has from the first been based on the understanding that the Commission is concerned with defining objectives, framing strategies, determining investment priorities and preparing coordinated investment programmes, but not with detailed sectoral or project planning, that being the responsibility of the technical ministries. What has not always been appreciated about this division of responsibilities is the necessity for the Planning Commission to have a preeminent position in policy formulation and coordination over the whole economy.

The Commission was organized with central units to deal with macroeconomic analyses and projections and the estimation of financial resources and sectoral divisions for agriculture, industry, infrastructure and the social services, each under specialist advisers. In addition, one or two senior officials were appointed as programme advisers to monitor the implementation of the states' public investment programmes. The Perspective Planning Division was created in the late fifties and became the focus of quantitative studies relating to planning. The next addition was a semi-autonomous Programme Evaluation Organization. The current monitoring of Plan projects was also carried out under a committee on Plan Projects, which later became the Commission's Monitoring Division. The capability for ex ante techno-economic appraisal of projects was developed and after that control over state plans was strengthened in the late seventies. The Commission has been free to recruit specialist advisers from all available sources in the country, and their total numbers have been kept fairly small.

Policy Analysis

The weakest part of the Indian planning system has been its inability to undertake sustained analyses of policy at different levels. Fundamental issues such as constraints development and strategies to overcome them are discussed, if at all, at the level of generality, in ways that have no impact on planning decisions. In the area of political economy the Planning Commission has always assumed that its position as a non-expert body precludes any consideration of specifically political constraints to development. Issues such as the oligopolistic structure of industry and political power, or the impact of tenurial conditions and agrarian relations on agricultural production, or the increasing pre-emption of resources for the supposed requirement of national security are not considered to be issues by the planners within their domain. In fact, all major structural changes in the economy such as the abolition of the zamindari system, the legislation of tenurial reforms and the imposition of ceilings on landholdings, the nationalization of banking, insurance and coal, and the attempt (not very effective) to limit the growth of large industrial groups were undertaken outside the ambit of the planning system and without much by way of policy contribution from the Planning Commission.

Again, the Planning Commission has not had any professional capability, either as member or as adviser to analyze social structures or to consider the problems of modernization of different groups of the Indian population despite the rhetoric of social transformation in the earlier plan documents. As a result, the Commission has had no considered response to offer when problems of social structure have come up in its programmes of economic development. These problems include access of drinking water supply to Harijans, impact of community landholdings on social forestry or exploitation of forest products, reservation of industrial opportunities for backward groups, the bias against vocational education in rural areas and lack of enthusiasm or motivation to promote girls' education or to limit family size in accordance with population control programmes. Where there were palpable planning failures as evident in the high proportion of children dropping out of primary schools or the failure of the rural health-care system to achieve even its limited goals because adequate health staff is unwilling to serve in villages, planners took little notice in the first twenty years or so.

Even when development planning is viewed in narrowly economic terms, it needs to go beyond investment programming to cover a range of policies and options. The Planning Commission has failed to develop the capability for analysis, i.e., preparation of background papers, marshalling empirical evidence and analyzing available choices. Responsibility for development-policy analysis has rested with the Commission's Perspective Planning Division (which is wrongly named, its main concern being the quantitative framework for medium-term planning), but the Division is hardly equipped for this task. The Economic Division is also concerned only with medium-term macroeconomic analysis and fiscal issues. Economists who are members of the Commission have contributed to policy analyses according to their own perceptions and capacities without the benefit of any professional staff support. Infrequent meetings of panels of eminent economists, a few sponsored investigations by individual scholars, or even research undertaken by associated institutions such as the Indian Statistical Institute or the Gokhale Institute have hardly compensated for the Planning Commission's lack of ability to adequately analyze the many critical issues that arise in development planning.

In the late sixties and again in the eighties, the government experienced working with Economic Advisory Councils independent of the Commission, but their work has been related mainly to macroeconomic policy or sectoral issues. In the area of macroeconomic policy, analytical capability does exist in the Economic Division of the Finance Ministry, the Reserve Bank of India and the Planning Commission, but there has not been sufficient appreciation of the usefulness of macroeconomic analysis in policy formulation. The analysis of sectoral policies such as energy pricing, or farm mechanization, or user charges for social services, has improved over time. Both the Planning Commission and the Finance Ministry need to be consulted by the ministries concerned, but the capacity of the central economic agencies for an independent examination of such issues is very limited. However, since the mid-sixties, the instrumentality of a Committee of Economic Secretaries (which reports to the Cabinet) has proved to be an effective coordinating device.

After the debates in the late fifties on the directions of India's development strategy, basic policy issues seem to have hardly concerned the Planning Commission till the early seventies when it came to consider the possibility of direct measures to raise the incomes and improve the living conditions of the poor (Rudra, 1978). It may be of some interest to enumerate those issues that have never been examined in a comprehensive or connected way either in the Planning Commission, or in any other part of the government, although they have been highlighted in academic discussions on India's plan priorities and have received attention from India's foreign-aid donors. Such a list would include defining: (a) the concept of self-reliance; (b) the overall changes in the structure of the economy that have resulted in shifting the balance between agriculture, industry and service sectors; (c) the impact of licensing and other policies on regional redistribution of industry; (d) the employment and income effects of input-intensive irrigated agriculture; (e) the effects of trade and exchange-rate policies on industrial structure and competitiveness; (f) the trade-off, if any, between inflation and growth; (g) investment priorities relating to wage goods and the consumption demands of higher income groups; (h) trends in income distribution above the poverty line; (i) changes in the rural-urban terms of trade; (j) the 'structural retrogression thesis'; and (k) the case for 'economic liberalization'. The absence of relevant empirical research and the ability for policy analysis has made the planning system vulnerable to shifts in policy initiated within the ruling party, as a whole or by individuals with strongly held views, by external mentors or by mere change in economic fashion.

The Planning Commission has never examined in depth the elements of the policy consensus we have referred to earlier such as establishing the rationale for public-sector investment in industry, putting curbs on private foreign investment and restraining the growth of consumption levels of relatively affluent groups.

Although the plan documents have referred to the issue, the Commission has made no analysis of the actual impact of agrarian relations on agricultural development in any part of the country. It has had a poor understanding of the structure of the rural debt and credit system and its impact on agricultural production. Non-farm employment has not been studied; nor has the informal sector of urban and semi-urban industry, or the linkages between small and large-scale industries. The entire area of the trade and services sector has been neglected in studies sponsored by the Commission, so that it has had no proposals to offer for appropriate policies in these areas.

The Planning Commission needs to concern itself with policy analysis and coordination but it has failed to equip itself for such a role. It has not even adequately asserted its right to be consulted beyond what is achieved by the deputy chairman's attendance in meetings of the central Cabinet. For instance, the now customary division of the domain of economic management into 'plan' and 'non-plan' has had unfortunate consequences. Social services, the maintenance of productive assets, efficient operation of irrigation, power and transport projects, and the policy environment in which all these operate, are treated as matters of small concern that are outside the purview of the planning process. The Planning Commission has, over the years, acquiesced in being a very junior partner of the Finance Ministry in fiscal decisions that are immensely significant for development. The division of public expenditure into current non-development expenditure and plan outlays should not mean that planners have no say in deciding the extent of pre-emption of resources for defence, administrative expenditure, the cost of borrowing or the impact of subsidies.

Planning Models

The basic quantitative framework for five year planning in India consists of: (a) a macroeconomic projection model for five years in which growth is linked to marginal savings assuming a Harrod-Domar relationship; and (b) to Leontief transformation linking the structure of production and consumption in the economy at the beginning and the end of the five year period. This approach, evolved in the sixties after many interesting and exciting discussions between Indian and foreign economists, aims simply at examining the implications and feasibility of the anticipated rate of expansion of the economy and ensuring consistency between sectors.

The planning procedure has remained unchanged since the Fourth Plan. First, on the basis of estimated incremental capital-output ratios prevailing in the main sectors of the economy and the anticipated distribution of both public and private investments between these sectors in the next planning period, the Commission determines the range of feasible aggregate growth rates at the professional level. The total investments required and the implied need for domestic savings and external resources are then estimated on the basis of the macroeconomic model, treating government consumption and foreign trade as exogenously determined. The resource implications of alternative growth paths are then considered by the entire Planning Commission—which includes the finance minister—and a target growth rate is chosen. In principle this is still a provisional choice, to be confirmed after a more detailed examination of the feasibility and consistency, but in practice the decision becomes binding on the planners. The input-output model of the economy is then used to calculate the production targets for goods and services; the model also produces sectoral investment estimates.

Separate exercises by ministries and working groups of the Commission produce estimates of demand for major goods and services based on the anticipated economy-wide growth rate, domestic output, imports and exports and new investment required during the plan period (taking into account projects in the pipeline and advance action needed for the next plan). Commodity balances are also drawn up. What the inter-industry model does is to serve as a check on these direct estimates of output and investment. Any large discrepancies between the results of the modelling exercises and the direct estimates are investigated and the process of reconciliation may serve to moderate sectoral demands for funds or to indicate a need for updating the coefficients of the model.

Consistency models have persisted in India because optimization concepts have not proved to be useful as far as economy-wide planning exercises are concerned. No advantage is to be gained either in enlarging the input-output table further.

Considerations of income distribution were incorporated into the technical planning exercises in the Fifth Plan by introducing a separate sub-model to simulate the result of the transfer of incomes from the highest to the three lowest deciles of the population (Chakravarty, 1987: 33–36). In the draft plan for 1978–83, employment effects of alternative investment patterns were estimated through sectoral sub-models.

In the Sixth and Seventh Plans, a sectorally disaggregated investment plan was incorporated into the macroeconomic model and a number of sub-models were used to check internal inconsistencies in the agriculture and industry sectors to examine the impact of demographic changes on employment and to estimate the likely effects of poverty alleviation programmes (Planning Commission, 1981).

Perspective Plans

The limitations of a five year horizon for development planning and the need for a larger perspective of social and economic change are obvious. India's first Perspective Plan of 1961–62 was an attempt to project a development path that would remove extreme poverty in fifteen years; it involved a 7 per cent continuous growth of the economy, then deemed feasible by planners. Subsequent perspective plans annexed to the Fourth Plan, the Draft 1978–83 Plan and the Seventh Plan have had a more limited objective of setting the Five Year Plan within a ten-to-fifteen years framework to demonstrate that the Plan's priority is to promote faster growth in the future.

The objective of perspective planning, however, should not be to set out a single set of projections similar to those in a Five Year Plan. Perspective planning should rather be directed towards more aggregative models which examine alternative development paths (including their impact on poverty and income distribution) and partial models dealing with long-term options in energy and environmental planning, demographic issues, regional imbalances, and choices in technological planning.

Medium-Term Plans

A system of five-year or any fixed period planning in the medium-term has inherent problems of lack of flexibility. There is a conflict between the plan as a normative document, designed to sustain the effort to mobilize resources for investment and the timely execution of projects and programmes, and the plan as a technical instrument coordinating the growth of different sectors of the economy, determining fiscal policies and forecasting the medium-term development of the economy. The latter purposes would be best served by a planning system which provides for an annual updating of the medium-term macroeconomic projections, adjustment of certain sectoral investment programmes in case recent developments in the economy indicate the need for significant deviation from the original plan targets, a continuous five year horizon for planning infrastructure, and detailed fiscal planning, again on a continuous basis. Annual adjustments of this sort, within the framework of successive Five Year Plans, were proposed in the late seventies and referred to as 'rolling plans'. The effort was abandoned as a result of political changes leading to the restoration of the older system of a single mid-plan reappraisal, together with lumpsum provisions for 'advance action' for the next plan. Fiscal planning still does not exist, so that the public investment programmes continue to be subjected to the vicissitudes of annual budgetary decisions on central and state resource mobilization, which are not part of any well considered medium-term financial plan.

Annual Plans introduced in 1967 represented some advancement on previous practice but they are simply yearly tranches of the public investment programme of the Five Year Plan. Recently annual plan documents have included a macroeconomic review but they make no attempts to assess or forecast developments in the private sector, whether in agriculture, industry or services. Nor is there any effort to evaluate inter-sectoral imbalances on a year-to-year basis.

At this stage, one may take note of the critique of the Indian planning system which generally emanates from the international financial institutions and liberal economists. The current orthodoxy of the World Bank, for instance, is that 'comprehensive planning' has not worked in any developing country and should be replaced by multi-year public investment programming supported by a macroeconomic framework (Baum and Tolbert, 1985: 20–22; World Development Report, 1993). It is not clear how public investments, which would cover at least the major infrastructural investments as well as support services for agriculture and the social sectors, would be determined without fairly detailed projections of sectoral growth in the economy. Inter-sectoral consistency and spatial planning of infrastructure would continue to require effective forecasting of the development of the private sector of industry. These critics would have no objection to the planning of social overheads. Detailed fiscal planning is also recommended. So what the criticism amounts to is that there should be no attempt to plan industrial output in the private sector. The objection is as much on the grounds of desirability as of feasibility. The Indian response to this continues to be that the structure of industrial production is as important as growth for the kind of development that is envisaged. It has implications for the consumption pattern of different income groups and for the call that it makes on domestic and foreign resources. It is also significant for long-term development goals including sustainability of growth and technological capability. While there may be need to be realistic and to avoid inflexibility in detailed industrial planning, planning itself is not something that should be abandoned.

Sectoral Planning

Planning according to sectors and sub-sectors, rather than simply the accumulation of investment projects and programmes, has been a feature of Indian planning since the Second Plan and has achieved a degree of sophistication since mid-sixties. Its main weakness has been the concentration on new investments rather than on related policies and the total outcome. In the social sectors particularly, this has meant that planning has concentrated on measurable inputs such as the number of schools, teachers, dispensaries, nurseries, and area coverage rather than educational quality or impact on health or nutrition. Investment planning capability has rightly been developed in the ministries and technical departments rather than within the Planning Commission whose role has been analytical and coordinating.

The largest planning organizations have been developed within the ministries dealing with the sub-sectors of industry. This began with the Development Wing of the Ministry of Commerce and Industry in the fifties, which was expanded to become the Directorate General of Technical Development. With the growth of the country's industrial base, separate specialist agencies have been established for investment planning and development of coal, oil, steel, ores, textiles, petrochemicals and electronics. Railways and telecommunications plan their machinery sectors independently. In some of these sub-sectors, the bulk of the productive capacity is in private hands, and overall planning relies on consultative bodies like the Development Council and working groups set up at the time of framing Five Year Plans. A weakness of the system of joint planning of industrial sub-sectors is that the ministries have inadequate knowledge of the investment intentions of the large industrial groups and the Planning Commission, unlike its counterpart in France, has hardly any contact with private industry.

Among the infrastructure sectors, railways, power, telecommunications and civil aviation have long established planning capabilities. The earlier tendency to overestimate demand by assuming unrealistically high growth rates for the economy as a whole have been substantially overcome and sophisticated projection frameworks have been developed. Planning in these sectors takes full account of the spatial distribution of investments. Sector-planning agencies have also developed adequate investment norms for aggregative planning and appreciate the need for phasing. These aspects of sectoral planning are carefully scrutinized by the Planning Commission. Some sectoral planning agencies have developed their own long-term planning models.

The Planning Commission is directly responsible for planning in areas, such as non-commercial energy or inter-modal choices in the transport sector which fall outside the purview of individual ministries.

The Ministries of Agriculture, Water Resources, Forests, Education and Health in the central government are organizations whose most important functions are nation-wide planning and coordination, since investments in these sectors are largely within the plans of state governments. An important issue, as we shall see, is the extent to which investment planning in these sectors can or should be decentralized to the state level and below. This problem is even more relevant in the case of the programmes devised in the seventies, and further elaborated since, for rural development and alleviation of poverty through specific schemes of income generation and the provision of basic needs. However, the point to be noted here is that these schemes indicate an increasing capability for detailed investment planning, part of which cuts across sectors. Planning capability has also been developed within the Indian system for science and technology, environmental impact analysis and the development of alternative energy sources.

Project Planning

When India's planning problems were considered at an international conference in Sussex in 1967, one of the main concerns voiced was that whereas the plans were well articulated at the macroeconomic level, the detailed preparation of investment projects and programmes was inadequate in many ways. Planning failures at this level were due to the absence of relevant data in some cases, insufficient technical and economic analysis and lack of impact evaluation (Streeten and Lipton, 1968). In the twenty years since, these deficiencies have largely been removed in such sectors as industry, power and transport. The ministries of the central government dealing with these sectors are now capable of project planning at an adequately sophisticated level. They are supported by the project-formulation capability developed in the various public sector corporations. Project formulation and appraisal, including the key problems of location, size, investment, timing and choice of technology, are carefully considered by the Project Appraisal Division of the Planning Commission and the government's Public Investment Board. Wrong decisions are still taken, as in the case of the Vishakhapatnam Steel Plant, but these are exceptions. In areas such as oil, fertilizer, telecommunications and power, the technological capacity of the public sector organizations undertaking major investments is no longer in doubt.

However, in sectors where investment decisions are more decentralized, the technical capacity for programme and project formulation still leaves something to be desired. In irrigation, crop production, forestry, nutrition, population control and the range of programmes aimed at creating employment through local development and conservation works, investment programmes may often still be inadequately designed and ineffective. This is partly because technologies in these areas are not always well established and often need to be matched with local conditions, but also because in these sectors the planning capacity has to be developed at the state government and lower levels throughout the length and breadth of the country.

Whereas in programmes of, say, social forestry or promotion of rural non-farm employment, the participation by intended beneficiaries is essential for effective project design, the gap between government functionaries at the village or block level and the rural population, and the constraints imposed by the social structure combine, resulting in poor performance. The effectiveness of these programmes is further reduced by uniformity of design imposed by planning from Delhi. Except in a few states, these disabilities have not been lessened by decentralized planning and implementation through panchayats or local bodies.

Policy Instruments

The most important tools of development planning after sectoral resource allocations and public investment programmes are the policy instruments directed towards attainment of specific plan objectives. The Indian experience with the more significant of these is reviewed here.

Fiscal Policy

The growth and composition of domestic savings, the extent to which these are available for financing public and private investment envisaged in the plans, and the ways in which savings are actually directed towards investment and their impact on production and distribution of incomes, are among the most crucial elements in implementing any development plan. The planners' role in this has been restricted to the quinquennial debates on finding a feasible level of resource mobilization to finance a particular plan. The year-to-year decisions on taxes, other public savings, government borrowing at home and abroad and deficit financing, and on the feasible level of aggregate public investment, have been the concern of the Finance Ministry and the state governments. When inflationary or balance of payments crises have supervened, as in 1963–65, 1973–75 and 1979–81, and in the interest of economic stabilisation public expenditure had to be curtailed, investment priorities were significantly revised by the Finance Ministry.

The central and state governments, in their efforts to garner tax and non-tax resources, have shown only moderate commitment to the fulfilment of targets laid down in successive plans. However, in the first thirty years of planning, tax revenues did rise from around 8 per cent of the GDP to 18 per cent of it. From the early seventies, the centre was able to tap the surpluses of nationalized banking and insurance systems directly, reducing the extent of reliance on tax receipts. Then in the eighties, the tax effort was significantly relaxed, narrowing the direct tax-base and lowering tax rates. The resource base for development has been steadily eroded with growing reliance on higher administered prices, and taxes on intermediate products, a rapidly rising level of government borrowing from commercial banks (leading to a domestic debt trap) and also unprecedented levels of budget deficits which the central bank is required to fund.

An important factor contributing to this outcome has been the absence of any medium-term fiscal planning. The forecast of resources incorporated in Five Year Plan documents have no operational significance; at best they are reviewed during a mid-term appraisal of plan performance. The annual budgetary process which determines the extent and manner of raising resources for public investment has no five year or other frame of reference. No forecasts of revenue yields or trends in current public expenditure on administration, security, maintenance of productive assets or the operation of social services are made; even debt servicing is not projected forward. In short, there is neither revenue nor expenditure planning by the centre or the states.[1]

The declining influence of planning on fiscal policy is also reflected in its approach to income distribution. In the early years of planning, efforts were made to structure taxes and fiscal incentives in a way that would reduce income inequalities. Even in the seventies, there was some discussion on the need for an income policy, though no effective action followed. These considerations have now simply disappeared from view and 'tax reforms' are directed towards producing incentives and export competitiveness and increased savings of upper income groups to the exclusion of distributional considerations.

Monetary and Credit Policies

From the outset, the planning system has been well equipped for the use of these policy instruments because it had, in the Reserve Bank of India, a strong central bank with jurisdiction over commercial banking, cooperative credit and long-term institutional credit, with an excellent backing of data and research capacity. The government's control over the utilization of credit by industry, agriculture and commerce was strengthened by the nationalization of the larger commercial banks in the early seventies, which was followed by a large expansion of the banking network in urban and semi-urban areas resulting in increased household savings in the form of bank deposits. On the whole, the Reserve Bank's use of selective credit controls and devices to regulate monetary expansion have been geared towards the achievement of plan objectives, subject to their inherent limitations. There are only two reservations. First, that the planners are not adequately associated with the making of monetary and credit policies by the Reserve Bank and the Finance Ministry. Second, as recent events have shown (and not only in India), monetary policy can be effective in supporting growth with stable prices only in combination with, and not as a substitute for, responsible fiscal policy.

The use of bank credit for speculative purposes in stock and commodity markets has been substantially curbed by extending the Reserve Bank's supervision of commercial banking loans through a system of credit authorization. From the mid-seventies, the nationalized banks have developed systems of functional credit allocations and area planning of credit which have been coordinated with the rural development programmes included in the Five Year Plans. Credit allocations are strengthened by a system of differential interest rates.

Pricing Policy

Plan documents have had little to say on prices beyond general observations about maintaining overall stability and planners have notably failed to articulate any pricing philosophy, but the pricing instrument has been widely used to attempt advancing various plan objectives. Administered prices may be resorted to for different purposes: to avoid exploitation by private monopolies; to determine appropriate prices for publicly produced goods and services when the government is the sole or dominant producer; to ensure supplies of essential goods to vulnerable sections of the population below market prices; to reduce commodity price fluctuations; and to serve as a brake on cumulative price increases under inflationary pressure. Over forty years of planning, India has relied on an extensive use of administered prices of industrial products, fuel, power, water and transport and on farm price supports. But price controls have been introduced piecemeal, abolished, reintroduced and modified at different times and not always with an adequate understanding of the aims to be achieved. The limitations of price control as an anti-inflationary instrument especially came to be recognized only slowly; in recent years administered prices have been adjusted with smaller time-lags in periods of inflation.

The Agricultural Prices Commission was established in the sixties, and then the statutory Tariff Commission was replaced by the Bureau of Industrial Costs and Prices as the agency for determining appropriate prices for industrial products. These bodies have established methods of cost analysis and principles of fair return on investment which provide a basis for flexible pricing policies. Weaknesses remain: the APC approach to agricultural prices does not deal adequately with relative pricing of competing crops; and BICP does not yet have the capacity to undertake comprehensive analyses of costs in the public sector on which a fully consistent public sector enterprise pricing policy can be based.

Power rates, railway fares and freights, port and telecommunication charges and air fares are important parts of the structure of administered prices which are not subject to regular external scrutiny. However, some improvements in rating systems have been introduced as a result of covenants relating to loans by the World Bank to these sectors. A notable case of the persistence of confused thinking in pricing policy relates to freight subsidies. These may be justified in the case of salt and kerosene supplies to remote areas, but not when applied to the equalization of steel prices all over India, leading to distorted industrial location and higher real costs for the economy.

Indian planning makes widespread use of discriminatory pricing: dual prices (cement and sugar), subsidies (food, fertilizer, power and water for farmers, urban transport, exports) and differential interest rates (agriculture, small producers, exports, backward regions). But the planners have not always established a clear rationale or an adequately researched basis for differentiation. And they have failed to attempt the targeting of subsidies to poverty groups or imposing differentiated user charges which would make for a more sustainable dual pricing system.

A part of the system of administered prices—controls under the Essential Commodities Act on the prices of salt, sugar, kerosene, drugs and many other consumer goods—actually dates from the

Second World War and was designed to deal with temporary shortages. According to public perception, these controls imply an obligation on the part of the government to supply goods of mass consumption to all people in adequate quantities at low prices, whatever the available supply or the general price level. Planners have done little to counter this misconception or the belief that prices of essential goods can be reduced by production or distribution through state-owned organizations.

India has, however, achieved a degree of success in commodity price stabilization. In the most important case—that of foodgrains—the buffer stocks and public distribution systems were designed to meet crisis conditions arising from monsoon failures and to ensure food supplies to vulnerable groups at low prices. The reduction of price fluctuations between and within seasons was a secondary purpose. These purposes have been largely achieved but at a very high cost because of the failure to discriminate between the poor and the non-poor as far as access to the public distribution system is concerned. Buffer stocks of raw jute, cotton and sugar have been established at various times but not always operated with adequate foresight or independent short-term commercial pressures. The continuous recourse to oilseed and vegetable oil imports in recent years to counter general inflationary pressure, however, is unsustainable as a policy instrument.

Industrial Policy

A plethora of instruments—physical controls, fiscal incentives and cooperative planning procedures—have been pressed into service to implement the industrialization programme. Apart from the public sector's leading role in plan implementation, these instruments comprise industrial licensing, controls on imports of capital, capital goods and inputs, allocation of foreign aid, licensing of technology imports, regulation of foreign-exchange transactions, capital issues control, legislation to limit concentration of economic power, and priorities imposed on long-term lending by the Industrial Development Bank and its subsidiaries.

This elaborate regulatory system was designed to direct private investment to conform to the detailed production structure and broad spatial distribution of industry envisaged by national planners at minimum cost in terms of deployment of capital. It has also been made to serve some subsidiary purposes such as phased indigenization of the production of intermediate products initially imported, reservation of certain markets for small-scale or household production of textiles and selected consumer goods, ensuring that new industrial units were at least of minimum economic size and encouraging the growth of small entrepreneurs.

The multiplicity of objectives makes the evaluation of the system as a whole quite difficult. Some major plan objectives have been achieved. Private investment, for most of the period under review, was channelled mainly into the desired directions, restricting to some extent the growth of production oriented exclusively towards affluent groups. Private sector output of cement, construction materials, industrial machinery, power and transport equipment, industrial intermediates and chemicals, drugs and pharmaceuticals was extended and diversified. The production of goods of mass consumption such as cheaper textiles, shoes and bicycles was encouraged and its growth was limited only by effective demand. New technology-oriented industries such as scientific instruments and professional electronics were established. Construction and engineering consultancy services were developed.

That certain costs were associated with the regulatory system is not disputed. Processes of clearance have sometimes been un-coordinated and time-consuming, the scope for corruption in government has increased and protection from both domestic competitors and imports has enabled relatively inefficient units to survive in many industries. The move towards 'liberalization' of instruments of industrial planning in the eighties has been aimed at increasing the flexibility of the licensing system, removing some disabilities imposed on the larger industrial groups, enlarging the area of competition and improving access of Indian manufacturers to imported inputs and technology. A concomitant of the liberal approach to industrial planning has been the perceptible shift of investment priorities in the consumer and intermediary goods sectors to automotive products, household durables, consumer electronics, and high value building accessories intended for the higher income groups (for a critique see Raj, 1986; Chakravarty, 1987).

Agrarian Policy

Abolition of landlords and intermediaries, recording and protection of the tenurial rights of small-holders, imposition of ceilings on landholdings and distribution of land held above ceilings to the rural landless have at least in theory, been among the most important tools for development planning in rural India. That only modest success has been achieved in the application of these policies must be attributed to the structure of power in the Indian state and society. State governments, other than those ruled by communist-led coalitions, have shown little enthusiasm for implementing tenurial reform or redistributive measures. Somewhat better progress has been made in the consolidation of scattered operational holdings and distribution of surplus lands held by governments to Harijans as homesteads. The sections on landlessness and rural poverty in recent plan documents are marked by an absence of any serious examination of these issues. The important issue of efficient and fair distribution of irrigation water has also hardly been considered except recently for new projects.

Labour and Employment Policies

These potentially valuable instruments of achieving development objectives have been used piecemeal and sometimes without forethought. Organized·industrial labour enjoys protection under legislation on rights of association, job security, safety conditions and compulsory insurance. It is able to protect wages against inflation although the trade union movement has been fragmented by union identification with narrow party and even factional interests. However, none of these rights and privileges have been extended to the self-employed or wage-labour in the large and growing urban informal sector; applicable minimum wage laws are not enforced; schemes of group insurance, disability relief and provident funds have not been attempted. Employment of two categories of labour has been partly protected, albeit at high cost. Workers in the handloom and household industry sectors have been protected by excluding organized industry from producing some types of goods, while those in inefficient or obsolescent textile and engineering units which have gone into bankruptcy, by nationalization of the units. These policies are being reviewed.

Policies for employment protection and enhancement are obviously more difficult to devise and implement in rural areas. Minimum wage legislation has existed for many years but the effectiveness of application varies from state to state. Its impact is felt the most in areas of high agricultural productivity or where it can be supported by government rural-work schemes.

Reservation Policy

An important tool of development policy forged in India is the earmarking of a proportion of jobs in the public sector and of educational facilities for especially deprived groups of the population such as the Scheduled Castes and Scheduled Tribes. This 'protective discrimination' has its critics and after forty years, opposition to its continuance is growing. A special threat to the system is the rising demand for extending the system of reservations to the middle-caste groups, the so-called 'Other Backward Classes'.

Federalism and Planning

The size and political structure of the country made it inevitable that the planning system would have to be designed to operate at least at two levels, namely, the central and state levels. If the constitutional division of functions had to be followed in allocating planning responsibilities, only broad indicative planning would have been feasible, since the exclusive responsibility of the centre was restricted only to small parts of the productive sectors of the economy, namely, mines and minerals, railways, ports and shipping, post and telecommunications and banking and insurance. The states' exclusive areas of responsibility cover many more sectors including agriculture, irrigation, and power and roads, besides health and education, urban development and all forms of social welfare. Under the Constitution industry was to be developed jointly between the centre and the states.

Immediately after Independence, even before the planning system was established, the centre took full control over the industrial sector by legislation as permitted by the Constitution, since it was agreed on all sides that industrialization would be at the heart of development and the necessary thrust could only be provided by the state operating through the central government.

Although (after some debate) the framers of the Constitution had placed planning on the concurrent list, as opposed to the central list, there was no dissension when, at the inception of planning, the system provided for comprehensive and detailed planning of all sectors of the economy by the Planning Commission, an agency of the central government. The National Development Council, chaired by the then prime minister and including the chief ministers of all the states and some central ministers, was designed as a forum for debate and developing a consensus rather than for exercizing any direct authority over the Planning Commission. The role of the states was envisaged as being implementing agencies for the national plan designed at the central level on behalf of the states.

The states' acceptance of the authority of the Planning Commission and their acquiescence in the investment priorities decided upon by the Commission and in executing programmes in the areas of the states' constitutional responsibility drawn up in detail by the central ministries were facilitated by a device that was not actually provided for in the Constitution. This was the system of loans and grants from the central government to the states to support plan outlays by the states. It was soon realized that the financial resources available to the states under the constitutional scheme of allocation of all tax sources were inadequate for financing major investment programmes in the sectors for which the states were responsible. Further, the centre had at its disposal not only the direct taxation of all income and the major commodity and trade taxes, but also controlled borrowing from the domestic market and abroad. As a result, the financing of successive Five Year Plans had to be mainly the responsibility of the central government.

Until the Third Plan, the central financing power was used in the form of scheme-by-scheme allocations to the states. This proved to be increasingly unworkable as well as contentious and was replaced by giving block loans and grants to the states. Allocation of financial resources to the states was determined by a formula which broadly followed the population criterion giving some weightage to relative backwardness in terms of availability of infrastructure and also taking account of the differing levels of average income in the states.

The sharing of financial resources between the centre and the states and between different states has thus come to be governed by two different systems of distribution. The Finance Commission, provided for by the Constitution, reviews the allocation of tax and non-tax resources every five years, but only from the point of view of the states' needs of additional transfers from the centre to meet their current expenditures. The Planning Commission makes independent allocations for each five year period to enable the states to finance their approved plans which are incorporated within the national Plan.

A lively source of controversy is the practice which grew after the system of block transfers of plan funds had been established, of the Planning Commission proposing new investment programmes to be included in the state plans but to be financed wholly or partly by additional assistance from the centre. These 'centrally sponsored schemes' include all activities in the field of population control, a number of programmes in the agriculture sector, the poverty allevi- ation programmes and certain innovative schemes such as those relating to low-cost rural health care and adult education. The increasing numbers of these schemes and the substantial outlays that they entail have raised the question whether such scheme-wise allocation of funds is essential for the maintenance of planning priorities. Going even further, the system begs the question whether this degree of uniformity in investment planning for agriculture and the social services across the country is either necessary or desirable.

Even with a division of planning responsibilities that left inter- sectoral priorities and major projects and programmes to be determined entirely by the Planning Commission, the need for adequate micro-planning capacity in the states was apparent quite early in the evolution of planning. The review of planning machinery by the Administrative Reforms Commission in 1967 emphasized the need to establish state-level Planning Boards. Even when these have been set up they have not been effective except in a few states. Project planning and programme formulation in the states continues to be undertaken by the line departments without any effective control or coordination, and the implementation of state plans is supervised by a senior official (the Development Commis- sioner). Implementation tends to be evaluated mainly in terms of the progress of expenditure against estimated outlays in annual and Five Year Plans.

During the seventies, some states have helped in the establish- ment of autonomous economic and social research institutes which have attempted to undertake analyses of the state's macroeconomy, empirical studies of agricultural productivity, poverty and employment, and urban development and industrial potential. This academic work has not, however, been integrated into state planning even in the more progressive states. Only some sectoral studies and programme evaluations have been entrusted to the Institutes.

The planning system as it has evolved so far is now facing a growing challenge, on account of three different, though possibly interrelated, reasons. First, the states—even those governed by the same party at the centre—are demanding more independence in economic decision making and larger unconditional transfers of resources to them from the centre. Second, the political dominance of a single party over the centre and most of the states has broken up and the states governed by non-Congress parties are more vocal in demanding a greater degree of autonomy in planning as in other fields (for a forceful statement of the states' discontent, see Hegde, 1988). Third, the consensus on development objectives, economic priorities and overall and sectoral policies, which has been sustained for nearly forty years of planning, is now showing signs of erosion. So far, the centralized planning system, the authority of the Planning Commission over the planning process and the allocation of plan resources have not been repudiated by any state. Dissatisfaction with the present system has been demonstrated by the adoption of major social welfare schemes, not approved by the Commission, by two southern states for funding outside the approved plan, by other states proposing to undertake power projects and industrial investments not accepted by the Commission, and through representations by almost all the states to the Ninth Finance Commission for curbing central government outlays in order to transfer more resources to the states.

The central government and Planning Commission now need to consider the following major issues:

1. To what extent can the planning system be decentralized to allow policies, programmes and specific investment decisions in certain sectors to be determined by the states?
2. What are the minimum requirements of national economic policy making which must be protected against devolution of authority to the states?

3. Are there any aspects of the present plan—for instance the emphasis on poverty alleviation programmes—which would suffer from decentralization of planning authority and would, therefore, need to be protected?
4. What are the areas where technology and economies of scale require investment decisions to be made centrally, even though the sector is constitutionally in the state's sphere of responsibility?
5. To what extent can transfer of funds from the centre to the states be delinked from the planning process generally and from specific projects and programmes in particular?

Below the State Level

From the very beginning plan documents have expressed concern for participation by the intended beneficiaries of planning in the process of plan formulation and implementation. The First Plan called for the revival of village panchayats and their involvement in the newly-established Community Development Programme and national extension service. The Second Plan proposed the concentration of rural planning effort at a higher level, namely the district, and indicated detailed guidelines for decentralized multi-level planning. Reviewing the position in 1957, the Balwantrai Mehta Committee noted that the least successful aspect of the local-level development programmes had been the inability to evoke genuine popular participation. It went on, however, to propose 'democratic decentralization' through an elective system of panchayats and panchayat samitis at the village and development block levels. The Third Plan proposed to assign responsibility for both preparation and implementation of rural development plans to the panchayat samitis.

Reviewing the developments twenty years later, the Asoka Mehta Committee in 1977 found that the institutions, after an initial spurt in the mid-sixties, had stagnated and declined. These institutions had not really been given any opportunity for planning or even executing programmes. In many states, panchayat elections were not held over long periods. The main programmes for agricultural development and poverty alleviation undertaken from the Fourth Plan onwards have not involved institutions even at the implementation stage.

As far back as 1969, the Planning Commission had issued comprehensive guidelines for district planning. The Commission's working group reported on the same subject in 1984 that there was hardly any decentralization of the planning process in any state and even administrative decentralization by way of implementing plan projects through district and block level agencies had made little progress. In states like Maharashtra and Gujarat where *zilla parishads* had been entrusted with some degree of investment planning in the sixties, the task had later been shifted to official Planning Boards.

When the Seventh Plan was being formulated, it was stated that decentralization of planning and full public participation in development would be among the plan's important features but as of today, district plans, where they exist, are no more than the aggregation of departmental schemes determined at the state level. Recently, the present government is understood to have instructed the Planning Commission that the Eighth Plan should be built up from below (presumably only for the rural development sectors) (for surveys on the history of decentralized planning see Kurien, 1987; Raj, 1988).

Ideas about what would constitute effective local-level economic planning remain ambiguous. District or block level development plans could be comprehensive area plans based on assessment of natural and human resources and prepared on the basis of state guidelines and indicated resource limitations; or they could be limited to locational decisions and restricted investment choices on the basis of detailed sectoral programmes laid down by the state; or they could, as now, simply be programmes of implementation, with a small allocation of free resources for local deployment. If the first of these alternatives were intended, it would have significant implications for the planning system as a whole, implying planning at three levels—central, state and local—with an iterative procedure to ensure consistency. It would mean greater flexibility in sectoral and subsectoral targeting of resources in the national plan. The extent to which investment priorities would be determined at the local and state levels would need to be decided, and possible conflicts between national policy objectives, and the states' perceptions of their own interests would need to be resolved.

The efforts that have been made to encourage public participation in planning and plan implementation have achieved little success, as the history of the Planning Commission's Public Cooperation Division shows. The Community Development programmes have proved unsuccessful in generating local investment efforts or freely contributed labour. Government-sponsored social service agencies like the Bharat Sevak Samaj have failed to take root. Ideas like creating a land army or organizations of the poor were bound to be wholly unrealistic under Indian conditions. Voluntary rural development and social service organizations established by the old Gandhian groups and some new social activists have achieved success in limited areas although government financial support to these agencies has proved to be a mixed blessing. It is clear that there are really only two choices: to continue relying on the delivery systems and agencies set up under the district and block level administrations, or to entrust these activities to elected local representatives at these levels.

The nature of decentralized planning would depend crucially on whether it is related simply to administrative decentralization—a further extension of the existing system—or to the devolution of decision-making to elective bodies at the district and possibly even lower levels. In West Bengal, significant devolutions have already been made to zila parishads and similar steps are being considered in Karnataka and Andhra Pradesh. However, there continue to be major reservations in the way of devolution of responsibilities for investment decisions and programme implementation at local levels. It is argued that socially and economically dominant groups would distort the distribution of agricultural inputs and access to services even more than is the case at present if rural development planning were left to elected local bodies. The contrary argument is that the subordinate or deprived groups would eventually be able to exert themselves under the elective system to get their fair share.

Present Status and Future Relevance of Planning

Forty years and where does the Indian planning system stand. The system of economic planning that was developed had reached a fair level of efficiency, at least from the seventies onwards, including capabilities for macroeconomic analysis, public investment programming and sectoral planning.

The system is not flexible enough to deal with sharp economic fluctuations when they arise but is able to adjust itself within a year or two after that. The network for economic planning with the Planning Commission at the centre is well established and coordinating procedures are adequate. Technical skills in planning, budgeting, coordination and plan implementation are not inconsiderable although policy analysis is sometimes weak and implementation delays persist.

If the aim of planning were simply to serve as an aid to economic decision making by providing a medium-term projection framework for budgetary decisions and the choice of public investments, ensuring reasonable balance between sectors and serving as a broad guide for directions of change in autonomous sectors of agriculture, private industry and trade, the Indian planning system could be considered well equipped for the purpose, needing only to shed some of its more regulatory features. The Planning Commission is also well equipped for its task of determining the distribution of surpluses of the central government to the states for their public investment programmes. Over the years planners have come to see these as their main purposes, so that most of their time is taken up with the preparation of Five Year Plans and annual capital budgets of the centre and the states, and the allocation of plan funds to the states. According to public perception too, this is what 'planning' has come to mean. Development planning, however, should mean much more than this.

A high point of the endeavour of development planning (as opposed to purely economic planning) was reached in the early sixties. Thereafter there was undoubtedly some confusion and a loss of direction. But to an extent, development planning was revived in the seventies, when planning objectives were redefined and the strategy of combining overall growth and diversification with a direct attack on poverty and unemployment was sought to be elaborated. In the eighties, however, there has been a steady decline in the commitment to development planning. The modernization of the industrial base and acceleration of the rate of growth of the economy are now seen as the primary objectives of planning, ideas of self-reliance and greater social and economic equality have disappeared from the view, and the outlays on schemes for poverty alleviation have come to be regarded simply as electoral necessities. The flagging interest in development is the basic cause of the decline in public savings, which has been especially pronounced in the period of the Seventh Plan. The planners have turned to search for development paths which would somehow require a lower rate of public investment.

The goals of development planning were conceived as the establishment of an economy capable of self-sustaining growth, and social transformation such as would ensure the end of poverty and rising living standards for all but with less unequal distribution of incomes and wealth. While recent plan documents continue to make ritual references to self-reliance and 'social justice', nothing in their policy or programme content bears on these objectives except the allocation of some resources to certain programmes for creating employment in rural areas, improving the incomes of small farmers and landless labourers and providing them access to safe drinking water, ruidmentary health care, etc. Relying on doubtful projections of a significant decline in the percentage of people below the poverty line, Indian policy makers now argue that the way ahead lies in increased duality, expanding the incomes of the middle and upper classes and expanding the production of the goods they would demand in order to achieve a higher growth rate, which they then assume will hasten the elimination of poverty.

Consistent with this outlook, the government has tended to play down the need for capital accumulation in the growth process. Implicit in recent policies on direct and indirect taxation, public salaries, and food and fertilizers subsidies is the view that the current consumption of the non-poor classes can be substantially increased since domestic-saving rates have already reached a high level. It is also assumed, with little public dissent, that the imperatives of national security justify the absorption of 5 per cent or more of the GDP on defence outlays.

Within the Indian system the Planning Commission may not fully accept the increased duality, the fall in tax yields, increased private and public consumption, or pre-emption for defence, but then they no longer have the status or authority enjoyed by their predecessors up to the mid-seventies. With the erosion of the resource base for public investment, even purely economic planning has now reached a point where fundamental conflicts cannot be resolved except by adopting one or the other of two policy stances.

One would be to take a limited view of planning possibilities, i.e., to accept that India should have only indicative planning. This would mean detailed planning of public investment in infrastructure, irrigation, agricultural support services and social services. A public sector of industry limited to existing enterprises (possibly with marginal privatization). Further, industrial growth would be left to the private sector with broad planning guidelines. This would reduce the need to transfer resources from the household sector to finance public investment. It would allow the structure of industrial production to conform to the existing distribution of incomes and free the planners from even a rhetorical commitment to greater equality. The alleviation of poverty would be recognized as only a subsidiary aim of planning, which is what it is in fact.

The other possibility would be to renew the quest for genuinely planned development with a commitment to early removal of poverty and the establishment of a more egalitarian society. This would require rebuilding the resource base for public investment, putting a restraint on the consumption of non-poor groups in our society-acceptance, in fact, of a degree of austerity and abandonment of any ambition for India to achieve the status of a regional power in South Asia. The reordering of investment priorities would involve greater selectivity in the industrial and infrastructure sectors in the process of being modernized. And it would mean a continuation of some direct controls over industrial investment despite the known costs of the system. It could well be that the overall growth rate of the industrial sector would be somewhat lowered under this option. Making a choice between these two approaches to development planning cannot be long delayed in the future.

Technical improvements in the planning system which could be considered are briefly listed here. In the general area of perspective planning, quantitative analysis needs to be directed to policy options rather than detailed sectoral and subsectoral projections over ten to fifteen years' horizons. Demographic issues, i.e., the impact of likely ranges of population growth on income, employment patterns, need for infrastructure and social services are a priority area. This analysis has to be regionally disaggregated. Comprehensive energy modelling and its impact on the environment could be valuable guides to future investment planning. Long-term water resources planning with appropriate models is a clear priority. Since the main medium-term planning models in use are not spatially disaggregated, a longer-term planning exercise in reducing regional imbalances is called for.

In the area of medium-term planning, the way forward would seem to be in formulating a number of policy models. It would be desirable to build these on the basis of 'SAMs' with functional groups and expenditure classes differentiated. Using these, the Indian economy could be simulated by computable applied GE models, with fairly aggregated sectors. These types of models could be used for fiscal planning, analysing the impact of alternative sectoral rates of growth, trade policy analysis and other policy options.

There is also need for better short-term economic forecasting models which can be used to improve annual plan and budget decisions.

The most important changes that will need to be made for a revitalized development planning system relate to greater autonomy for state level investment planning and effective decentralization of certain kinds of development activities below the state level, as have been indicated earlier. The appropriate division of sectoral planning between the centre and the states will have to be considered completely afresh, without trying to derive it from the distribution of functions in the three lists appended to the Constitution. Thus, a high degree of centralization in framing energy policy chosen between alternative sources and in the operation of electrical power generation and high voltage distribution are all justified even though power is in the state list. The location, size, phasing and choice of technology in the major sectors of industry have to remain a central responsibility. There needs to be a national water policy to guide the broad distribution of available water between agriculture, industry, power and urban consumption use, besides overall conservation. Similarly, a national forestry policy binding on the states is essential for environmental protection. But subject to these overall controls in the national interest, the area of state discretion in agriculture and industrial planning could be considerably wider.

Macroeconomic policies are generally within the purview of the central government. Pricing for both agriculture and industry needs to be also retained for central decision making. But it will be necessary for the centre to educate the states on the use and impact of these policy instruments so that the policies to be implemented are national rather than purely central. A broader inter-state council, with responsibilities that are at present entrusted to, but not exercised by, the National Development Council is the obvious instrument of national planning and consensus building (see Government of India, 1988).

Some weaknesses of sectoral planning will have to be remedied quickly. For instance, the water management side of both large and medium irrigation schemes should be improved by detailed planning which takes holding-sizes and actual and potential cropping areas into account and optimizes water use. The concepts used for watershed development and dryland farming would be given much greater relevance if applied to local soil and water conditions and topographical features through detailed planning. The production of oilseeds, pulses and coarse grains needs to be expanded, partly by technological developments and partly by adjusting relative prices. Effectively targeted nutrition projects and insurance schemes have to be devised for groups in the lowest decile of income. Schemes of population control should be restructured, taking note of recent motivational research and should be designed specifically for local areas rather than on an all-India basis.

For effective development planning, some improvements in the coverage, quality and timeliness of planning data are called for. Important gaps need to be filled in direct estimates of private investment in different sectors of industry and indicators of growth in housing and construction. Many coefficients used in the input/output tables require updating. There is need for greater coverage of social indicators, regionally disaggregated. Above all, the coverage of the National Sample Survey could be increased to yield usable results, first statewise, and then by subregions within states. The NSS could also be expanded to identify poverty groups, including the very poorest, by areas and demographic and functional characteristics for local planning of poverty amelioration schemes.

To conclude, the infirmities of Indian development planning have arisen less from the deficiencies in the planning system than from a diminishing national consensus on development goals and a decline in the commitment of governments at the centre and in the states to sustain the development process. It is possible that this could be reversed by a shift in the balance of political forces within the country. In that case, it should not be beyond the capacity of a future Planning Commission to build a new consensus on the basis of clearly defined development priorities to support a further effort spread over three or four plan periods to remove destitution

and malnutrition altogether while raising general living standards
at the same time and moving the economy towards self-sustaining
growth.

Note

1. The Long-Term Fiscal Policy issued by the Ministry of Finance in December
   1985 was an inadequate first attempt. It was weak on forecasting current
   expenditure and concentrated on assurances of stabilising taxes at lower levels.
   The exercise was abandoned after the first year.

References

Baum, Warren and Stokes Tolbert 1985. *Investing in Development: Lessons of
World Bank Experience.*
Chakravarty, S. 1987. *Development Planning: The Indian Experience*, New Delhi,
Oxford University Press.
Government of India 1952. *First Five Year Plan*, New Delhi, Planning Commission.
———— 1981. *A Technical Note on the Sixth Plan of India 1980–85.*
———— 1988. *Annual Report of the Planning Commission*, 1987–88.
Hegde, Ramkrishna 1988. *Planning and States Rights*, Bangalore, Government of
Karnataka.
Kurien, C.T. 1987. Development Planning: The Indian Experience, in P.R. Brah-
mananda and V.R. Panchamukhi (eds) *The Development Process of the Indian
Economy*, Bombay, Himalaya.
Paranjape, H.K. 1964. *The Planning Commission: A Descriptive Account*, New
Delhi, Indian Institute of Public Administration.
Raj, K.N. 1986. New Economic Policy.
———— et al. 1988. *Development Perspectives*, Delhi, Institute of Economic Growth.
Rudra, Ashok 1978. *The Basic Needs Concept and its Implementation in Indian
Development Planning*, Geneva, International Labour Office.
Streeten, Paul and Michael Lipton (eds) 1968. *The Crisis of Indian Planning.*
World Bank 1983. World Development Report, 1983, Washington DC, World
Bank.

4

Agriculture and Rural Development in the 1990s and Beyond: Redesigning Relations between the State and Institutions of Development

TUSHAAR SHAH

In the India on the threshold of the twenty-first century, orthodox economic planning is unlikely to prepare the nation to meet the challenge of rapid agricultural and rural employment growth, which it has failed to tackle so far. More is wrong with the Indian approach than just the planning of its resource generation and allocation. What India needs to do most is to focus, above everything else, on devising radical and innovative strategies that can yield and sustain 5–7 per cent annual growth rate in the value of output of the agricultural sector. Recent experience shows that in nations which have secured anywhere near such high growth rates, the state and its institutions of economic development have done more than just orthodox economic planning. This seemingly unachievable goal can be achieved, but only by reorienting the relationship between the state and the institutions of economic development—our legal framework, our markets and our economic organizations in the private, public, cooperative and informal sectors.

Parts I and II respectively review the Indian agricultural and rural development policy, and how it actually operates. Part III assesses the performance of the Indian state as a 'player' in the development process. In contrast, Part IV highlights the contribution of institutions of development as 'players'. Part V explores what all is involved in rolling back the present 'awkward' state and rolling forth the 'subtle' state.

I

Historical Underpinnings

Indian agricultural policy and planning in the post-Independence era can be divided into two segments: the pre-1965 and the post-1965 periods. During both these phases, our national outlook towards agricultural and rural development planning and policy was guided by different mindsets, ideological postures and world-views, as also of different assumptions about what works and what does not work in our particular context. In the first phase or the structuralist–institutionalist phase, the dominant goal was that of creating a modern, progressive and egalitarian rural society, a grand Nehruvian blend of Gandhian and Marxian visions. The instruments of policy devised therefore stressed land reforms, community development programmes, co-operative farming and so on. The second phase or the technology–investment phase emerged primarily out of the disillusionment with the structuralist–institutionalist approaches and a dire need to rapidly augment food production. It was also considerably spurred by the recent availability of high-yielding Mexican wheat and maize varieties as a godsend which, if nothing else, alleviated our apprehensions about the capacity to grow our own foodgrains.

Much has been achieved during this period. However, growth in rural population and unemployed labour force have kept pace with our achievements. Besides, the world around us has changed at a relentless pace. As a result, we are relatively worse off today on many counts than we were at the dawn of Independence. Moreover, forty-two years of experience of agricultural and rural development planning has fostered much national learning for us to reassess the limits of both structuralist–institutionalist as well as technology investment–led approaches. Using a broad-based approach, this paper suggests that the time is now ripe for a paradigm shift,[1] for us to undertake a fundamental re-examination of our past strategies and goals, and question our assumptions about cause-effect relationships. We need to focus much more on how we, as a nation, do things rather than on what we do. We argue that if India's rural economy has to keep up with the times (and of course, its growing population and rural labour force), we need to break out of both these approaches and pursue a different goal and a different strategy which are more in keeping with our new realities and new times.

Impressive Achievements?

During the last four decades, India's agriculture has grown. While during the fifty-five year period before Independence (1891–1946) the area under cultivation, average yield and total output of all crops grew at rates of 0.4 per cent, 0 per cent and 0.4 per cent respectively, during the 1949–50/1983–84 period covering thirty-five years, these quantities grew at rates of 6.8 per cent, 1.4 per cent and 2.6 per cent per year respectively. In case of food production, area yield and total output grew in the pre-Independence period at rates of 0.3 per cent, 0.2 per cent and 0.1 per cent, but in the post-Independence period, these grew at a rate of 0.7 per cent, 1.6 per cent and 2.6 per cent per year respectively (Rao and Deshpande, 1987). During the post-Independence period, the rate of growth of foodgrain yields rose from 1.5 per cent per year before 1964–65 to 1.8 per cent per year during 1967–68/1983–84 because of the rapid propagation of green revolution technology in north-western India. Total irrigation potential was expanded from 9.7 mha in 1950–51 to 30.5 mha in 1984–85 and nearly 50 mha by the close of the 1980s although the actual utilization of irrigation fell far short of the potential created. During the first thirty-five years of Independence, the area under high-yielding varieties shot up from less than 2 mha to 56 mha; the use of chemical fertilizers increased from just 0.1 mmt to 8.4 mmt; of pesticides from 2,400 mt to 50,000 mt. Food production has increased from 55 mmt in 1950–51 to 170 mmt in 1990; and, in keeping with the historical experience of other industrializing nations, the share of agriculture in GDP has suitably declined from 56 per cent in 1950–51 to 38.2 per cent in 1984–85.[2] Dairy production has increased rapidly from 17 mmt at the time of

Independence to 52 mmt in 1990. Thus, once heavily dependent on dairy imports, India became self-sufficient in dairying by the turn of the 1980s. Sugar production increased from 11.5 mmt to 110 mmt; and so did the output of the plantation industry. The production of tea increased from 27 mmt to 70 mmt; that of coffee from 2.5 mmt to 22 mmt up to 1989; and rubber from 1.4 mmt to 35.8 mmt. As for cash crops, cotton production went up from 3,044 m bales to 8,686 m bales; jute from 3,300 m bales to 6,625 m bales; and tobacco from 26.1 mmt to 49.1 mmt.

Many scholars laud these as impressive achievements; so they may appear, but only when compared to a handful of nations in the world which during the last five decades have performed worse than we have. Worse still, these achievements have just not been good enough when compared to the growth of our population. As a result, converted to per capita terms, many of these optimistic-looking, steeply rising output curves become flat when they do not actually stoop down. Mahalanobis, Nehru's economic wizard, had asserted the primacy of heavy industrialization and investment in a powerful capital goods sector as the route to high growth rate in agriculture, and consumer goods sector two decades later. Four decades have passed since then; and the rural economy has stayed the same, more or less.

The moot point is that all these achievements have done little to improve the condition of the large and growing mass of our rural poor, and much less to enhance their capacity in order to improve their lot in the long run. Indeed, when compared to what we need to achieve, what we have already achieved pales into insignificance. If the going continues to be what it has been like in the past, India will enter the twenty-first century a miserable nation with an army of 300 million half-clad, hungry rural unemployed and under-employed; a per capita rural income of no more than Rs. 900 per year; an average landholding of about 1.5 ha; a 55 per cent literacy rate; and little or no rural social infrastructure to speak of. Certainly not Prime Minister Rajiv Gandhi's idea of an India entering the twenty-first century.

Several things went wrong. Land reforms, on which much stress was laid during the first phase all but failed. In the 1960s, much euphoria was created when the government passed a special act of the Parliament to take away the power of the judiciary to slow down the implementation of ceiling laws; but the same government helplessly watched the administration and political elite making a mockery of the laws. The move from the sublime to the ridiculous took but a few years. Many social researchers of yesteryears who believed that structural change was the basic precondition to creating an egalitarian society were completely disillusioned by what followed. M.L. Dantwala, who had argued that 'a direct attack on (rural poverty) without an equally direct attack on the (socio-economic) structure which has bred poverty . . . is an illusion at best, fraud at worst . . .' wrote years later, 'Except Zamindari abolition and tenancy legislation (that too in only some states), on all-India scale land reforms have not been effective. This is particularly true of ceiling legislation' (Dantwala, 1987: 152).

The experience of land reforms has been an important lesson in the political economy of structural reform and the limits to efficacious state intervention in executing such reforms. Like in Japan and Korea, land reforms in India too would have perhaps worked if they had been enforced by some British McArthur in the late 1800s; but even if occasional lip-service is paid to them, it is unlikely that effective land reforms can be the part of any serious strategy of rural development in the India of the 1990s.

Anti-poverty programmes are essentially an act of penance performed by the Indian state begging remission from the nation's poor whom it had let down on structural reform. The 1970s and 1980s have witnessed the launching of several of these programmes—IRDP as a non-land asset transfer programme; Employment Guarantee Scheme (EGS), Rural Labour Employment Guarantee Programme (RLEGP) and National Rural Employment Programme (NREP) as wage employment programmes; (TRYSEM) as a skill-building and HRD type programme for artisans and unemployed youth and a number of other specialized programmes. Numerous studies and scholarly reports produced claims and counter-claims about the proportion by which all these programmes have raised the below poverty line (BPL) families above the poverty line.

At more informal levels, numerous stories of the 'stolen bore-wells', and of the 'circulating IRDP buffalo', of the devastating vetpatwari-bank officer-trader-beneficiary combine began doing the rounds in development folklore. By the mid-1980s, however, the nation came to a near consensus that only a tiny fraction of the resources earmarked for target groups actually reach them; Prime Minister Indira Gandhi conceded this, somewhat guardedly, as

early as 1984. Prime Minister Rajiv Gandhi conceded this categorically, owning up that no more than 15 per cent of the money
that his government had earmarked for anti-poverty programmes
had actually reached the poor.

Anti-Poverty or Pro-Rich Programmes?

Even if all their money reaches the poor, anti-poverty programmes
may not necessarily help the lot of the poor. Indeed, they may
actually worsen it, or at least that is what some researchers argued.
In a 1988 paper, Nilkantha Rath argued forcefully that IRDP just
cannot do 'garibi hatao'; he suggested instead, more of wage
employment programmes a la EGS (Rath, 1985). But reports of
massive corruption in EGS, RLEGP and even JRY began appear-
ing. Let alone doing good, detailed studies began to question
whether anti-poverty programmes are not in fact decisively pro-
rich. A few years ago, Professor Dantwala quoted the conclusion
of a simulation model thus: 'A spill over effect of a net injection of
one rupee to the rural bottom class would result in an overall
increase in income of Rs. 1.916 in rural areas, distributed in
Re. 0.213 to the bottom class, Re. 0.520 to the middle class and
Rs. 1.183 to the top class (apart from an income generation of
Re. 0.640 in the urban class)' (Dantwala, 1987).

And if anti-poverty programmes are just an act of expiation, it is
fruitless to expect them to resolve enduring problems of society;
India is not the only country which has tried anti-poverty programmes; many nations have. Even in other developing countries,
somewhat better administered than we are, evidence about anti-
poverty programmes is not very different. Through such programmes, it seems it is a lot easier to make income distribution
worse than to improve it. A study by Adleman and Robinson of
the Korean anti-poverty programmes concluded: 'Most anti-poverty
policies eventually help the rich and the middle income groups
more than they help the poor . . . (and this is true) even when the
rich are taxed progressively to finance the anti-poverty programmes
and there is no graft, corruption, diversion or stupidity in their
execution'.

Thus, all is certainly not well with our agricultural and rural
development policy; as a consequence, rather than becoming the
engine of economic growth, the Indian rural sector has become a

liability on the economy. As India struggles, over the coming decades, to pull itself up by the bootstraps, it is unlikely to find much success unless it succeeds in turning around its agriculture and rural economy. What all this would involve is a matter of much conjecture and analysis. But one thing is clear: even if well-administered anti-poverty programmes can provide succour to the poor, they cannot remove poverty.

Linear thinking and projections do not inspire hope for a bright future. It is unlikely that population growth rate will fall perceptibly below 2 per cent for quite some time; there are no technological breakthroughs on the horizon, nor do we see such élan vital in the agricultural research establishments. In the meanwhile, under inexorable pressure of rising rural population and workforce, the average holding size displayed a secular decline from 2.69 ha in 1960–61 to 1.82 in 1980–81 and even further to 1.5 ha in 1990–91. And counter-intuitively, crowding at the bottom of the landholding ladder rather than at the top has emerged as the major source of growing rural economic inequality. In the fiftieth annual conference of agricultural economists at Hisar, V.M. Dandekar asserted that the central problem we need to tackle in rural development is how to make a marginal farm into a viable economic unit. Significantly, study after study has pointed out strong and immediate inverse relationship between agricultural growth and rural poverty indices. Montek Ahluwalia's time series analysis of all-India data found such relationship in 1978; and a rerun of the same exercise on a larger data set by the author 10 years later confirmed it once again (Ahluwalia, 1978; 1986). Hanumantha Rao (1986) too found the same relationship. Using district-wise cross-section comparisons in Andhra Pradesh, Radhakrishna and Reddy (1985) too concluded that the proportion of BPL families fell as the pace of agricultural growth increased; and so did Mundle (1983) through an inter-state comparative analysis. This growing evidence seems to suggest not only that there may be no conflict between growth and equity, but as a matter of fact, rapid agricultural growth may be the only sustainable answer to the plight of India's rural poor.

What India's rural economy seems to need most is to break out of what the late Raja Krishna called the 'Hindu rate of growth' of 2.5 per cent per year. Above everything else, what we need is to gun for the real value of agricultural output to growth at 5–7 per cent per year for fifteen to twenty years, for only then would we have broken out of the 'poverty trap' by around 2000. With an employment elasticity with respect to the value of agricultural output of even 0.3 to 0.4 per cent, we will have cleared the backlog of the rural unemployed by the early years of the next century. Even then there is no hope for a decent livelihood for every Indian. However, even as crowding at the bottom continues, being a plain agricultural labourer or a marginal farmer in much of India will be half (or less) as bad as it has been in recent years. This kind of growth in the agricultural-rural economy cannot come from economic planning of the kind we have pursued so far. It can neither come from tinkering around with resource allocation nor from a sterile search for technological miracles. Rather, it can come only from a quantum jump in the way we as a society think and work.

II

Planning and Command Economy: 1950–90

The classical view of public policy assumes that public intervention[3] in economic affairs takes essentially three forms: taxes and subsidies, regulation, and public production. Besides revenue generation, taxes serve the important purpose of guiding incentives at different levels of economic structure; contrariwise, subsidies (negative taxes) stimulate economic activity that is considered socially or economically desirable. The state also intervenes through law and quasi-legal instruments, which are better at 'regulating' than at 'stimulating'. When the state cannot 'stimulate' economic activity to desirable levels in certain sectors either through the tax/subsidy approach or through the legal approach, it turns into an entrepreneur/economic player itself and undertakes 'public production' of that activity. In this view, planning would essentially involve planning of public investments and supportive incentive and regulatory structure.

The Indian state has extensively used numerous combinations of all these three categories of public intervention in economic activity. The state has assumed the role of an entrepreneur in establishing co-operative organizations; it has played the role of an entrepreneur–manager in creating organizations like the Food Corporation and the State Trading Corporation; it has undertaken public production of rural development services through myriad forms—organizations (like the District Rural Development Agencies), programmes (like the Jawahar Rozgar Yojana or JRY), and campaigns (such as the various technology missions and literacy campaigns). A major input in all these interventions had been investment of resources. However, by no means have resources been the decisive input in determining the success or failure of these interventions.

The failure of the Indian agricultural and rural development policy is to be explained not so much by inadequate or malallocated investment as by the indifferent performance of the state in devising and deploying all these three sets of instruments of public intervention in a way that would achieve overall goals of policy. There are four common drawbacks which characterize this institutional failure in all state interventions:

1. goal confusion—most interventions end up trying to achieve more than one, and often conflicting goals;
2. mistargeting—most fully or partly miss their target groups or objects;
3. redundancy—most tend to survive long after they stop serving their original purpose. We have singularly failed in devising an 'exit procedure' for interventions/organizations no longer relevant to their original goals; and finally,
4. negative loops—most end up in the centre of a new political economy that gets created as the consequence of their implementation with deeply entrenched pressure groups and vested interests (the 10 per cent-wallahs, as these have come to be popularly known).

These are not peculiar to India. Indeed, these are general features of state intervention in economic sphere in modern economic development everywhere (see, e.g., Lipton 1991). What is peculiar to India is that we have failed to recognize and manage these drawbacks as effectively as some other nations have (often by abolishing such interventions). Often there are, within India or in countries with comparable conditions, superior and more efficient examples of achieving the same goals for which state intervention was planned in the first place. As a nation we have tended to learn little from these, much less to make mid-course corrections on the basis of such new learning.

Subsidies

Subsidies have been extensively used in the Indian agricultural–rural economy as a means to guide incentives and as means to effect direct or indirect resource transfer to weaker sections. Fertilizer subsidies are an example of the first, food subsidies exemplify indirect resource transfer, and the Million-Well Scheme illustrates attempts at direct resource transfer to poor. There is much formal research and investigation on the effectiveness of subsidies in the Indian agricultural–rural development field. The Dagli Committee Report (1967) on controls and subsidies highlighted the general evils that are engendered by subsidies and non-market controls. Minhas's recent analysis (1991) of the public distribution system (PDS) is a good example of the mistargeting of food subsidies; Rajagopalan (1982) showed long ago that 44–60 per cent of the subsidized sugar leaks out of the PDS into the open trade. Phansalkar (1990) has explored very recently how the subsidized sale of edible oils through PDS is diverted by trade for adulteration and how the rents so generated lubricate Gujarat's political machine. Gulati's analysis (1990) shows how hidden subsidies allow Punjab to be nation's largest rice growing state although it makes no economic sense to do so. Most recently, the chairman of the Commission on Agricultural Costs and Prices has strongly argued for reducing the 'retention price' of fertilizer. He has convincingly shown that in the name of subsidies to farmers, it is the fertilizer companies which walk away with the 'cream' by overpricing their plants and equipment and stashing away hundreds of crores.

The broad conclusion of this corpus of research is that subsidies always tend to outlive their utility, seldom fully reach their target groups, and are almost always used as instruments of patronage. Each new subsidy springs to action a new class of 'rent seekers'—the 'per cent-wallahs'—who earn their living not by productive activity but as specialists in mastering the procedures and cultivating the 'contracts' needed to secure their 'cut' in subsidies. Finally and most importantly, subsidies interfere with the normal processes of development even when they are diligently planned. This is most evident in biogas programmes. A 1988 study by IRMA of biogas programmes implemented by NGOs suggested that cash surplus available from biogas subsidy was often the prime beneficiary goal in installing a biogas plant. Very often, the plant was not even meant for use; and therefore, naturally, the digester was never filled.

Regulation

The state regulates actions of private organizations and individuals through a legal framework consisting of laws, quasi-legal instruments and GRs. The legal framework is the foundation of modern civilized society. However, if this framework is not adaptable to the needs of a modernizing society, it can stifle development. Laws are the primary instrument that the state uses to operationalize ideology; the legal framework of a society at a given point in history therefore provides a strong indication about how sensitively the state is able to adapt the vision of the society that it wants to create to its understanding of how laws actually influence the course societies take. Thus the Nehruvian socialist state enacted MRTP as an instrument to contain excessive concentration of wealth and economic power; it enacted the Industrial Policy Resolution of 1956 to place state at the commanding heights of the economy; it enacted land reforms acts to restructure property rights. That the land reforms acts remained on paper and that the other two laws were very nearly scrapped by the present government is an indication that the Indian state was not adept at judging how laws could affect people, institutions and society. Worse, it took very long to learn and to devise better instruments.

The Co-operative Societies Act is a classic example of how a legal framework can stall the growth of a whole movement for four decades. In the apparent fear that an independent, member-controlled co-operative movement would be prone to sabotage by local vested interests, the law has perpetuated the hegemony of the government and the bureaucracy over co-operatives. Our present Co-operative Act, enacted in 1904, is a colonial act reflecting the natural propensity of the alien ruler to control native institutions, and hence provides enormous powers to the registrar of co-operatives. In recent decades, rather than protecting co-operatives from petty, sectional interests, in numerous instances the law has been unabashedly used by politicians and petty bureaucrats to stifle their growth by superseding their boards and suspending elections to their boards for decades. In Tamil Nadu, elections to co-operatives were not held for fifteen years; and in Andhra Pradesh, for ten years.

The prevailing legal framework formulates the immediate legal environment within which people and institutions operate. A farmer plants and protects trees if the law upholds his right to be its owner—which would include the right to use, cut, sell, transfer, lend, gift or do whatever he wants with his tree. When laws curtail private property rights even partially, they hit incentives in economic activities. Worse, when laws/regulations are made without appreciating the dynamics of implementing them on the ground, they create a complex maze of criss-crossing impacts—the strong and the smart turn the new regulation to their maximum advantage; the weak and the conscientious end up as suckers. In this context, the destructive power of GRs has been extensively studied in recent times in the context of natural resources. Several scholars including Saxena (1990), Shah (1986), Singh (1988), and Chambers et al. (1990), have highlighted how numerous restrictions on harvesting, transporting and marketing of privately owned trees induce rent seeking by petty forest officials, depress incentives in tree cultivation and protection, and hit forest-based tribal economies in many states including Orissa, West Bengal, Maharashtra and Gujarat.

When laws fail to curb economic activity of the forbidden class, they result in a parallel economy operating on its own devious logic. Shah (1991) has documented such phenomena in the case of citing and licensing restrictions for installing wells. In this case, since direct implementation is impossible, the electricity board and financial institutions enforce the norms before granting power connection and loan respectively. The norms do not affect the resourceful rich, who use diesel pumps and are able to self-finance their investment, or who can get both power connections—loan as well as subsidy—by making what economists euphemistically call 'side payments'. As with subsidies, here too tight a linkage between instruments and targets is not possible, and therefore numerous regulations produce unpredictable impacts which typically hit economic activity as well as poor people.

Direct Action

A recent analysis by Liberman and Ahluwalia (1990) of the state's direct intervention in markets has confirmed the conclusion of several other such earlier studies. Through such direct intervention, the society buys an indifferent social outcome at prohibitive social price. The instruments the state creates to intervene in the markets end up, in less than a decade, as monolithic, inefficient, self-serving white elephants. The Food Corporation of India is but one example. Created in 1957 in response to the recommendation by the Ashok Mehta Committee, the FCI grew into a colossus employing nearly 80,000 workers. In its chequered history, the FCI was never viable, its staggering losses cumulating to several hundred crores during the 1958–89 period. Directionless and without a long-term strategy, the FCI became a den of corruption and inefficiency. With strong labour unions, the operating costs shot up to unheard levels. To cite an example, the FCI's average loading cost is Rs.200/mt compared to Rs.25 for private grain handlers; its storage losses have averaged to 3 per cent as compared to 0.5 per cent for private handlers; its grain losses due to moisture alone are what private handlers tolerate under all categories. Organizations like the FCI are beyond redemption; they are difficult to manage and impossible to turn around.

Providing support prices to farmers and building a food-grain bufferstock is an important task for the nation. But FCI may well be paying too high a price for achieving such a task particularly since recent times have witnessed several new institutional innovations in market intervention in which the state plays a supportive role but autonomous network/organizations enforce market interventions. Two examples of such interventions are mentioned later. Both are strikingly different from state intervention in foodgrains; both are more efficient in economic terms and more effective in achieving their goals; both are more professionally executed; and finally, both have produced dramatically improved producer incentives. Above all, neither has needed a monolith like the FCI.

III

The State as Player

Americans use the term 'smart' for someone who appears idealistic and sensitive but is also pragmatic and practical. In American slang, the Indian bureaucracy, politicians, rent seekers and organized labour have been very 'smart'; while talking constantly of the poor and their development, they have never lost sight of which side of the bread is buttered. But the Indian state—and, of course, its poor—have been far from 'smart'. If the Indian state had been 'smart' and had sincerely desired to serve the larger interests of its people, it would have played its cards better. But as a player in the field of development, rather than going about its business in a brisk and business-like manner, the Indian state has continually got detracted by scholarly discourses of socialism here and of free market there. In the process, it has got its priorities all mixed up and ended up doing bad jobs of what it ought not to have done in the first place. We identified four roles that the Indian state has consistently mal-performed; the first two, it could have largely done without, but not the other two, where the state as a player will have to do better.

Throughout this paper, we have used the term 'monitor' to denote the governance structure of any human system.[4] In all organized human activity apart from professional and technical staff, there is always need for a 'monitor', whose primary task is to ensure that the organization functions in keeping with its goals. In broader terms, the role of the 'monitor' is to establish and maintain consonance between the interests of those with direct stake in the performance of the organization and the actions of the managers/administrators of the organization. In classical business corporations, this role was played by a board elected by shareholders who are its owners; in a co-operative, it is played by a board of directors elected by members who are the owners as well as users of the services of the co-operative. This is so presumably because a corporation and a co-operative exist to serve well-defined groups of people who own them and who therefore have a more enduring and direct interest in ensuring that professionals manage them in long-term interests of their owners.

The sterling principle was violated with great success by the American corporations, which by the 1950s had established the practice of separation between ownership and control. It succeeded, among other things, because the constant threat of decline in the market value of the share—the key index of a management team's performance—was control enough on the managers to perform; there was also constant threat of takeover bids, which kept corporate managers on their toes. Be that as it may, the success of managerial capitalism reduced owners of business corporations to mere suppliers of capital entitled to moderately rising market value of the share. It also extruded them from the governance structure of the corporation—its board of directors, which increasingly became a dummy of the professional manager. The success of the corporation established the practice as a principle that left to themselves, professionals and civil servants will manage organizations in the best interests of their owners and stakeholders. The role of the 'monitor' was merged with that of the 'manager' and was entrusted to the hired professional. This was a complete reversal of the classical owner–manager stereotype in which the owner, the biggest stakeholder, sank along with the organization if he failed as a manager.

The success of managerial capitalism did incalculable damage to our understanding of how human organizations are governed best. Luckily, however, this success lasted for less than fifty years. The onset of the 1980s witnessed the rise of the Japanese competition which has beaten the American corporation hollow. Moreover, increasing takeovers of corporations by Lead Bank Organizations (LBOs) and pension funds have created fundamental crises in America's industrial capitalism; and uppermost in the agenda of business leaders and researchers in the US during the 1990s is how to get owner control back into its corporations, many of which have become huge, flabby, bureauctratic and self-serving organizations, unable to compete in the market place. *Harvard Business Review*, the most prestigious of American business journals, recently led an open debate on owner control in corporations as the major vehicle to restoring America's competitive edge.[5] The sterling principle—that a human system is best governed by those who have greatest stake in its performance—is back in circulation.

Unwittingly, the command economy back home has negated this principle ab initio. This has meant that regardless of whether it is a co-operative of farmers or a canal authority created to serve the needs of irrigators or a DRDA created to 'deliver' development to poor, or an electricity board, the state plays 'monitor' to the organizations it creates; and in this capacity, the state is represented either by a politician or a civil servant who neither represents (potential) owners, not users, nor the principal stakeholders of these organizations. Happily enough, there is also no market valuation of these enterprises so that there is neither market control nor any obligation to provide information (except that provided by managers) that can enable the society to learn about the performance of these organizations. Separation of stakeholding/ ownership and control is complete right from the beginning.

It is no surprise therefore that most of these organizations are born flabby, bureaucratic, self-serving organizations. How well the crucial 'monitor' role is performed is determined not so much by personal stake (and the motivation that only personal stake can foster), but by how conscientious the ruling politician/bureaucrat happens to be towards his job, and how long he is given before he is transferred to some other job. The result has been there for us to see: in the low plant load factors, high transmission and distribution losses and the pathetic balance sheets of our state electricity boards; in long delays and cost overruns, low irrigation intensities, large shortfalls in actual versus design commands of canal irrigation projects; in our fraudulent rural development programmes and our moribund agricultural co-operative system—all of which have the state as the 'monitor'. It is evident in the miserable performance of numerous organizations to which the state plays monitor or worse, monitor-cum-manager: National Seeds Corporation, State Farms Corporation of India, State Trading Corporation, Cotton Corporation, Jute Corporation, Central Seeds Certification Board, Hindustan Vegetable Oil Development Board, National Horticulture Board, and so on.

Two points are being made: first, the state's primary job is to be 'monitor' to the nation or region. However, when the state assumes the role of 'monitor' to a co-operative or a business organization, it in effect transfers this crucial function to someone who is neither accountable to the owners nor the principal stakeholders of that business but to someone/agency who often has even less stake in the business. Second, as a result, there is no way those affected by good or bad performance of the organization can influence/improve its management.

In its role as 'monitor', the indifferent performance of the state results from the structural difficulty in linking performance demand system with governance structure of state-operated organizations. But besides being the 'monitor', the state is also usually the manager in many such organizations; in DRDAs, the state plays the role of rural development manager but is not accountable for its performance to the poor people for whom it is created to deliver the wherewithal for development; in canal irrigation authorities, it plays irrigation manager, but the executive engineer in charge of a system is not accountable to the farmers, who are the principal users of the irrigation service; again, in the agricultural research system, the state plays research manager but is not able to make the research system directly accountable to farmers, the ultimate users of the output of their effort.

Problems of stake are also acute here, be it the executive engineer in charge of a canal project or a DRDA director. When an IAS officer is the top manager, there are additional problems: his planning horizon seldom exceeds two years (six months or less is more common). For most IAS officers, postings to DRDAs, CADAs, co-operatives and tribal development corporations are opportunities for 'cooling their heels' before they proceed to more meaty postings. Even as they absent-mindedly help a few poor here and uplift a few tribals there, the eye is constantly on a probable posting in finance and economic ministries, and if possible, in Delhi. If this is not possible, State Industries Corporation or even the Electricity Board would do, thank you. Search for such preferred postings can take substantial effort and frequent visits to the state capital. In any case, since CRs are not written by tribals or poor people, it is easy to take it easy.

In the arena of development policy, the important contribution needed from the state is in terms of creating a congenial, stable, long-term macro-policy environment within which institutions of development can emerge and operate. This would include stable long-term economic policies based primarily on economic logic and devoid of chauvinism of any kind; it would include the state projecting itself as the protector of certain basic and inalienable values and of institutions; finally, it would include stability and predictability in the legal framework of society. In the case of the last, we include not only the laws of the land but also the credibility of the legal system and the effectiveness with which laws actually deter citizens from the actions they bar. Repeated failure to enforce legal provisions impairs this effectiveness of the legal system; and to that extent, the rule of law gives way to the rule of the jungle. In this respect, Gunnar Myrdal considered India to be a 'soft' state; we legislate far more than we enforce. Land reforms and their tardy implementation, which we discussed earlier, is an example of this argument.

The most important role of the state is as protector of institutions of development; when it fails in this regard, the impact on the institutional fabric is incalculable even when not apparent. The

Indian state is notorious in devouring the nation's institutions of economic development often for paltry and short-lived political gains. Two examples will suffice to make the point. Tamil Nadu and Andhra Pradesh had among the more vibrant rural co-operative movements in the country. Indeed, Tamil Nadu was a pioneer in dairy co-operatives as also in weavers' co-operative movements. An important role of the state vis-à-vis co-operative movements is to protect the spirit of democratic governance, which is the hallmark of co-operatives. The state failed to perform its role as protector of these democratic local institutions. In both these states, throughout the 1970s and the 1980s, the ruling state governments used our archaic co-operative act as a political weapon and suspended elections in co-operatives as well as panchayats. Compared to the political capital it created for the ruling parties, the long-term damage it imposed over the institutional fabric of these two states is enormous and can be gauged only by comparing their co-operatives 'with those in states like Gujarat and Maharashtra, where the ruling elite, howsoever different in their political outlook, protected the state's local democratic institutions.

The second instance of the state delivering a lethal blow to an institution of development is the loan-waiver decision of the government of Prime Minister V.P. Singh. Today, nearly two years after that decision was taken, it is clear that co-operatives will find it impossible to recover even those loans that were not waived; that the recovery percentage of many well functioning PACS, LAMPS and FSSs has tumbled from 60 per cent plus to less than 5 per cent; that in Maharashtra and elsewhere, co-operatives themselves have denounced and opposed the measure; that the principal beneficiaries of loan waiver, once again, are the well-off borrowers at whom it was not targeted; and that the only way hundreds of thousands of our PACS, LAMPS and FSSs can continue to function as economic entities is by permanently severing their credit operations which would otherwise make them completely unviable; and that at one stroke, this measure has destroyed the credibility of the entire rural credit system which it will take decades to rebuild.

The Constitution of India guarantees certain fundamental rights to all the citizens of India. The Preamble to the Constitution also sets out the vision of the society that our leaders wanted to create.

One of the principal functions of the state is to protect the rights of individual vis-à-vis the society; at the same time, it is also the task of the state to protect the right of the totality of the Indian people against individuals or groups. It is often said that law is an ass; whoever finds the stick to beat it with, enslaves law and makes it serve his purpose. As individuals, we often come across cases of poor people, tribals, women and children who are not able to secure the stick and therefore suffer at the hands of law. Trade unions, consumer associations, producer organizations, etc., are institutional devices, which inter alia, strive to make the law work for their respective patrons.

The totality of a nation's citizenry—and its unborn future generations—is often as weak as a child or a tribal in getting the law to protect its rights. Mancur Olson's thesis applies with maximum force when it comes to the totality of a society protecting its rights against individuals or powerful pressure groups.[6] Since the protection of the rights of the totality is a public good, it would always be in under supply; therefore, the totality will always be exploited by resourceful pressure groups unless the state judiciously strikes a balance between the rights of the totality versus the rights of individuals and pressure groups. In actuality, the Indian state has ended up protecting the rights of sections that are articulate and/or politically active; these include labour unions in organized sectors, kulak organizations such as the *kisan sabha*, and vocal urban consumers. Indeed, some of these organizations have become so powerful that they have begun to affect the performance of institutions of economic development.

The increasing conflict between organized labour and productivity and efficiency gains in the organized sector is a direct consequence of this hiatus. There is no need to belabour the point that one of the principal beneficiaries of post-Independence Indian economic development has been the organized labour. There has been mounting evidence that the contribution of organized labour to nation building has not been commensurate with the increasing share of the national cake that they have usurped for themselves. In many large organizations, particularly in the public sector, the prevailing labour environment—dominated as it is by the power of the unions and the labour laws—is getting increasingly inconducive to rapid productivity increases, efficiency gains and performance improvements. Occasional and feeble outbursts by consumer organizations pose very little challenge to some of the well established bureaucracies in public sector organizations. Leave alone goal achievement, it has become impossible to maintain a rudimentary sense of discipline in many of these organizations. While it is nobody's case that the rights of labour should not be protected, the Indian state has far greater responsibility towards the several hundred million of unorganized rural labour and, of course, the unemployed than the powerful tiny minority of organized sector employees. The point is that a state whose primary concern is to nurture and strengthen institutions of economic development cannot afford to allow the balance to be so tilted in favour of organized labour that it can eat into the vitals of its institutions and the economy.

IV

Institutions as Engines of Development

The most devastating impact of the Indian state intervention in rural economy has been on our national mindset; it has bred a powerful, unerasable 'sarkar mai-baap syndrome' pervading the entire development scene. When a social researcher interviews a rural citizen—landless, large farmer, artisan, teacher, nurse—about any problem, be it personal, organizational, social, political or professional, the dialogue will continue until it concludes with something that the 'sarkar' should do. Regrettably, often the researchers also end up writing only what sarkar should or should not do; even more regrettably, through the length and breadth of its vast presence, the sarkar functionaries too have begun to believe in this self-fulfilling prophecy. At the policy-planning level, this syndrome has reinforced the notion of the state as the sole generator of developmental impulse and led decision makers to ignore or understress the powerful role institutions can and do fill as development players. The creation and sustenance of new economic organizations, particularly of farmers, put into operation powerful engines of local economic growth. The skill and sensitivity with which the state interacts with these in their formative stages has an indelible impact on the patterns of their life cycle.

Energizing a Local Economy

The history of Indian development is replete with examples of new organizational structures having produced powerful growth stimuli. We begin with the example of the dairy co-operatives of Gujarat which started with the Kaira Co-operative in late 1940s and spread to other districts in central and north Gujarat. Much has been written about the economic impacts of these co-operatives and the fact that because of the institutional structure for procurement, processing and marketing, and for production enhancement and technical change that they provided, Gujarat's GDP from dairying has consistently increased at a rate of above 8 per cent, and in several spells, of well above 10 per cent over the last two decades. The direct annual capital investment made by the state and para-statals in these co-operatives has been less than 1 per cent of the value of annual milk output of co-operative members, although the members themselves and their primary co-operatives have been systematically investing in cross-breeding and other technologies of production enhancement. In Gujarat's GDP of approximately Rs. 10,000 crore, dairying accounts for some Rs. 1,200 crore, supporting livelihoods of some 2.5 million of Gujarat's rural households.

In many other regions better endowed for dairy development than central Gujarat, dairying as an economy has lagged throughout the 1960s and 70s and continues to do so. As prime minister, Lal Bahadur Shastri tried hard to figure out why dairying was not doing as well in western UP as it was in Kheda. A major explanation was that milk producers of western Uttar Pradesh did not have the institution of economic development that the farmers of Kheda had built for themselves. Alternatively, the state in Gujarat was wise and foresighted enough to support, nurture and enable a young Amul with milk producers themselves as its monitor. The state in Uttar Pradesh was less subtle and assumed itself the role of the manager as well as the monitor, and refused to learn ever since. Much as Shastri tried to create Anands in Uttar Pradesh, his home state and many other states could not create institutions of dairy development with the same élan vital as Gujarat's dairy co-operatives had. And a thousand crore worth of state investment cannot do for dairying in those states that a few tens of crores did in Gujarat through the dairy co-operatives.

Similar is the case of the role played by sugar co-operatives in the evolving economies of south Gujarat and Maharastra. In 1990, south Gujarat's twelve sugar co-operatives paid over Rs.250 crore to their members as payments for cane, employed over 5,000 workers in cane crushing and over 25,000 more in cane harvesting. The cane yield in the area has grown at a rate of 6 per cent since 1975, when cane cultivation began in a big way; rapid technological changes—in the form of new varieties, cultivation practices, new inputs, etc.—have been ushered in by the co-operatives, which are their fountainhead. Over a short period of fifteen years, an otherwise modest looking economy based on inferior cereals, vegetables and cotton has been transformed into a booming economy based on sugarcane. The sugar co-operatives have served as the engines of this growth, and their tremendous economic significance in the local economy is signified by the skyrocketing prices of the right to supply cane to them, which range between Rs. 10,000 to Rs. 1,25,000 (Rajagopalan and Shah, 1991).

The dairy and sugar co-operatives of Gujarat and Maharashtra are exceptions that prove the rule that the power of co-operatives as engines of economic growth varies inversely with the extent to which the state treats them as instruments of statecraft. Many theories have been propounded to explain why co-operatives have succeeded only in these two states; there may be elements of truth in each of these. However, the principal factor that explains the poor performance of co-operatives in many other regions is the oppressive and overbearing influence of the state.

In managing a developing agricultural economy, commodity and input markets play an important role. When the capacity of markets to provide suitable price signals to producers and consumers and to clear the demand and supply on a periodic basis gets impaired due to imperfections, a modicum of market regulation becomes an important precondition for productivity growth and technological change. The problem is that regulating the market is a fine art which can be performed with specialized skills and resources far more easily and effectively than with brute force of the state. This we learnt the hard way by taking over the wholesale trade in grain, and then by quickly retracing; by creating monoliths like the Food Corporation of India and the STC; and through the experience of the Agricultural Prices Commission whose support prices for most commodities other than foodgrains are seldom higher than the minimum level that open market prices ever hit.

What most of our past state effort at market regulation failed to recognize is the simple fact that the intervening agency must alter the expectations of millions of independent private traders. In order to do this, the intervening agency needs to have moderate resources, skill and credibility amongst the traders. What the state often attempts to do using its coercive power and resources, some institutions of economic development achieve with far less effort. We illustrate this with two recent examples.

In 1979, when the Government of India asked the National Dairy Development Board (NDDB) to work out a programme on co-operative modernization of the Indian oilseeds sector, the Dairy Board realized that the major obstacle in this task is the highly unstable, volatile and speculative character of the edible oil market. At the end of a detailed exercise, the NDDB concluded in 1979 that any agency which controls 15 per cent of the total edible oil supplies in the country can, through limited but skilfully executed open market operations contain the market prices of edible oils within carefully computed, pre-specified upper and lower limits.

Ten years later, the Government of India asked the NDDB to launch their Market Intervention Operation with limited commitment of financial and commodity support. The NDDB initiated two steps: they launched 'Dhara', a national brand of consumer-packed oil, which in its maiden year became a runaway hit and one of India's greatest consumer marketing successes in modern times. The second, the NDDB launched open market operations involving the newly created oilseeds growers' co-operatives in the procurement and processing operations. During 1989–90, the price band given by the government to the NDDB was Rs. 20,000–28,000/mt; not once did the market price in Bombay move out of the price band.

There were several lessons. First, while the government provided much moral support, it went back on most promises of financial and commodity support. Second, contrary to its earlier analysis, the NDDB concluded that it needed not 15 per cent, but less than 5 per cent of the market share to regulate the prices in most years.

Third, for launching Dhara as well as for its open market operations, the NDDB added less than ten men to its staff. Finally, the
government could hardly have done what the NDDB did and with
the flair it did it, for no civil servant would have had the heart to
take the risks it entailed. At the same time, the NDDB would not
have been able to do what it did if it had not commanded complete
support of the Government of India.

Similar is the case of the National Egg Co-ordination Committee
(NECC) established in 1982 as a loose organization of poultry
producers. The NECC's charter is to provide market information
and to undertake price support to poultry producers of India. With
a staff of less than sixty professionals, the NECC has done this
without having to undertake any open market operations. All it
does is to collect daily market prices through its three-tier structure
from various markets and to stipulate on a daily basis a support
price for each of its eighteen zones; since 1982, rarely has an egg
got sold by a poultry producer below the NECC declared price. In
1990, the NECC declared its own 'home-made' Market Intervention
Operation (MIO) to maintain the egg price above Rs.40/100; to be
sure, the egg price was stable during the entire year. The impact of this
extremely 'cost effective' MIO—on egg prices and on national egg
production—is carefully documented in NECC's annual reports.
Once again, it is certain that the state would never have been able to
achieve what the NECC did as quickly and cost effectively; at the same
time, the NECC would not have performed as well as it has done but
for the intensive and high quality state support and patronage.

Indian development thinking has traditionally been suspicious
of markets; it has painted the private trader as the villain of the
society. Usury practised by money-lenders and the role of grain
traders in accentuating famines in the pre-Independence era contributed to this attitude. There are, however, two aspects of informal
commodity and factor markets which need to be noted: first, they
have proved highly resilient institutions. Seventy years of regulatory
efforts and forty years of effort directed at replacing them through
organized financial institutions have not been able to curb informal
capital markets in India; if anything, in absolute terms their business
has expanded. In relative terms too, institutional financial agencies
have come nowhere near replacing them. The second important
aspect is their on-demand nature: while in abnormal times they
tend to exploit, in normal times, informal markets provide services

that the organized sector is seldom able to match. At the end of a micro-study in West Bengal, Samar Datta concluded that informal and organized credit institutions were more complementary to each other than competitive in nature. In any case, for many of our isolated rural communities, 'the suffering caused by the exploitation by a market is nothing compared to not being exploited at all'. A recent exploration of the increasing popularity of formal and informal chit-fund organizations in Kerala, Tamil Nadu and other states as savings and loan associations too suggests that these derive their energy and drive from their ability to constantly adapt their character to fit the needs of the people. While the state views these as evil, people have taken to them increasingly. In the eighties apparently, 20 per cent of Kerala's household savings went into chit funds and these provide twice the amount of credit provided in that state by the organized sector. Predictably, the various chit-fund acts passed by state governments have, instead of regulating their working, in effect forced them out of the purview of law since many chit funds have begun to operate in the informal sector. The rest operate in southern states from their branch offices in Jammu where no chit-fund law exists (Shah and Johnson, 1991).

Another example of market as a growth stimulator is available in the ground-water irrigation sector, where private local initiative and indigenous institutions have played a far more important role—in terms of scale as well as quality—than official programmes. Several social researchers (including those at IRMA) have over the last few years studied the powerful role that fragmented, village-level ground-water markets have played in forging irrigation-based local agricultural economies in the whole of western India. The emergence of the water market has enabled numerous small holders, who would otherwise continue with rain-fed farming, to switch to irrigated farming with purchased water. Likewise, the potential opportunity to sell water to neighbours ensures a potential investor in a tube-well of high levels of capacity utilization; this assurance is very important in several areas of the country where tube-wells can cost several lakhs. The existing evidence suggests that since well owners have a stake in building long-term clientele, the irrigation service provided by private well owners is of a very high quality, and in any case, uniformly better than that of either state tube-wells or of canal systems.

There are several complex dimensions of this important indigenous institution. However, for our present purposes, it is important to note that over 13 million private well owners in India have created larger and superior quality irrigation potential than all of the large state-sponsored canal and public tube-well irrigation programmes together. In doing so they have mobilized some Rs. 25–33 thousand crore of capital. Shah (1991) recently estimated that India's private well owners may well be serving an irrigated area as large as around 40 million ha (of which nearly 15 mha may be water buyers' land) compared to the combined irrigated area of all major irrigation projects placed at 26 mha. The most important feature of this is that the state has played no direct role in forging these water markets; indeed, the state has still not even recognized their existence.

There are other examples from other fields, far too numerous to describe here. They all illustrate the powerful role law, markets and organizations can play in producing developmental impulses by facilitating, organizing and fostering technical change and by removing bottlenecks. Research institutions are known to have changed the local economies. The role played by Punjab Agricultural University in ushering in the green revolution in Punjab is well documented. Less well documented is the contribution of Karnataka Agricultural University in promoting outstanding yield growth in the predominantly drought-prone agriculture of that state. This can also be said in the case of the Deen Dayal Research Institute in eastern Uttar Pradesh, which sank 30,000 bamboo tube-wells in two districts in just one year. In Gujarat 'remarkable growth in fertilizer consumption in rain-fed areas (during the 1970s) was due to . . . certain strengths in the fertilizer distribution system and the pressure from the fertilizer supply side' exerted by the Gujarat State Fertilizer Corporation, a joint sector company (Desai, 1986). The exemplary work of Campco, a small co-operative of cocoa growers engaged in an unequal battle with Cadbury's, a multinational monopsony, in safeguarding the economies of its 16,000 members was recently documented in the *Economic and Political Weekly*.

One feature common to all these examples has been that they have either been unnoticed by the state and therefore left alone, or they have invested in building a very beneficial relationship with the state in which the latter has provided support and resources but has been discreet in exercizing control. As an economic institution, water markets fall in the first category. Private tube-well investments benefited from state-supported credit programmes; water markets have been sustained by state investments in power supply and distribution as also of power pricing policies followed by state electricity boards. However, private pumpers are too numerous and water markets too slippery to be easy prey to state control. There are many researchers who believe that the rise of the water markets as a powerful institution—one which widely diffuses access to ground-water to resource the poor, enhances manifold the overall productivity of private sector investment in minor irrigation, and erects an efficient and highly equitable on-demand irrigation demand system—was possible primarily because the state failed to take cognizance of their existence. The apprehension is that if the state had taken cognizance of the total extent of the 'business' that private water sellers are doing, in a fit of misconstrued chauvinism it would have clamped down numerous restrictions on curbing this business without discovering the massive growth and equity stimuli they produce in much the same way as it has done all these years on the informal credit markets and more recently in case of the chit-fund companies. True, some of these companies have been unscrupulous and exploitative; but instead of regulating these, what the state has done is to try to demolish the institution itself.[7]

Sugar co-operatives in Gujarat as well as Maharashtra used state support—financial as well as political—in the initial stages, but ensured that the state did not replace members' elected boards as 'monitor'; many sugar co-operatives insisted that they be allowed to repay equity contributions made by the state so that the spectre of state's direct control is eliminated. In developing dairy co-operatives all the states were able to use state support in one form or another. But only Gujarat was able to retain the 'monitorship' within the co-operatives; in most other states, the state took over as monitor. As a result, although milk collection and marketing by the government controlled co-operatives grew, dairy co-operatives outside Gujarat could not develop the same character and dynamism of Gujarat's early co-operatives. In case of the NDDB's MIO, enlightened state support was critical in whatever success the programme achieved. In case of NECC, the state had little direct role to play, yet the NECC's many activities enjoy enlightened state support. Significantly, both the NDDB and the NECC are extraordinarily skilful organizations in dealing with the state apparatus.

V

'Awkward' versus 'Subtle' State

After several years of modelling and econometric research, the World Bank recently pointed out what is wrong with Indian development planning. According to it, our investment priorities are distorted; our pricing policies mess up the incentive structure; we give too many subsidies; the rate of capital accumulation in agriculture is tumbling; we are not completing our irrigation projects on time; our agricultural research system is not coming up with new technologies fast enough; we need to spend less on anti-poverty programmes and more on irrigation; and that if we correct all these and invest more in irrigation and agricultural research, our agricultural and rural economy will soon be OK. Right?

Wrong. Even if we do all that the World Bank is saying, it is extremely unlikely that we will be OK. May be all that the World Bank is saying is wrong with us is true. But there is far more to what is wrong with us than just that. Therefore it is unlikely that correcting these wrongs is going to put us on the right path. It is unlikely that more of the same—more investment of money in irrigation and in research and greater subsidy reduction—is by itself going to help. This is because what is critically wrong with us has something to do with the chemistry between the state and our institutions of economic development.

This is not to suggest that resource generation and its allocation to sectors of national priority have no role; these are certainly necessary, but they are not sufficient. For investment to generate the desired output growth, it is important that accompanying social, economic and institutional processes of change take place. This is true not only of a complex organism like a nation's economic system, but also of economic micro-organisms such as an individual farmer or a business organization. When a farmer invests in a new technology, he himself, and often his whole family, have to change before the full benefits of new investment accrue. When business organizations generate and invest resources for growth, good business leaders also carefully devise organizational structures and processes that support and foster growth. At all levels of economic hierarchy and in all forms of economic organizations investment is certainly crucial to growth, but it is not the sole determinant of growth. One is not saying that the Indian Planning Commission is so naive as to believe that desired growth rate can be obtained by dividing the projected savings rate by the ICOR, but then we seldom see a plan document (or, for that matter, a World Bank document) which says much else.

Our development planning must recognize that people find their own resources when they come across attractive opportunities and dependable institutions; that engines of economic development cannot be created by merely allocating more 'plan funds'; that institutions can be fountainheads of modernization and growth impulses; and that subsidy and investment cannot do the institution's job. We need to recognize that without any public sector investment, powerful developmental impulses can get generated by the reform of a stultifying law; that, unobtrusively, a market can open up new opportunity sets and harness private capital; and that a co-operative or an NGO or even a research institution can revolutionize a local economy. Our development planning needs to reconsider its position that all development springs from its urn of plan funds, and to adopt a more pluralistic, institutionalist approach to development. If all these are to happen, the Indian state has to make a fresh beginning.

A major aspect of Indian plans has been the multiplicity of goals they have pursued. This is as it should be, for no society can engage in unfettered pursuit of only one goal, be it growth, equity, self-sufficiency, environmental sustainability or giving women their due in society. However, multiple and often conflicting goals are the principal source of poor implementation, low productivity and lack of viability in state initiatives. If an initiative is not justifiable on productivity/viability grounds, it is always possible to find other plan objectives—rural employment, self-sufficiency, equity, environmental benefits, improved conditions of women, or finally, the interests of the people employed by the project—that it can be shown to have contributed to. In economic analyses of projects, since one can use wage rates anywhere between zero and the government minimum wage rates, it is often easy to make an unviable project/policy appear viable and vice versa. The national

planning objectives do not offer a single talisman which can integrate the actions of the state with the actions of all the institutions
of development. We often come across the innuendo that our
plans are all right; the problem is with their implementation. As the
first step to improving plan implementation, what we need is this
single talisman. It appears that this can be best done if the state
adopts as the superordinate goal of its policy continual and sustained
enhancement in the wealth producing capacity of the agricultural
and rural sector. This would include more than just raising incomes
or even livelihoods. It would mean raising the productivity and
quality of the output of products and services, changing product
mix to match our distinctive strengths with the needs of domestic
and international consumer, and constantly improving the managerial and technical competencies and skills of our rural workforce.
It would mean creating new supportive institutions and an environment within which our agricultural and rural production systems
can establish competitiveness not only within the economy but also
on a global scale; it would mean continuing 'creative self-destruc-
tion', i.e., regular and systematic dismantling of structures, technologies, policies and organizations which have outlived their
purpose; and finally, it would include uniform and sustained increases
in the efficiency and productivity of public and private sector
investments in asset creation.

Other important goals of public policy such as equity, employment,
environmental sustainability and self-sufficiency should certainly
be there, and public sector resources should be allocated to these
in accordance with the priorities the government may wish to
assign to these goals. However, the approach here too must be one
that constantly stresses productivity, efficiency and long-term
viability. Moreover, in assessing tradeoffs, the superordinate goal
must never be sacrificed. Finally, the pursuit of this superordinate
goal cannot end with plan implementation; it would require economy-wide changes that must fundamentally alter the way we live,
think and work. Above all, it must alter the nature of the equation
between the state and the nation's institutions of development.

Institutions of Development

This last would essentially involve the state acting in a cohesive
and understanding partnership with the nation's three principal

institutions of development: the legal framework, the markets and organizations. The primary condition of establishing such a synergetic partnership is to cleanse our national mindset of all the chauvinistic beliefs and attitudes that colour the way we think about institutions and development actors, and to make a realistic assessment of who can contribute what in the task of building India's agricultural–rural economy. We must take a fresh look at our laws and the way they assign property rights, and modify them in such that they become consistent with the superordinate goal. High priority should be given to the reform of our antiquated Co-operative Act, which is long overdue. Much work has already been done on drafting a new bill by the Planning Commission. This must be passed expeditiously, especially because farmer co-operatives, with an enlightened, high-quality state support can play major role in the new strategy. At the economy-wide level, it is also important to institute a legal reform which contains the damage organized labour and trade unions can do to nation's institutions of development without abrogating their constitutional rights. This is important not only because the present hegemony of the organized labour is unfair in itself to the unemployed and unorganized, but because it has already begun to have two potentially devastating effects: first, it is beginning to have a telling effect on the productivity of organized labour as well as on large organizations; and second, it is systematically driving the organized sector towards labour-saving technologies and to casualization of labour. This last is evident in the stagnant employment growth in the private organized sector throughout the 1980s.

There is also a dire need to reconsider several of our stereotypes about markets. Forward markets in farm commodities, banned in the 1980s as a vestige of capitalism, have a great potential to contribute to the modernization of processing and marketing. Our inability to devise effective regulatory devices has in the past led to some periodic aberrations in their functioning; but by banning them, we have thrown the baby out with the bath water. There is a need to resurrect and legalize this important economic institution. In any case, such markets seldom get abolished by legal ban; they continue to function but fail to perform their useful role. A more practical method of dealing with them would be to strengthen the regulatory and disciplinary authority of the exchanges that operate these markets. These suggestions apply to informal credit markets as well; much research has shown that institutional credit agencies cannot replace these. It appears that it is not even necessary to do so. What is necessary is to bring them within the RBI's overall regulatory framework and to create countervailing powers—to some extent, this has already been done through the spread of RRBs, commercial banks, and credit co-operatives—which can contain their exploitative tendencies.

Knee-jerk reactions based on ideological or populist consider- ations do incalculable harm by destroying institutions of economic development. Nations which have witnessed impressive agricultural and overall economic growth have enjoyed long periods of stability not so much in their political leadership but in state's outlook towards institutions of development. Indeed, these are considered so important that broad national consensus has been built around the relationship of state with these institutions. It is high time we also began working towards a new national consensus on these issues. However, the progress on this front will surely be slow if our political leaders fail to break out of their old ideological bastions and to take a fresh look at new realities. In particular, in a new national code of conduct, political parties of various hues need to consider the long-term damage caused by measures like loan waivers—even by private money-lenders, as was done by Indira Gandhi—to the credibility of institutions.

Rather than assuming control over operations, which often results in bureaucratization, the state must hold strategic organizations responsible for performance budgeting and audit as a determinant of the extent of state support that the organization would qualify for. Zero-base budgeting for financial planning needs to be introduced in the government sector without further loss of time. This is most urgently needed in public sector organizations like the FCI, STC, CCI, NABARD, NDDB and various state-level organizations; in anti-poverty programmes like the IRDP, JRY, NREP and TRYSEM; in agricultural research establishments; in government departments dealing with major and minor irrigation, animal husbandry and dairying, forestry; and in the agricultural extension system. In all these institutions, their superordinate goals need to be redefined or reconfirmed, and performance budgeting and audit needs to be undertaken against these goals. This has to be a mature and constructive process or it would end up in a target-chasing exercise. For such mature and constructive audit to be possible, the state and its machinery needs to change from the political–bureaucratic to a development ethos. This in turn would mean that the state and its apparatus would have to improve its performance in five capacities: as monitor, as manager, as organization builder, as designer of interventions, and as micro-monitor.

Playing 'monitor' is serious business; the primary function of the monitor in any organization/human system is to supply governance. A 'monitor' can produce requisite supply of governance if he has the skill and the competence to understand and guide the functioning of the system and if he is concerned enough to ensure that the system works towards its mandate. The state or its deputy playing the monitor usually has neither, and therefore, his performance as monitor is, as a rule, indifferent. The reasons why the state assumes monitorship in organizations/systems are: (*a*) the state is the creator of the organization (as in public sector units) and supplier of equity capital; (*b*) there is perceived need to exercise tight control; (*c*) no one else *prima facie* appears better qualified to play monitor; and (*d*) to protect the interests of the society at large. Even where the state does not directly play monitor, as in universities, it retains the power to appoint and fire the top manager. Over the years, many governments have used this power for narrow political ends, and this has been one of the most important reasons for the erosion of institutions.

When the state plays monitor, two things happen. First, the awesome power of the state makes the top management authoritarian, that is, the management becomes excessively submissive to state machinery and oppressive towards the rest of the organization and its client system. And second, since the locus of control is shifted from within the organization to a ministry/department, the top management easily develops despondency; it is neither able to generate the drive and energy for positive action, nor is it able to easily assume responsibility for the consequences. Rapid transfers of officers from managership as well as monitorship breed a myopic view and further intensify directionlessness and lack of drive.

Since this is a systemic feature of state monitorship, a plausible solution is for the state to be extremely careful in assuming this role and to devise procedures to create self-governing systems. Co-operatives are an example of self-governing systems; in PSUs and educational/research establishments, self-governance and autonomy must be strongly encouraged. To ensure that these function as engines of development, the state may link its support to the contribution made by these institutions in larger developmental processes. However, even if the state succeeds in curtailing its monitorship, it will still have to play monitor in some organizations. For this reason, it is important that the state improves the competence of its apparatus to function as monitor.

In most public systems, dramatic improvements in performance can be achieved without any significant resource commitments simply by the top managers stressing performance improvements and defining clearly what they want; further improvement is possible if they desire it strongly enough. This is because performance improvement is the last concern of everyone engaged in a moribund public system; by the time a new man takes over as the top manager, he has but a few months before retirement and the others down below know that whether they rise in the hierarchy or not will have little to do with their performance. This is a familiar story, but no analysis of the state and institutions of development can be complete without repeating it. And undoubtedly, no significant development can occur, even with thousands or crores of investments, unless we crack this malaise.

Again, a practical way out is for the state to avoid playing manager unless it is absolutely important for it to do so. There is no reason why canal system has to be managed by the state, neither is there one for the state to manage public tube-well programmes. There is no reason why the state should play vice-chancellor of a university or a social forestry, manager of private or village lands, or, for that matter, as a rural development manager. Particularly so, if past evidence suggests that the state has not particularly distinguished itself in this role.

Where it does have to play that role, it can perform better if: (a) the state deputy to managership is professionally equipped to play manager; (b) he is given a sufficiently long tenure; and (c) he is made accountable for performance to the principal stakeholders of the organization.

In the new national ambience that we are trying to describe, the state will continue to be a major shaper of and intervener in the processes of economic development. However, the state will play this role with increasing effectiveness if it becomes a 'learning state'. By 'learning state', we mean a state which continually and critically evaluates the consequences of its action, builds an ongoing corpus of such institutionalized learning and incorporates this learning into its design of future interventions. The performance of the Indian state is pathetic as a designer of interventions and even more so as a learner from past follies. Despite forty years of experience, our interventions continue to be grossly mistargeted, and the state is usually way off the mark in predicting the impacts of its new interventions. In many cases, this is not easy to do, but we often fail to incorporate the simplest of political economy lessons in our design of interventions. Rajagopalan's analysis of the complex dynamics of the cobweb of subsidies and controls in the use of alcohol and molasses is a classic example not only of inept intervention design but also of high-level political–economic tomfoolery. The recent muddle about fertilizer subsidy is a case in point; anyone could have predicted what would happen to the restoration of the subsidy to small farmers. If it was done unknowingly, it reflects naivete, but if it was done knowingly, it is callous.

The Indian state needs to master the fine art of managing subsidies and controls and of outsmarting—or at least steering clear of—the army of rent seekers waiting in the wings that our licence-control raj has bred. It is nobody's case that these should be abolished forthwith, but it is certainly important for good statecraft that those subsidies and controls which are there should in fact continue to serve the purposes for which they were introduced in the first place. High-level 'rent-seeking' is, of course, the deplorable game played by successive state governments that have increasingly been eating into the vitals of our society. Containing or stopping this would be an ideal that the state as an institution of national governance must steadfastly pursue. However, what can be done readily is to take explicit cognizance of such games and to redesign and retarget interventions.

The key to correcting the relationship between the state and institutions of economic development lies in the state switching to the institution-building role. Rather than direct action, a 'subtle' state can create and use strategic organizations as instruments of change. A strategic organization is one which has 'the potential to produce large positive change and development in its respective domain or sector' (Khandwala, 1988: 27). Khandwala further classifies three types of strategic organizations in rural development: apex strategic organizations such as the Planning Commission,

NABARD, NDDB and others; 'spearhead organizations' such as agricultural research organizations, management institutes and IITs, which can fundamentally change the way we think and do things; and change agent-type strategic organizations such as PRADAN, Tilonia, Myrada, and other such development NGOs.

The state can and must play a major role in building these and similar institutions. There are numerous ways the state can play this role effectively; these do not include back seat driving and remote-control ruling from Delhi. Conditions of birth and formative years are crucial in determining the nature of a strategic organization as an adult. The Indian state's record as a midwife and nurse has so far been indifferent: 'if individuals with bureaucratic or political orientation are made in charge of the fledgeling strategic organiz- ation, the chances are that the organization will get "set" as a bureaucracy or as a "spoils system" . . . the resource dependence of the strategic organization on the government takes its toll and [it] degenerates into a sick organisation, heavily bureaucratised and politicised . . .' (Khandwala, 1988: 43).

Building strategic organizations is a complex game. A good deal of it generally involves letting the young organization have the cake and eat it too—which demands great magnanimity and subtlety. However, in broad terms, the state needs to consider two positions: first, the state's consultative role should focus on a careful structur- ing of the consonance between the goals of each of the strategic organizations and the superordinate goal of the state; second, when state becomes a resource provider to these organizations, it must match high 'performance demands' by high 'performance support'. Performance linkage is the key; the interaction between the state and the strategic organization can become nationally and organizationally productive only if control as well as support are linked by a shared understanding of performance needs. As Khand- wala points out, this relationship must be a nurturant in times of crises and demanding in times of peace (1988: 38).

Finally, if India decides to gun for a 5–7 per cent annual rate of growth in its agriculture–rural sector output, we need to look at who is going to buy that output. For if relative prices fall with the rising output, we will end up in a zero sum (or even a negative sum if recent evidence is anything to go by) game (see, e.g., Nadkarni, 1988). In a steady state equilibrium, growing rural incomes and food demand itself will provide expanded food markets, and forward linkages with agro-industries will need to be structured to absorb the changing product mix. But ultimately, a rapidly growing Indian agriculture will have to turn global to support sustained output and productivity growth. Regrettably, Indian planners have never seriously thought through this option. As a result, rather than capturing new international markets, we have lost out even on those markets which were, for long, our traditional forte. This is a failure that needs most urgent correction; and there is no 'smart' way of doing this; it needs a sustained and painful globalization of the Indian agricultural system.

Michael Porter, a well-known student of strategy, recently explored in a popular article why firms that dominate world markets in specific industries happen to come from the same country. He considered several alternative hypotheses: balance-of-payments policies of national governments, cheap and abundant labour, bountiful natural resources, management practices in different countries, and finally, well-targeted national government policies calculated to launch certain industries as export leaders (Porter, 1991: 29–34). Porter found that none of these explains the competitive success of nations in different industries. He argued instead that 'nations succeed in industries if their national circumstances provide an environment that supports improvement and innovation, . . . where local circumstances provide an impetus for firms to pursue such strategies [of innovation and improvement] early and aggressively . . ., [where] their homebase advantages are valuable in other nations and where their innovations and improvements foreshadow international needs' (p. 31). These circumstances are a product of skills and competences, cultural ethos, institutional structure and related variables operating as a mutually reinforcing system that Porter euphemistically calls the 'national diamond'). 'Policies implemented without consideration of how they influence the entire system of determinants (or, the "national diamond") are as likely to undermine the national advantage as enhance it' (ibid.: 32).

The cutting and polishing of the 'national diamond' is the primary task of the state as the macro-monitor or monitor of the whole economy. What Porter has identified is as much true of the nation as it is of any organization; the organizational governance structures have the primary responsibility of shaping the 'organizational diamond'; and the national governance structures, of the 'national diamond'. Like successful organizational governance structures, the state as the economy's governance structure too needs to function as a strategic planner for the nation, orchestrating the nation's long-term economic strategies by constantly analysing our national strengths and weaknesses in the light of opportunities and threats held out by the global economic environment.

According to Porter, competitive advantage grows fundamentally out of improvement, innovation and change, and involves the entire value system of the host society. It is also sustained through relentless improvement and a global approach to strategy. The national diamond that the Indian state has created in its first forty-three years of governance promotes none of these at either the farmer level or the organizational level or the national level. Our national diamond encourages farmers, workers, firms and markets to look for surpluses not by productivity improvements but by collective bargaining; through lobbying rather than through market-place; by seeking protection from global competition and from domestic rivals than by quality and efficiency gains; through concealing mediocrity rather than through open pursuit of excellence. All these fundamental changes are not easy to accomplish, but if we want enduring solutions to the problems of our agricultural and rural sector, we have no alternative. We can waste a few more years struggling with the political economy's populist policies, but time will soon run out.

In achieving all these, the Indian state has to be the prime mover. There is a groundswell of recent opinion that what we need is less state. This is wrong. In our view, it is neither possible nor desirable. It is not possible for a modern welfare state to go back to what Rousseau called the 'state of nature'. Moreover, in the most ardent of today's free market economies too, the state plays a pervasive role in economic affairs. What we need is not less state, but better state. What we need is to roll back the 'awkward state', the 'soft' state which legislates far more than it can enforce, the stifler of initiative and creativity, the 'usurper' which takes upon itself what others can do better. Instead, we need a more comprehensive but 'subtle' state—a 'hard' state which legislates judiciously but enforces vigorously, a state which skilfully deploys the power of suggestion, one that governs through policies rather than direct and shoddy action, and one which is concerned more with enabling rather than regulating. What we need is a 'paradigm shift' in our entire outlook about the equation between the state and society.

Only by fundamentally altering this equation can India continually enhance its wealth producing capacity and find enduring solutions to the problems of its people.

Notes

[This paper is the result of an effort to which many faculty members of IRMA contributed ideas and suggestions. Special thanks are due to R. Rajagopalan, who read the paper with great care and offered extensive comments. The author also acknowledges comments by R.P. Aneja, Pankaj Jain, Akhileshwar Pathak and Rajagopal. V. Kurien provided some valuable ideas. While in many respects this paper represents the thinking of many scholars at the IRMA, the responsibility of efforts and misjudgements in articulating this thinking rests entirely with the author.]

1. We use the term 'paradigm shift' in a loose sense and not in the 'history of science' sense. The liberty taken is regretted, but so commonly is the phrase misused that there is no better way to stress a change in framework of thought except by calling it 'paradigm shift.'
2. This is in keeping with the well-known Kuznets studies. What is disturbingly not in keeping with the international experience is the extremely limited transfer of labour from primary to secondary and tertiary sectors. In most economies, the process of labour transfer invariably accompanied industrialization and material progress; in the Indian case this has not happened to the same extent (see Kuznets, 1966).
3. The term 'state' has been used to imply several things. Throughout this paper, we have meant by 'state' the institution of national governance. While the state is an 'institution', the government is an organization.
4. This usage of the term 'monitor' is recent and was introduced in the economic theory by transaction cost economists (see Furubotn and Pejovich, 1981).
5. See, for example, Taylor (1990); Jensen (1989); Johnson (1990); Rappaport (1990); Drucker (1991).
6. One of the central theses of Olsen's work was that all those efforts at collective action which result in the production of a public good cannot work except through coercive elicitation of member participation and contribution (see Olsen, 1967).
7. In many states, electricity boards do specify as an explicit clause in their contract a new power connection for irrigation that the well owner will not use his well to supply water to his neighbour. This sounds incredible,particularly when there are numerous small holders who can hardly afford their own well and who can derive enormous benefit from an opportunity to buy irrigation from a neighbouring well owner.

References

Ahluwalia, Montek S. 1978. Rural Poverty and Agricultural Performance in India, *Journal of Development Studies*, 14(3).

Ahluwalia, Montek S. 1986. Rural Poverty, Agricultural Production and Prices: A Re-examination, in Mellor and Desai (eds), *Agricultural Change and Rural Poverty*, Delhi, Oxford University Press.

Chambers, R., N.C. Saxena and **Tushaar Shah** 1989. *To the Hands of the Poor: Water and Trees*, New Delhi, Oxford and IBH.

Dantwala, M.L. 1987. Growth v/s Equity in Agricultural Development Strategy in Brahmananda, B.R. and V.R. Panchamukhi (eds), *The Development Process of the Indian Economy*, Bombay, Himalaya Publishing Company, pp. 147–60.

Desai, G.M. 1986. Market Channels and Growth of Fertilizer Use in Rain-fed Agriculture, Ahmedabad, IIM (mimeo).

Drucker, Peter 1991. Reckoning with the Pension Fund Revolution, *Harvard Business Review*, March–April.

Dagli Committee 1979. Report of the Committee on Controls and Subsidies, New Delhi, Ministry of Finance.

Furubotn, Eirik G. and **Svetozar Pejovich** 1981. Poverty Rights and Economic Theory: A Survey of Literature, *Journal of Economic Literature*, Vol. XIX, December.

Gulati, Ashok 1989. Input Subsidies in Indian Agriculture: Some Policy Implications, *Economic and Political Weekly*, 30 September, pp. A124–A132.

Hanumantha Rao, C.H. 1986. Changes in Rural Poverty in India: Implications for Agricultural Growth, *Mainstream*, 11 January.

Jensen Michael C. 1989. Eclipse of the Public Corporation, *Harvard Business Review*, September–October.

Johnson, Elmer W. 1990. Saving the Corporation by Shaking Up Its Board: An Insider's Call for Outside Direction, *Harvard Business Review*, March–April.

Khandwala, Pradip N. 1988. *Social Development: A New Role for the Organisational Sciences*, New Delhi, Sage Publications.

Liberman, S. and **D. Ahluwalia** 1990. Review of GOI Agricultural Product Market Interventions, New Delhi, World Bank (mimeo).

Mundle, S. 1983. Effect of Agricultural Production and Prices on Incidence of Rural Poverty: A Tentative Analysis of Inter-state Variation, *Economic and Political Weekly*, Review of Agriculture, June, pp. A48–A52.

Minhas, B.S. 1990. Brief Notes on Access to Subsidised Food and Social Services in India, Washington, World Bank, (mimeo).

Olson, Mancur 1971. *The Logic of Collective Action: Public Goods and the Theory of Groups*, Cambridge, Harvard University Press.

Porter, Michael E. 1991. The Competitive Advantage, *Span*, Vol. XXXII, No. 9, September.

Phansalkar, S.J. 1990. Draft Agricultural Policy Resolution: A. Critique, Institute of Rural Management, Anand.

Radhakrishna, R. and **S. Reddy** 1985. Class Composition, Poverty and Agricultural Development, Hyderabad, Centre for Economic and Social Studies, (mimeo).

Rajagopalan, R. 1982. The Sugar Economy: A Cowed of Policies, Ahmedabad, IIM, Fellow Programme Dissertation.

Rajagopalan, R. and **T. Shah** 1991. Co-operative or Member-controlled Corporation: Sugar Cooperatives in South Gujarat, Institute of Rural Management, Anand (mimeo).

Rappaport, Alfred 1990. The Staying Power of the Public Corporation, *Harvard Business Review*, January–February.

Rao, V.K.R.V. 1983. *India's National Income: 1950–80*, New Delhi, Sage Publications.

Rao, V.M. and **R.S. Despande** 1987. Agricultural Growth in India; A Review of Experiences and Prospects, in B.R. Brahmananda and V.R. Panchamukhi (eds), *The Development Process of the Indian Economy*, Bombay, Himalaya Publishing Company, pp. 161–99.

Rath, N. 1985. Garibi Hatao: Can IRDP Do It?, *Economic and Political Weekly*, 20(6) 9 February, pp. 238–46.

Nadkarni, M.V. 1988. *Farmers' Movements in India*, Bangalore, Institute of Social and Economic Change.

Saxena, N.C. 1987. Common Trees and the Poor in Uttar Pradesh Hills, London, ODI Social Forestry Network, Paper 5f.

Shah, Tushaar 1987. Gains from Social Forestry: Lessons from West Bengal, London, ODI Social Forestry Network Paper, October.

——— 1991. *Water Market and Irrigation Development*, Oxford University Press.

Shah, Tushaar and **Michael Johnson** 1991. Informal Institutions of Financial Intermediation: Social Value of Vishis, Chit Funds and Self-help Groups, Institute of Rural Management, Anand (mimeo).

Taylor, William 1990. Can Big Owners Make a Big Difference?, *Harvard Business Review*, September–October.

5

Organization for Policy Formulation

Ishwar Dayal

Although there have been intermittent periods of economic and social growth and stability in many of the developing countries, the overall development in most of them has been much below the desired level. Among the reasons for unsatisfactory development, the most noticeable are: inadequacy of administrative machinery; inability to develop the collective will to achieve results amidst diverse interest groups and political parties; lack of mass involvement in the process of development; and inappropriateness of policy formulation. A more satisfactory level of achievement could perhaps be ensured by overcoming all these weaknesses.

After the initial phases of national development, the interdependence among its many segments becomes sensitive and demands the fullest consideration in policy formulation. The economic, social, technological and political areas exert a strong mutual influence, and the impact of policy in one area calls for examination of its simultaneous impact on the related areas as well. The lack of a holistic perspective in policy formulation becomes an impediment to growth; policy decisions in one area stall progress in another. Certain kinds of incentives for the growth of small industry, for example, may seriously jeopardize long-term research and development in certain sectors of the larger industries or push up prices of certain goods and commodities. In the early years of development planning, the scope for growth may appear to be substantial enough in all aspects of national life, and interdependence between the various segments may not seem so critical. At one time the interdependence between agriculture and industry may not have seemed crucial. With progress in growth, however, the interlinkages among the several sectors of national development have come to exert much more influence on overall growth.

The imbalanced economic growth in different sectors and growing aspirations of people among different groups, especially the economically deprived groups, exert pressures to bring about more egalitarian systems. These pressures, in turn, cause further imbalances and often aggravate negative feelings among the groups. There is yet another problem of considerable significance. While policy relating to customs and excise duties may assume that the bureaus, say Labour, would take suitable action, the Labour Ministry may not be able to, or want to, take the supportive action. As a result, the policy measures taken by the Finance Ministry would fail to yield the expected level of outcome. The success or impact of the policy measures in this highly complex social and economic environment would rely on achieving harmony in policy measures in many interdependent activities. Research in business organizations shows that while differentiation between functions is necessary in areas where knowledge is growing rapidly, the success of the enterprise depends equally on creating integrating positions. Hence, positions that encourage both differentiation and integration have to be created in order to derive the best advantage from specialization. These measures become critical when the markets or the external factors become sensitive. Inter-sector influences have to be fully considered in policy formulation, as in administration. The complexity of the situation compels the formulation of an appropriate integrative organization purpose that can effectively respond to the many demands of the changing social and economic situation. Inter-sector influences have to be fully considered in policy formulation, and an appropriate organization for policy formulation has become necessary.

Problem Areas

Policy formulation is taken to comprise five aspects here: (*a*) predicting and defining the areas where policy formulation is needed; (*b*) the process of formulating a policy; (*c*) planning programmes and projects to achieve the purposes of the policy; (*d*) reviewing the policy by setting operational measures of the effectiveness of the policy; and (*e*) revising the policy if the review shows that new measures are needed.

One of the major strengths of the policy-making process in India is the vast consultation and involvement of experts, administrators, public men and interest groups. After reviewing the policy formulation process in the Government of India, Dayal and his colleagues (1975) summed it up as follows:

> The style of policy formulation involves extensive advice and consultation. The outstanding feature of policy making is characterised by accommodation and settlement, involving the political, administrative and specialist groups as far as possible.

While the basic approach is generally followed, the ruling elite have used their individual style to follow this, and suspend the process for periods of time under certain circumstances. These circumstances broadly cover the periods of Emergency or periods when the government is subject to a defensive approach with respect to certain public issues such as a specific corruption charge.

Although I consider the process of consultation and accommodation to be a major strength in policy formulation, it still has certain problems, as the authors quoted earlier have pointed out in their critique. Often radical policies are difficult to formulate and do not easily invite acceptance. These policies seem to come out of the initiative of top political leadership and not through the formal machinery that is set up for the purpose. Committees invariably try to seek agreement among its members and attempt to find a common basis among them. This tends to perpetuate the existing difficulties rather than offer new policy options. The members' tendency towards compromise and accommodation has cultural relevance. In our relationships, social and work roles are rarely distinguished (Dayal, 1977; Kakar, 1978). Disagreements in specific work situations are often extended in all other areas of social interaction. In meetings, unless there are other specific reasons, a member ordinarily tries to minimize anything that gives the impression of being 'difficult' or 'hostile' unless his role justifies it, as in the case of a trade union leader in management–union meetings. In such situations the member often withdraws, either by writing a minute of dissent, or by resigning from his membership. It is not unusual to come across members of committees who criticize the report and blame it on the autocratic handling of the chairman, even when they had given no indication in committee meetings that they had reservations about the decisions made by the chairman. It has also often been noticed that members who are seen to be difficult are dropped from the membership of other committees. At times committees give recommendations that are unrealistically 'radical', as often seen in international gatherings, as if saying that effect is more important than substance. Thus, the dynamics of committee functioning are complex and the quality of their outcome depends on a number of different factors, especially in matters that concern the public. In a developing country such as India, where radical approaches are necessary to tackle serious social and economic problems, the prevailing strategy for policy formulation is not always unsatisfactory. It is frequently mentioned that the policy is sound but the implementation is poor. I believe that the soundness of the policy can only be judged by the results achieved, i.e., achieving the purpose for which the policy was set out. If the policy fails to solve the problems that it is expected to solve, it could hardly be considered sound. I recognize that government organization and systems of working are complex, but this may be an added reason to consider that an organization for policy formulation is all the more necessary in the government.

As mentioned earlier, another weak spot in policy formulation is the lack of interdependence in some important areas of public policy. The success of policy in small scale industry, for instance, must depend on the finances made available by financial institutions, the availability of services and technology, infrastructure development, the nature of development of large-scale industry and a variety of other interlinking policy factors. While framing policy for the growth of small-scale industry, a series of support policies must also be framed and implemented. Each of these policy areas happens to be a subject of other ministries besides the one that deals with small-scale industry. An integrated policy is difficult to evolve since the government resorts to setting up a committee to examine the problem, let us say, the growth of small-scale industry. The committee would recommend various interrelated factors for development. These recommendations would be examined by various concerned ministries or a committee of secretaries. The final shape of policy recommendations would emerge from extensive interministerial consultations. A paper for the

Cabinet or the minister concerned, depending on the nature of the issue, would be prepared. The decision of the Cabinet would be implemented by the various ministries.

The procedure is cumbersome, time-consuming and expensive. Moreover, it does not ensure the best quality of output. The understanding of issues by the implementing departments may be different and the sequencing of the various programmes may become distorted or, the follow-up may receive inadequate attention. What's more, midcourse correction is rarely possible if the results are not being achieved. For the policy to serve its purpose, the set of activities and programmes have to be seen as a package and reviewed as such. The integration of components is necessary at several stages of policy formulation including those of identifying problem areas, developing policy goals, formulating a policy, planning programmes and projects and reviewing the policy. This task cannot be carried out fully at the level of the individual ministry. In the present system, the Planning Commission is expected to perform an integrative role with respect to development projects, but in fact the job rarely gets done. There are two reasons for this: (a) organizationally the Planning Commission is itself fragmented into functional divisions and is in no way better equipped to handle this task than the ministries in the government; and (b) the programmes and projects are framed by the individual ministry concerned, which is likely to go by its own priorities. Because the job was poorly done by the Planning Commission, a new Ministry of Plan Implementation was created. There is no evidence that the new ministry has contributed anything significant to either policy formulation or policy review. I believe that the problem of poor achievement of results lies in the areas mentioned earlier and that the creation of a new bureau can hardly improve the results.

The use of policy formulation experts in the government is inadequate. The effort on the part of members of a committee is invariably to find agreed solutions rather than to apply expertise in search of the best action alternatives. Diverse groups set up to look into the problems and suggested solutions often find it difficult to get out of the existing frame; as mentioned earlier, the suggested solutions end up perpetuating the problems, perhaps in another form, instead of offering workable radical changes. Occasionally some members may write minutes of dissent on specific issues without having much effect on the policy.

A more useful way of using experts is to get them to analyze and diagnose the problems in hand and to seek alternative action choices by applying their particular knowledge and training to this search. This approach is being increasingly used to advantage in the United States and some countries in Western Europe. The growth of knowledge in every field of study is phenomenal, and diagnostic and predictive tools have become available. The government system appears to be more concerned with acceptability and consensus, though in public administration, as indeed in any large organization, these considerations are important rather than the optimality of a decision. Taking into view the growing complexity of the social and economic situation, I believe that *both* the acceptance and optimality of the decision would be important. Without any one of the two, either the government would become irrelevant or the society would lose its dynamism.

Another major difficulty thrown up in the absence of an organization for systematic policy formulation is that up-to-date data on the areas under examination is not easily available. For each single problem, the data has to be gathered from several sources. Massive data generated by committees in their deliberations, or data used for purposes of planning is shelved after the committees finish their deliberations. This data is not easily found. Operating data is published by the Central Statistical Organization or the Reserve Bank of India. It is aggregative in content and is often published too late for current use. This data is needed for decision making and policy review and has to be built up at the administrative level. Data from special agencies such as the Central Statistical Organization or the Reserve Bank of India has limited usefulness for managerial reviews of policy effectiveness. Hence, the data used in making operating decisions gets outdated. Data is generally updated by review committees (and not too often by administration) in the normal course of their work.

The structure of the government is such that the interlinking of policies presents a perpetual problem. The work of the government is organized on a functional basis, each minister being independently responsible for the subject of his ministry. The coordinating point for decisions is the Cabinet and its committees. With the increase in work and the complexities of problems, the Cabinet's examination can exert minute care only on those policy issues that are selected as the most important. There is considerable informal consultation among ministries, the Planning Commission and the Finance

Ministry, especially with respect to development policies. Formal coordination on certain policy issues is provided by the committee of secretaries, but a large number of issues that have a significant impact on the totality of national development remain primarily within the functional purview of the ministry concerned. Hence, the structure of the organization itself and the size of each ministry makes coordination difficult. Special ways have to be found to enable closer examination of the interlinkages between different ministries in policy formulation.

Role of Policy Analysis Cluster

What should be the nature of the unit that can help both sectoral and interministerial policy formulation and what should be its characteristics, i.e., what role does it have to perform? Generally, the support system—I shall call it the policy analysis cluster, as it is known elsewhere—should perform the following roles:

1. Identification of Policy Needs: The documents on long-range plans are the source for identifying policy needs. Another very important source is the review of the effectiveness of the policies in the given field of study. A review of effectiveness would throw light on what really needs to be done. This can be called the *development role*.
2. Policy Formulation: Policy options that are proposed by the government are to be analyzed with special emphasis on their effectiveness in totality, including choices of alternatives, costs, availability of subsidiary or support systems and any special features that appear necessary. I shall call this the *analyzing role*.
3. Examination of programmes and projects: This would enable the purpose of the policy to be realized. The examination would have to consider how well the economic and social goals are served by the policy. I shall call this the *implementing role*.
4. Policy Review: There has to be a continuing review of policy to evaluate its effectiveness and to assess the need for new measures to serve the policy objectives. This shall henceforth be referred to as the *reviewing role*.

The policy analysis cluster will thus have to assume a prismatic role, the sides of the prism being development, analysis and diagnosis. The skills needed for carrying out these roles to the greatest effect would vary from one situation to another. The emphasis, however, is on diagnostic expertise and application of analytical tools and skills, and not merely on subject knowledge. These roles cannot be performed by any one person as the expertise needed in the task is many sided. The policy planning cluster would need to have a strong base of behavioural and mathematical sciences since the task requires the prediction of events and the testing of the validity of options.

I believe that the glaring failure in all countries, especially the developing countries, is the great lag between the planned and achieved levels with respect to the development of the individual citizen and the growth of a healthy society. In this respect, the experiences of the developed countries of the West as well as of the developing countries show that man, in spite of being the central focus of all development, has increasingly become merely incidental. He is not central to social development, and achievement is far removed from the stated goals of most governments.

Western countries have assumed that an increasingly better standard of living and greater availability of goods and services would by itself lead to contented, complete citizens. The emphasis has been firmly placed on economic opportunities, better environment and availability of more goods and services.

In the developing countries too, the assumption is made that legislation to create an egalitarian society and provision of education, health and social services would develop a happier citizen. However, though a great many programmes are taken up for the well-being of the individual, the development of the total citizen continues to remain a vision of the distant future.

I believe that part of the failure to provide a better life for the individual and create a better new society lies in ignoring the social and the psychological aspects in the planning of programmes and projects. The intentions of the social policy have to be translated into action plans through major programmes and projects. Since the translation of policy into action is of such extreme importance in the process of policy formulation, an illustration will perhaps make the meaning clearer.

While planning a large fertilizer plant or steel plant in an underdeveloped rural location, questions such as the following need to be raised and their solutions incorporated into the planning of the project. The questions are:

1. How will the location of the plant affect the values, the mode of life and the social relationships of the community in which the plant is being located?
2. How should indigenous social values be incorporated into the management of the project?
3. How should the management and the local population be educated to develop a better understanding of each other, of old values and of unavoidable changes in the value system?

These questions are raised in discussions but are rarely included in the programme of action. Studies have shown that people who had to vacate their lands for a large factory to be established in that location have been given compensation but this is spent on drinks, and the family is forced to live in abject poverty. Training or counselling centres were proposed to be established to help workers who seek voluntary retirement, but three years after the announcement of the policy, no counselling or vocational centres had been established. The workers have to make repeated visits to the office from their villages for more than two years to claim their dues. The various bits and pieces that should hang together with the retirement policy are in fact detached and lost in the maze of administrative non-action.

Social changes in terms of new attitudes, values and ways of life would come about if programmes and projects consciously took into consideration the best means of inducing these changes. The government's stated policy that the nation should nurture the traditions and culture of the local society would have to find visible expression in the way a fertilizer project or steel plant is established in a completely rural setting. The day-to-day administration will have to give special consideration to the local traditions and values. Of course, if the organization fails to act on the stated policy of nurturing tradition and culture, the policy goal would not be achieved because of the inherent conflict in practice and precept.

Social policy goals cannot be achieved merely through legislation nor can they be achieved through the formulation of broad policy statements. They have to be given a place and form in the planning of programmes and projects and in their implementation.

A common approach of the government to social evils is to proscribe certain traditional practices by legislation, or to appoint special agencies to look after the interests of underprivileged groups. Legislation against untouchability, dowry, etc., and commissions set up for tribal welfare, or welfare of minorities are examples of typical policy approaches. While legislative measures are necessary for achieving certain goals, they are not enough to affect the overall development of the individual and the society. Several aspects of this development must also be planned at micro levels, as, for example, in the planning of programmes and projects. The planning of policy must include looking at its options at several levels—the overall level, the sectoral level, and the programmes and projects level.

With the increase in the volume of work, several ministries have been fragmented, leading to tunnelled perspectives. The Agriculture Ministry has been separated from the Rural Development Ministry and each has been further sub-divided. These measures have also had an impact on policy formulation. Drought policy, for example, cannot be separated from rural development, and the emergency measures have to be integrated with long-term plans of development, which in turn would have to include non-farm occupation. While these interlinkages are discussed in many fora and also written down, there is overwhelming evidence that such a holistic perspective is seldom translated into an action plan.

A policy cluster has to be integrative. The total development policy for rural development has to integrate seeds, water, fertilizers, agriculture production, non-farm development, literacy and many other related areas. The data for policy formulation for rural development must invariably come out of many specific studies in each component of the policy in order to determine what its individual and collective problems are and how different regions may need different approaches or emphases in the policy.

The policy analysis cluster does not in any way replace the responsibility of the administrative departments to achieve results. The cluster is a specialist group equipped with the skills (identified earlier) to perform the respective roles of developing, analyzing and diagnosing in the process of policy formulation. To perform these specified roles, the cluster is attached to the minister and the secretary. Decisions concerning plans and action choices must be exercised by the concerned administrative machinery of the government and not by the cluster. The policy analysis cluster is provided to improve the quality of policy choices by a more reasoned, analytical, and holistic approach, and by the use of improved techniques in policy formulation.

The Experience Abroad

Most countries in Western Europe and the United Kingdom have planning at two levels, the central and the sectoral. Strategic studies and forecasts are carried out by the Ministry of Finance, or designated councils, taking into account the constraints of the situation such as availability of manpower, and finance, and the capacity of critical industries like building or energy.

Most ministries have their own respective research and planning units which carry out planning studies on various aspects of the department's activities. Policy reviews are carried out to determine new objectives and to set new standards for the department's activities. A unit in one ministry has useful contact with the other ministries.

It is not unusual to set up special groups to study certain problems that are considered critical. For example, during the preparation of the country's Sixth National Plan, the French Government set up a special group for forward planning of research and development in the building industry. There was a steering committee of forty leading builders, architects and sociologists, together with officials from the main government departments concerned. This group tackled the main tasks of:

1. long-term consideration of the various ways of life and types of housing;
2. forecasting of the techniques of building; and
3. defining the aims of research and experiment in housing.

In 1972, the French Government set up an interdepartmental group for the evaluation of the environment. The task of the group was to obtain better quantitative information about the state of the environment and the factors bearing on it, as for example, the damage done by pollution, in its widest sense.

Sectoral forward planning is also carried out in Belgium and the UK. At the central level, a unit is responsible for preparing an expenditure plan. Mrs. Thatcher brought in an advisory group reporting directly to the prime minister. Generally, the British system relies more heavily on Cabinet sub-committees and the minister draws heavily on the staff members in his ministry. Traditionally, the civil services have employed and relied on the talent drawn from the best universities in the country. This is why the in-service training of civil servants was greatly emphasized in the UK. In the last ten to fifteen years, the quality of in-service training of civil servants has been considerably upgraded. There has also been a substantial shift towards developing areas of specialization among civil servants. In these respects, the system appears to be close to the organization of French and Japanese civil services. There is also a widely accepted practice of consulting various ministries or local bodies in the process of planning.

In the United States, the Office of Management and Budget and various councils and special advisers that form the Executive Office of the president are concerned with policy options. The National Security Council is concerned with policy in such fields as international relations and defence. There has evolved a systematic process of preparing expert papers for presenting carefully developed policy options. These are developed both by staff members from the concerned departments and specialists employed by the Council.

The executive departments (ministries in other countries) and several independent agencies have policy analysis units reporting directly to the secretary or the under secretary of the department. Generally, these units provide an impetus for effective policy making among the various programme elements of a department and integrate different policy elements from the various sections of the department. This effort is necessary for better integration of the policy and to ensure that the efforts of the various component units have a consistent direction. Briefly, the experiences of most countries show that:

1. there are specified agencies for forecasting national expenditure on a long-term basis. The institutional arrangements and the period for which forecasts are made vary from one country to another;

2. planning and forecasting is generally done at two levels, the national level and the sectoral level;
3. the involvement of specialists is increasing and varies with the nature of the problem. In Western Europe, committees are set up for specific subject matters. There are also inter-ministerial committees, as in India. The increasing use of policy analysis specialists in the ministries or the Cabinet or both is becoming common; and that
4: in the USA an extensive use of policy analysis specialists and researchers is made both at the departmental and national levels.

The Indian Situation

Most elements of European practices in forward planning and forecasting, and policy making exist in India. The planning process is more formalized and incorporates the overall and sectoral components. The Planning Commission has the responsibility to perform several tasks in formulating development policy and its role has to be examined before a suitable organization for policy making can be discussed. The role of the Planning Commission was laid down and established by the Cabinet Resolution No. I-P(C)/50 of March 1950. Its functions as laid down in the Resolution are:

1. to make an assessment of the material, capital and human resources including the technical personnel of the country, and investigate the possibilities of augmenting those resources that are found to be deficient in relation to the nation's requirements;
2. to formulate a plan for the most effective and balanced utilization of the country's resources;
3. to define the stages in which the plan should be carried out and propose the allocation of resources for due completion of each stage once the policy's priorities have been determined;
4. to indicate the factors which tend to retard economic development and determine the conditions which, in view of the current social and political situation, should be established for the successful execution of the plan;

5. to determine the nature of machinery which will be necessary for securing the successful implementation of each stage of the plan in all its aspects;

6. to appraise from time to time the progress made in the execution of each stage of the plan and recommend the adjustments of policy measures that such an appraisal may show to be necessary; and

7. to make such interim or ancillary recommendations as appear appropriate either for facilitating the discharge of the duties assigned to it or on a consideration of the prevailing economic conditions, current policies, measures of development programmes or on examination of such specific problems as may be referred to it for advice by the central or state governments for facilitating the fulfilment of duties allotted to it.

The Planning Commission has to analyze the economic, financial, social and political situation, diagnose reasons for successes and failures in performance and evaluate capabilities to execute and recommend improvements. One important component of its task is policy formulation. In carrying out its assigned tasks, the Planning Commission appoints a large number of technical, sectoral and special committees, thereby involving experts, administrators and public men in the framing of national policies. The notes and papers for the guidance of the committees are generally prepared by the special staff of the Planning Commission. The plans lay down the national goals to be achieved and the strategy to be followed.

The Planning Commission has no direct involvement in non-development policies. The ministries formulate policies in their area of responsibility. Some policies need the clearance of the Ministry of Finance and the Cabinet. Not all policies, however, require discussion and approval of the Cabinet.

In the area of development, the Planning Commission was intended to serve as an idea body, helping also in the task of policy formulation. The Planning Commission was to be a nodal agency for assessing the areas where policy formulation was needed, evaluating the strengths and achievements of the policy and evolving an integrated perspective. It was linked with the government through the top structure of the Commission and the Minister of Planning, leaving the planning body independent under the deputy chairman, who need not have been a member of the government. The Com-, mission could employ experts and organize itself to perform its role in the best way possible. Over the years, the central role of the Planning Commission has become diffused. Briefly the factors that contributed to this shift are:

1. The Commission developed a segmented structure and became a shadow organization of the ministries of the government. Hence, the Planning Commission has a separate bureau to deal with agriculture, and other bureaus to deal with industry, education, etc. The perspective is as fragmented as it is in the operating wing of the government.

2. Authority and power has shifted from the expert groups to full-time civil service personnel. The secretary of the Planning Commission, who is a civil servant, has become the nodal point in plan formulation as opposed to the expert bodies. In fact, barring a handful of persons drawn from academia or industry or scientific institutions, all central tasks are manned by civil servants on temporary transfer. They bring their experience from the government.

3. The evaluation of policy in some areas is done on a routine basis. Some of these studies are useful but a large number would contribute little to policy review.

4. The Planning Commission provides a perspective; policy formulation remains the task of the concerned ministry. The Planning Commission involves many people, including experts in their respective fields, to serve in committees. In most cases, the consultative process follows a *form* but rarely provides the *substance*, which is generally provided by the departments within the Commission.

5. The members of the Commission, who are invariably drawn from among the best talent available in their area of expertise, seem to contribute very little to policy formulation. By and large, the structure of the Commission and the dynamics of how it functions preclude decisive contribution by the members.

Sectoral policies in major areas are formulated in two distinct ways:

1. Commissions are appointed to review and recommend a policy frame; and
2. the concerned ministry puts up recommendations to the minister out of a necessity to handle day-to-day problems. At times the need for a policy is pointed out by the Cabinet. Based on certain events or recurring issues at the centre or in the states, the minister may ask for a fresh approach or policy in that area. Most ministries have economic advisers whose role is determined by the minister or the secretary from time to time. It is rare for them to perform a critical role in policy formulation, except, perhaps, in the Finance or Commerce Ministries.

In public matters, however, committees would always have an important role in the examination of certain types of problems such as the following: (a) issues where several interest groups have to collaborate to arrive at solutions, (b) reviewing work carried out by government, or by projects, etc., and (c) examination of certain alternative action choices, especially when public acceptance of the decision is important. On technical issues, however, committees have worked with less success than was anticipated.

In brief, the dynamics of policy formulation in India have the following characteristics:

1. The Planning Commission is responsible for development policies and reviewing what is achieved by them.
2. Sectoral policies, programmes and projects are mainly the responsibility of ministries and attached offices of the government.
3. The most dominant style of policy making is that of appointing committees or commissions for direction on important public matters. The interlinkages between sectors and among ministries are often achieved through the appointment of such bodies. At times the recommendations are reviewed among the ministries and changes are made to suit the practical problems of administering the recommendations.

Organization for Policy Making

As discussed earlier, the Planning Commission is a vast body but its contribution to policy formulation would hardly justify its existence. That such a body is needed in a country like India is, in my mind, not a matter of conjecture. If it were a compact body consisting of independent people with strong research support, it would be able to help in the task of policy formulation. In the present context, it is mainly an extension of the government. The question may well be raised whether it can be transformed to serve the policy formulation function. Judging from the experience of reform in administration brought about by the government from time to time, it is most doubtful that the government can deal with fundamental changes in administration. Even Morarji Desai, with his invaluable experience of having held key ministerial positions, failed to bring about a change. As Prime Minister, Rajiv Gandhi succeeded in breaking the ice, but he, as other ministers over the years, was unable to bring about reform in many areas of administration. Hence, changes would have to be introduced in addition to the existing machinery and not in lieu of such bodies, in the hope that reforms would also continue to follow their own pace.

Over the years, the Planning Commission has broadly functioned as a wing of the government. It would be difficult to believe that the contribution it has made to development policies and strategies is the contribution intended in the Cabinet Resolution quoted above. Many efforts have been made to reorganize the Commission, but it has become so unwieldy, as indeed is the government system, that every effort has achieved only marginal changes which have soon been wiped out under the weight of its internal dynamics.

One added problem is that policy formulation in the government is generally seen to be a set of prescriptions to solve a set of problems. It is meant to provide direction and, at times, to lay down the boundaries of action for concerned parties. There are many variations of the policy, but rarely is it conceived to include the aspects that have been stated in this paper. This paper conceives that organization for policy formulation has to be concerned with identifying the need for policy in different regions, framing a policy, planning programmes and projects to achieve the goals of the policy, reviewing results and revising the policy where required.

What should be the role of the policy planning cluster? It should have a perspective of the totality. Different perspectives including economic and social, and immediate and futuristic are essential for policy formulation. The members of the cluster must have knowledge and understanding of the ground reality. They would also have to avoid the mind-set that is likely to develop in an administrative situation when certain approaches or constraints are taken as given. The cluster has to consist of a group of people and not the person. Placed as it is, the Planning Commission would have to have a policy planning cluster.

The central policy planning cluster has to function as a single unit and not in sectors. If the policy planning cluster loses perspective of the totality and views policy in sectoral terms, the cohesion sought in policy formulation would be lost. Sectoral policies must also be seen at an overall level. The analysis and diagnosis should suggest how, aggregatively, the policies, programmes and projects framed under the plan would achieve the national goals, and identify the alternative choices that could be considered with advantage.

Besides overall policies and central policy planning clusters, sectoral formulation is important. However, as discussed earlier, sectoral policies must have a perspective of the totality in order to ensure that the national goals are achieved. Considering the significant impact of sectoral policies on national development, large ministries would have to set up policy analysis clusters. It has to be emphasized that policy planning clusters lower than the ministry level would be dysfunctional. The policy should be viewed from an interlinking perspective, which would be lost if the policy analysis clusters operate at lower units of administration than the ministry.

The inter-ministerial policy making would only be handled by setting up special groups for specified purposes. The important requirement for such clusters to function well is the recognition of their need by ministers and senior civil servants. No permanent groups can function for inter-ministry policy linkages.

The use of policy analysis clusters and the quality of their contribution depend largely on how much use of the scientific or systematic approach the government makes in the task of policy formulation. At present such clusters function erratically, depending upon the individual minister or secretary seeing the need for them.

As soon as the interested person leaves his post, the clusters lose their role and become useful for odd assignments until they are finally phased out. This experience is repeated in several ministries. The policy planning clusters will fail to make the necessary contribution unless the system is institutionalized. The important question for consideration is what needs to be done to institutionalize the system of policy planning clusters in the government.

During the 1960s, the Home Ministry under the then Home Secretary, Mr. L.P. Singh, had started a research wing. During his tenure, this wing did extremely useful work by way of examining many issues independently and providing the feedback to the government, which was used in policy reviews. Soon after Mr. Singh left the ministry, the research wing remained only in name, till the key people were shifted to other positions. Such experiments have been done in other ministries and bureaus as well, but the function has not been institutionalized.

Many administrators believe that the idea of policy clusters is impractical in the context of the government. There reasons to hold this reservation may be summarized as follows:

1. Each ministry is responsible for results in the functional area it deals with and has to determine its own priority. The need for confidentiality adds to the problem of sharing data before a policy is formulated.
2. The administrators are trained over a period of time to understand what is feasible and what is not. Outsiders who lack the experience in public administration cannot contribute much to policy formulation. Besides, the best talent is available to the government, and experts from outside are not needed.
3. The interlinkages are complex and policy clusters cannot serve the purpose of integrating them.

The problems that an open democratic government faces in a developing country are extremely sensitive and no single measure such as a policy cluster can solve them. The point is that we should use the analytical and predictive tools that have developed over the years, which the government is not doing at present. The second point is that the policy perspective has to be essentially integrative. The results can only be achieved if the components of the problem situation are identified and simultaneous action is taken to deal with them. A third point is that policy alternatives should be explored meticulously to seek the best policy option possible. These issues can perhaps be handled more adequately by policy clusters.

The first step towards such an institutionalization is to recognize at the top levels of the government that there really is a national need for formalizing policy making functions. The second step is to recognize the problems of policy formulation and of the usefulness of specialist groups in the process of policy formulation. If these aspects were accepted, the first firm step towards improving the policy making process would have been taken.

References

Dayal, I., Kuldeep Mathur, Abhijeet Dutta and **Utpal K. Banerjee** 1975. *Dynamics of Formulating Policy in Government of India—Machinery for Policy Development*, New Delhi, Concept.
——— 1977. *Change in Work Organizations*, New Delhi, Concept.
Ink, Dwight A. 1975. *Policy Making in the United States, Policy Analysis and Development*, ACDA, United Nations, 345–406.
Kakar, Sudhir 1978. *The Inner World—A Psychoanalytic Study of Childhood and Society in India*, Delhi, Oxford University Press.
Nodder, T.E. 1975. Institutions, Practices and Problems: France, Belgium and the United Kingdom, *Policy Analysis and Development*, ACDA, United Nations, 2: 323–44.

6

Institutional Framework for Policy Advice: The Cabinet Secretariat and the Prime Minister's Office

KULDEEP MATHUR
JAMES W. BJORKMAN

The policy relationship between cabinet ministers and their secretaries exists in an institutional framework. The channel through which a minister must operate is the secretariat, which is organized pyramidically, with the secretary to the ministry acting as the principal policy adviser to the minister. Originally, the concept was that the secretariat only looked after policy formulation, execution being the job of non-secretariat field organizations. During the colonial rule, considerable authority and power resided with the field officers, who were the men on the spot and were usually British. This created a sense of trust between the headquarters and the field, so necessary for the efficient functioning of a government in a geographically large country like India, whose topographical diversity did not allow for easy transport or communication. But the increasing ease with which a secretariat could reach district collectors quickly was probably one important factor that made it take greater interest in the execution of policies. In the current administrative milieu, the situation is mixed. Much executive work is handled in the secretariat; on the other hand, several non-secretarial organizations participate in policy formulation to a greater extent than would have been considered appropriate previously.

To coordinate the work of the secretaries so that contradictions in advice do not occur, there is a cabinet secretary, who is the seniormost civil servant in the country. He presides over the Committee of Secretaries, which examines inter-ministry matters as well as issues that concern the government as a whole. Often the Cabinet refers matters to it for comment and advice. Since the early 1950s, the cabinet secretary usually does not prepare papers for the Cabinet or its committees; nor does he take upon himself the responsibility for a comprehensive scrutiny of agenda papers for the Cabinet. Rather, he ensures that all notes are self-contained and that appropriate details for discussion are provided, occasionally seeking clarification or raising points for modification with the ministry concerned (Limaye, 1989).

On rare occasions, the cabinet secretary prepares a paper at the Cabinet's specific request when, for instance, a tangled issue drags on and various views expressed in meetings need to be combined. At times, the issues raised in the notes and in meetings are referred back for reworking or for further discussions to the ministers concerned. Sometimes the cabinet secretary is asked to discuss these matters for resolution with the ministers concerned.

The cabinet secretary is present at all meetings of the Cabinet and its committees. He is responsible for preparing the agenda, the priorities of items, and the allocations of subjects to cabinet committees. Although these are approved by the prime minister, the cabinet secretary must exercise his judgement, taking into account national priorities as well as what the ministries consider important. The cabinet minutes are prepared by the cabinet secretary and decisions are communicated to the ministers by him.

The role of a cabinet secretary is crucial in the cabinet system of government. As head of the civil services, he provides a vital link between the political and permanent functionaries of government. As policy advisor to the Cabinet and its committees, he must remain informed about the urgent socio-economic and political problems, about the bottlenecks in the implementation of government programmes, and about the issues of which the prime minister should be aware. While a prime minister may ask him for greater details on any official matter, he is rarely briefed by the cabinet secretary about items placed on the cabinet agenda. The need for personal briefing was acutely felt by Nehru's successor, Lal Bahadur Shastri, who became the prime minister in 1964. Shastri was indeed 'first among equals' and not very familiar with issues concerning foreign policy or science and technology (Dhar, 1989). He established an independent secretariat and appointed as head, a secretary-level civil servant who doubled as his principal private secretary. Three joint secretaries and a number of deputy secretaries were also appointed. Since then the prime minister's secretariat has grown in size and importance.

The background and experience of the key personnel in the prime minister's secretariat are not specified in a formal manner; incumbents are appointed to this office to provide 'secretarial help' to the prime minister. Whoever heads it may or may not come from the civil services. His essential qualification is the trust of the prime minister. Thus no fixed duties are laid down, and depending on what the prime minister wants, the secretary's role can be both political and administrative. But his responsibilities include dealing with all papers routed to the prime minister and making briefs for decisions. The secretary to the prime minister can also initiate action on behalf of the prime minister and write directly to ministers. Thus, with access to data from different sources, he can become an autonomous source of independent policy perspectives.

During the prime ministership of Nehru, greater reliance on the ministries and their secretaries was the characteristic way of working and the cabinet secretary provided the primary link. In subsequent periods, the prime minister's office intruded on many functions and practically snatched the initiative from the cabinet secretariat. It has been a widely held view that, as the Principal Secretary to Prime Minister Indira Gandhi, P.N. Haksar virtually ran a parallel government from the prime minister's secretariat (Limaye, 1989: 129). But the kind of interventionist role played by him has been justified by his successor in office, P.N. Dhar (1989), who argues that the assumption of the office of prime minister by Mrs. Gandhi was accompanied by significant changes in the economic and political environment. The leadership of the Congress Party had become weak and fragmented. The country was hit by two successive droughts. The economy was in a state of crisis; economic plans had decelerated to what was called a 'plan holiday'.

The devaluation of the rupee, a decision taken earlier but implemented in the first months of her regime, became a political fiasco that did not help the economy in any way. The authority of the central government had eroded considerably. Mrs Gandhi's Cabinet did not have the capability to respond to such problems because it did not consist of like-minded persons.

As a result, Mrs. Gandhi faced a twofold challenge. The first was to establish her pre-eminence in the Cabinet; the second was to forge a coherent set of policies and to develop a credible political stance. To meet these challenges, she could not depend on the cabinet colleagues. Some of them were her political rivals. She needed to devise ways to develop or choose leaders who would be personally loyal to her and also needed aides who would provide professional advice and assistance. The prime minister's secretary fulfilled this role of designing political strategy and mobilizing professional advice. Because Mrs. Gandhi wanted to become an assertive prime minister, she needed an activist secretary. Such a role could not be played again. The future role of secretaries was that of being the prime minister's confidantes, thereby providing confidential briefings on policy or other matters that could be trusted. Such briefings were not necessarily dispassionate or neutral; indeed, under the circumstances, they were likely to be just the opposite. In this context, Dhar (1989) emphasizes that the prime minister's office (PMO) is not a think-tank. While it certainly does assemble ideas on policies from other parts, the PMO rarely generates ideas on its own. More often, it serves as a transmission belt for ideas that constitute part of the inputs that go into policy formulation.

Two Inferences

The above discussion suggests at least two inferences. One is that the PMO is essentially an extension of the political role of the prime minister and that so much depends on how a prime minister prefers this role to be played. The second is that the PMO does not seek advice that may or may not be professional; rather it seeks advice that is trustworthy. These two features of the PMO determine the relationship sought to be established with the cabinet secretariat.

It can be productive to the extent that the congruence between the two functions leads to galvanizing policy inputs from the government and outside. In a situation of power plays, the PMO will fare better because its secretary is someone who has the confidence of the prime minister and reflects the latter's political style.

There is another feature of the PMO that adds to its mystique. The prime minister takes on portfolios that are either important or are lying vacant due to ministerial resignations or reshuffles. In matters relating to work in these ministeries, the prime minister tends to seek advice from the PMO. The role of the PMO expands when the portfolios with the prime minister increase. Prime Ministers Indira Gandhi and Rajiv Gandhi had kept some departments under their charge for long periods during their tenures in office. Atomic Energy has traditionally been directly under the charge of the prime minister since Jawaharlal Nehru began the practice. Mrs. Gandhi added the Department of Electronics in 1970 and that of Space in 1972. This practice was continued by Rajiv Gandhi, who added Science and Technology as well as Ocean Development to the list when he became prime minister. Morarji Desai, however, did not follow this practice.

Prime ministers have usually held portfolios during interim periods when vacancies have occurred. Sometimes these periods have been long and not so 'interim', particularly when a critical ministry is involved. Mrs. Gandhi, for example, held the home portfolio from 27 June 1970 to 4 February 1973; Information and Broadcasting from 18 March 1971 to 7 November 1973; Finance from 16 July 1969 to 26 June 1970; and Defence from 14 January 1980 to 15 January 1982. Similarly, Rajiv Gandhi held portfolios like Environment and Forests (31 December 1984 to 22 October 1986), and Defence (25 September 1985 to 25 July 1987). Some of these portfolios were held by the prime ministers for nearly two years or even more. Mrs. Gandhi held the portfolios of Home and of Information and Broadcasting at a critical period of her political career when she was asserting her supremacy and removing obstacles in the way of her leadership.

The Home portfolio provides direct access to a coercive machinery and crucial investigative agencies that provide classified information on men and events in the country. During the Janata Party interlude of 1977–79, it was for no small reason that the Bharatiya Jan Sangh (now the Bharatiya Janata Party) chose this portfolio in the

Table 6.1

Temporary Charge: Portfolios held by Prime Ministers (for over one year)

Indira Gandhi:	1. Atomic Energy (1967–71, 1971–77, 1980–84)
	2. Planning (1967–71, 1975–77)
	3. External Affairs (1967–69)
	4. Home Affairs (1971–73)
	5. Information and Broadcasting (1971–73)
	6. Space (1972–77, 1980–84)
	7. Electronics (1971–73, 1980–84)
	8. Science and Technology (1975–77, 1980–84)
	9. Defence (1980–82)
Rajiv Gandhi:	1. Environment and Forests (1984–86)
	2. Defence (1985–87)
	3. External Affairs (1987–88)

coalition. The prime minister can also lend prestige and importance to a portfolio in the government. Probably this was Rajiv Gandhi's intention in keeping Environment and Forests for a long time.

These arrangements cannot be termed as interim arrangements. Additional responsibilities undertaken by prime ministers have expanded the role of the PMO and stimulated perceptions of its increasing accumulation of power. By routing decision through the PMO, which provides trustworthy advice, the cabinet secretary gets bypassed because matters are handled directly by the prime minister.

Evidently the PMO is a reflection of a prime minister's personality. Mrs. Gandhi needed a political secretary upon whom she could rely for evolving policies that would establish a pre-eminent role for her in both her party and the government. The prime minister's secretary became her strategist as well as tactician and advised her in the formulation of such public policies as would secure the prestige needed to return to power in the first elections held. But the PMO lost its political lustre when Mrs. Gandhi shifted her trust to another set of policy advisors who were led by her younger son and were not in the formal set-up of the government.

The interventionist image of the PMO is strengthened as prime ministers attempt to make their influence all pervasive. One way for this to happen is through controlling all crucial appointments in the government. A cabinet sub-committee chaired by the prime minister confirms appointments to high-level positions proposed by ministeries, the Public Enterprises Selection Board, and other agencies. In effect this clearance means approval by the prime minister, who in turn seeks advice on these matters from the PMO. Critics contend that such advice should be sought from cabinet secretary, who is the head of the civil services. In fact, delays in obtaining such critical approvals have led many to believe that the 'PM Secretariat has become a very serious bottleneck in the way of smooth functioning of the government' (BM, 1982: 1843). The PMO also appears to be a 'powerhouse of influence' when it takes initiatives in matters which legitimately fall within the realm of ministers. For example, the permission to import colour TV sets as 'gifts' during the 1982 Asian Games was allegedly taken without the knowledge of the Department of Electronics (BM, 1982: 1844).

However, even without the encumbrances of the formal minis-terial set-up, the PMO has taken policy initiatives that may be termed innovative. Policies that strengthened Mrs. Gandhi's poli-tical power, such as abolition of the privy purses, bank national-ization and *garibi hatao* (abolish poverty) emanated from the PMO. Similarly, Rajiv Gandhi had a secretary in the PMO who did not belong to the civil service in the conventional sense but was a professional technocrat instead. He expanded the PMO to include professional advisors who had his trust and who promoted the technological thrust which he favoured.

There is another side to the picture. While the PMO has un-doubtedly become a source of powerful influence in policy matters, some centralization has occurred due to the way the Cabinet itself has functioned. Cabinet ministers have increasingly become sub-servient to the wishes of the prime minister because of the latter's preponderant role in their party. After 1971 Indira Gandhi, and after 1985 Rajiv Gandhi, systematically undermined the institutional mechanisms of the party and chose ministers on the basis of personal loyalty rather than party standing (Bjorkman, 1987; Manor, 1988). One way to ensure such loyalty was to sustain a constant threat of displacement or replacement. Mrs. Gandhi re-shuffled her council of ministers thirty-nine times between 1966 and 1977 and twenty-eight times between 1980 and 1984. From

1984 to 1989 Rajiv Gandhi changed his council no less than thirty-six times. As a result, ministers were loathe to disagree in cabinet meetings because they did not want to risk displeasing the prime minister. A former secretary of the prime minister asserts that Cabinet ministers unnecessarily sent papers and drafts to the prime minister for clearance; files often came with an attached note saying, 'PM may also kindly see before orders are issued' (Alexander, 1991: 50). A similar view is expressed by another secretary when he says that the PMO was constantly besieged with pleas such as: 'It can only be done through your office', 'How will the PM feel about this?' or 'What is his mood like?' (Dhar, 1989–54).

The strength of the PMO lies in the trust placed in it by prime ministers and is reflected in the types of behaviour cited by former secretaries. Since 1977, the PMO secretaries have been retired civil servants whose professional competence would not differ much from that of the contemporaneously serving Cabinet secretaries. Obviously this competence is not of crucial importance to differentiate between these two sets of civil servants. What is important is that the PMO can organize alternative sources of policy inputs. When the prime minister intends to initiate innovative policies or is interested in certain issues that have wider implications, then she or he can include advisors of her/his choice and professional background in the PMO. Mrs. Gandhi used the PMO to retain professionals who would offer her the 'balancing' opposite view (Basu, 1992).

Thus, power politics apart, the PMO offers a prime minister an opportunity to obtain professional advice elsewhere than from normal government sources only. It serves as an institutional base for eliciting views that may counter those offered through regular government channels. The PMO can enhance the prime minister's ability to push forward major policy initiatives. But it has earned a bad name, not because of the concentration of excessive power, but because of the injudicious use of that power (Gill, 1990). However, in a policy set-up within a parliamentary system of government, the PMO can be used effectively as a source of alternative policy advice. Interestingly, Mrs. Gandhi had also provided for a Council of Economic Advisors. This Council consisted of economists of different political persuasions and thus provided an opportunity of having contrary opinions before making a choice.

154 / KULDEEP MATHUR AND JAMES W. BJORKMAN

References

Baru, S. 1992. The 'Development' Prime Minister's Task, *The Economic Times*, November 12.

Bjorkman, J.W. 1987. Party, Personality and Dynasty, in *Political Parties: Electoral Change and Structural Responses*, London, Basil Blackwell.

Dhar, P.N. 1989. The Prime Minister's Office, in Bidyut Sarkar (ed.) *P.N. Haksar: Our Times and the Man*, New Delhi, Allied Publishers.

Gill, S.S. 1990. The PM's Office Has a Valid Role, *The Times of India*, January 5.

Limaye, M. 1989. *Cabinet Government in India*, New Delhi, Radiant Publishers.

Manor, James 1987. Party Decay and Political Crisis in India, *The Washington Quarterly*, Summer.

7

The Prime Minister and the Bureaucracy

David Potter

Any state in modern society includes two core components—a political leadership and a bureaucratic apparatus. Each component is powerful and also dependent on the other for survival over time: political leaders need the apparatus to collect necessary revenue and maintain their positions (if need be, through the use of force) and bureaucrats need the political leadership (obtained through periodic elections or in some other way) to legitimize on a continuing basis their coercive and other activities. These relationships of dependence contribute both to the continuity of the state and to its changing nature. Leadership roles continue even as particular leaders are replaced by others, and bureaucratic structures and procedures remain similar as one generation of bureaucrats is gradually replaced by another. Bureaucracies also change over time, sometimes quite radically, as the two basic components of the state both struggle and cooperate with each other and as the political project of the state evolves in response to changing class and other social forces.

These very general propositions regarding the state in modern society provide a framework for examining relationships between the occupants of the leadership role of the prime minister within the Indian state and civilian bureaucratic structures. I can only touch on certain aspects of these relationships in a chapter like this, but the analysis does bring out elements of cooperation and conflict, continuity and change, and the importance of broader social forces in Indian society and beyond. The chapter opens with a section that briefly sketches the most distinctive feature of India's civilian bureaucracy—the continuation, from 1947 to 1991, of an ICS (Indian Civil Service) tradition of administration within a changing bureaucratic structure. The next two sections trace the ambiguous story of how India's prime ministers during this period relied on and supported the ICS tradition within the bureaucracy while also being, at the same time, more or less hostile to its continuation. The final section suggests rudiments of an explanation of the story.

India's bureaucracy has been profoundly marked by the ICS tradition of administration. This tradition derived mainly from the way the colonial state was organized. Most colonial bureaucrats in India were Indians, and to control them, a few ICS administrators, mostly recruited in Britain, were sent out to India to work as trusted agents of the British government in posts especially reserved for them in the districts and secretariat in each province and at the centre. Setting aside strategic posts for an elite group of administrators in this way had a profound influence on the entire structure of the colonial bureaucracy. The main features of the tradition were:

1. dominance of ICS elite generalists in policy making within secretariats at central and provincial levels;
2. extensive controls over policy implementation placed with ICS district officers;
3. extremely wide disparities (and pay differentials) between the few trusted elite administrators and the many subordinate administrators;
4. separation of policy making by elite generalists in secretariats from policy implementation by subordinate experts—elite generalists on top, technical experts on tap;
5. division of subordinate administrators into many discrete services (fragmented bureaucratic structure);
6. detailed procedural rules and red tape binding most subordinate administrators to routine tasks, with decisions of consequence normally referred to trusted elite generalists; and
7. frequent rotation of ICS men (women were not allowed in the ICS) from post to post (the 'tenure system'), from district to secretariat and back; the system brought field experience to bear on policy making in secretariats, but it also led to

much paperwork and noting on files so that each ICS man, on arrival at his next post, would have the background to policy issues at his fingertips.

These distinctive bureaucratic structures and attendant procedures that characterized colonial administration in India required the presence of an administrative elite like the ICS and only made sense as long as there was such an elite.

Sine Independence, this tradition has been regularly criticized as being administratively inappropriate in the changed circumstances. For example:

> The ICS has contained some outstanding individuals, but it is a symbol of inequality, casteism and amateurish dilettantism in our administration. The tradition may have been appropriate to a colonial regime when the functions of government were limited and comparatively simple. But with the increasing complexity of functions and the technical nature of many of the problems faced, the continuance of this tradition is bound to affect the successful conduct of our attempts at planned development (Paranjape, 1966).

The tradition has also been repeatedly criticized as being inconsistent with India's federal democracy: the Indian Constitution 'has the facade of a democratic formulation but its interior design reflects imperial hauteur' (Mitra, 1991). Despite such criticisms, in the early 1990s the bureaucracy in India, as a whole, was still marked by the ICS tradition of administration. It was still very elitist; members of an all-India elite, the IAS (Indian Administrative Service), dominated the administrative input into policy making in secretariats at the central and state levels. India was still divided into districts for purposes of policy implementation and each district was presided over by a district officer (normally IAS). The pay differentials between top IAS administrators and lowly subordinates were extremely wide. The subordinate bureaucracy over which the IAS presided was still fragmented into numerous separate services. For example, in Rajasthan state in 1981 there were 319,567 bureaucrats (not counting those in all-India services like the IAS) divided into 109 separate services, each with their own pay scales and conditions of service (Government of Rajasthan, 1981).

Numerous studies have also found that subordinate bureaucrats were bound tightly by detailed rules and red tape, leading (according to probably the best such study) to the overriding importance which subordinates placed on obeying elite superiors and procedural rules (Mook, 1982). I have argued elsewhere that lower level bureaucrats in India are not innately deferential and rule-bound, but rather that they have been made so as a consequence of having to work within an institutional structure organized to accommodate an ICS tradition of administration (Potter, 1986, esp. Chaps 1 and 6).

As for the tenure system, it still existed in 1994 despite the federal structure of democratic government. Like its predecessor, the IAS as a whole was made up of state (formerly provincial) cadres. There was no central government cadre. What made the IAS all-India was that during the course of a member's career, he or she might work for the central government from time to time; and, if so, the person was placed on deputation to the central government for a period of years, and except in unusual circumstances, he or she reverted to the state at the end of the period. While servicing under a state government, an IAS officer was formally under its control. However, he or she was governed by service rules made by the central government, and these could only be altered or interpreted by the centre. In effect, what the central government was doing was recruiting an elite group of officers and sending them to the states to hold key administrative posts in the secretariats and districts there. Such an arrangement, appropriate to a colonial regime, was hardly likely to delight political leaders in state governments, particularly those state governments formed by political parties opposed to the party(ies) controlling the central government.

The ICS tradition continued even while the bureaucracy as a whole changed in many ways. For one thing, the bureaucracy ballooned in size. The data in Table 7.1 shows that the size of India's bureaucracy in 1989 had more than quadrupled since 1953. The figures for 'state government' include those persons who worked in the districts. The 'quasi-government' figures refer to those who worked for public enterprises or nationalized industries accountable either to the central government or to a state government. The 'local bodies' figures include those who were employed by Panchayati Raj (or village council) institutions in rural districts

Table 7.1

India—Growth of Public Sector Employment 1953–89
(in millions, rounded)

	1953	1973	1989
Central Government	1.5	2.9	3.4
State Government	2.2	4.6	6.9
Quasi-Government	0.1	2.5	6.0
Local Bodies	0.3	1.9	2.2
Total	4.1	11.9	18.5

Sources: For 1953: data derived from GOI, Directorate General of Employment and Training, Census of Central Government Employees, 1961, mimeo, which uses 1953 as a base year; for 1973: GOI, Ministry of Finance, Economic Division, Economic Survey, 1973–74 (1974), p. 28; for 1989: GOI, Ministry of Labour Handbook of Labour Statistics, 1991, p. 8.

or by metropolitan and other urban governments (most of which were also within districts).

The government and the bureaucracy had also become vastly more complex by the early 1990s. In the central government, for example, the number of ministries had just about doubled between 1947 (seventeen) (Indian Institute of Public Administration, 1958) and 1991 (thirty-three) (Government of India, 1991), and the remit of each one had also expanded. The ministries in 1991 were as follows:

1. Agriculture
2. Civil Aviation
3. Commerce
4. Communications
5. Defence
6. Energy and Non-conventional Energy Resource
7. Environment and Forests
8. External Affairs
9. Finance
10. Food
11. Civil Supplies, Consumer Affairs and Public Distribution

12. Food Processing Industries
13. Health and Family Welfare
14. Home Affairs
15. Human Resources Development
16. Industry
17. Information and Broadcasting
18. Labour
19. Law, Justice and Company Affairs
20. Parliamentary Affairs
21. Personnel, Public Grievances and Pensions
22. Petroleum and Natural Gas
23. Planning
24. Programme Implementation
25. Railways
26. Science and Technology
27. Steel and Mines
28. Surface Transport
29. Textiles
30. Tourism
31. Urban Development
32. Water Resources
33. Welfare

Many of these ministries had oversight of various separate departments. P.V. Narasimha Rao involved himself in a number of them. Besides being prime minister and chairman of the Planning Commission, his portfolios in October 1991 included four ministries (Industry; Science and Technology; Personnel, Public Grievances and Pensions; Civil Supplies, Consumer Affairs and Public Distribution) and six departments (Atomic Energy, Electronics, Fertilizers, Ocean Development, Rural Development, and Space). Previous prime ministers also took on a number of such portfolios. To add to the growing complexity, there was a tremendous expansion in the number of public sector undertakings. For example, those accountable to the Government of India rose from fifty-three in 1958 (Ramanadham, 1964) to 214 in 1991 (Government of India, 1991). The ICS tradition ensured that the top civil servants in most of the ministries and departments were IAS officers and that these IAS officers were involved in many of the public sector undertakings as managing directors or in some other leading capacity.

Coordinating this increasingly complex array of governmental activities involved the Cabinet and the Cabinet Office, the PMO (Prime Minister's Office), interdepartmental committees and informal networks of IAS officers and ministers in different ministries, departments and public sector undertakings. The power of the PMO has varied considerably under different prime ministers. Jawaharlal Nehru had only a small personal office and coordination of government activity occurred mainly through interdepartmental committees and networks, the Cabinet, and to some extent the Ministry of External Affairs, of which he was also the Minister. During his brief tenure, Lal Bahadur Shastri set up a Prime Minister's Secretariat to service the papers submitted to him. Indira Gandhi then greatly expanded the scope and power of this Secretariat; it began to issue directives to departments and ministries, and sometimes even ministers learned what their policies were from their senior administrators who had received the news from the Prime Minister's Secretariat. Morarji Desai changed the name back to the PMO and began to reduce its size and power. Although Indira Gandhi's second term saw the PMO become powerful again, Rajiv Gandhi reversed that somewhat, and V.P. Singh and Narasimha Rao continued this trend by trying to achieve coordination in more traditional ways and giving more autonomy to ministries and departments. Again, the ICS tradition has ensured that whatever the particular constellation of forces under a prime minister, the IAS officers were always prominent within it, holding key posts in the PMO, the Cabinet Office and the ministries.

Important as the IAS was within this complex and growing bureaucracy at different levels, it remained minute in size; in 1991, it contained 4,881 persons (not including the 1990 and 1991 recruits), roughly .00003 per cent of the bureaucracy as a whole. Table 7.2 sets out the principal administrative units into which India as a whole was divided in 1991, together with the total strength of the IAS for each unit (a few of whom from each unit were on deputation to the central government). It shows 466 districts in twenty-five states and seven union territories in 1991: the number of states and districts has increased as the size of the population and the bureaucracy has grown (for example, 233 districts in eight provinces in

Table 7.2

Principal Administrative Units and IAS Distribution in India, 1991

States	Population	Number of Districts	Number in IAS Cadre
Andhra Pradesh	66,304,854	23	312
Arunachal Pradesh	858,392	11	196
Assam	22,294,562	23	196
Bihar	86,338,853	42	383
Goa	1,168,622	2	a
Gujarat	41,174,060	19	241
Haryana	16,317,715	16	206
Himachal Pradesh	5,111,079	12	129
Jammu and Kashmir	7,718,700d	14	98
Karnataka	44,817,398	20	258
Kerala	29,011,237	14	161
Madhya Pradesh	66,135,862	45	378
Maharashtra	78,706,719	30	339
Manipur	1,826,714	8	135
Meghalaya	1,760,626	5	b
Mizoram	686,217	3	a
Nagaland	1,215,573	7	51
Orissa	31,512,070	13	202
Punjab	20,190,795	12	171
Rajasthan	43,880,640	27	241
Sikkim	403,612	4	44
Tamil Nadu	55,638,318	21	305
Tripura	2,744,827	3	c
Uttar Pradesh	138,760,417	63	530
West Bengal	67,982,732	17	298
Union Territories(7)	11,370,267	12	197
All-India total	843,930,861e	466	4,881f

Notes: a) The figure is included within the figure for Union Territories.
b) The figure is included within the figure for Assam.
c) The figure is included within the figure for Manipur.
d) The 1991 Census had not yet been conducted in J & K, so this figure is a projection.
e) Provisional figure.
f) This figures does not include 1990 and 1991 recruits.

Sources: Ashish Bose, Demographic Diversity of India, 1991 Census: State and District Level Data (Delhi, 1991). For the IAS figures, GOI, Ministry of Personnel, Public Grievances and Pensions, The Indian Administrative Service Civil List 1991 (New Delhi, 1991).

1919, 324 districts in fifteen states in 1962).[1] The IAS has grown accordingly and has continued to occupy an increasingly wide range of control posts at the district, state and central levels.

Table 7.3 shows the location of the IAS in 1991 as compared to the location of the ICS in 1919. Considerable difficulty was encountered in classifying the data on which the comparison in this table is based. Nevertheless, even if one allows for errors in classification, the data does suggest a broad ICS/IAS continuity.

The changing proportions between those in the districts and those in the state (provincial) secretariats are not as great as they

Table 7.3

Distribution of ICS/IAS Officers in India, 1919 and 1991

Level	1919		1991	
	Number of ICS	% of Total ICS	Number of IAS	% of Total IAS
District	497	38	1,294	27
Province/State	415	31	2,145	44
Govt. of India	182	14	815	16
Other	224	17	627	13
Total	1,318	100	4,881	100

Note: 'District' level includes commissioners of divisions, district officers, and officers within district (e.g. subdivisional officers). 'Province/State' level includes officers working in 'Provincial/State' headquarters and the 1919 officers on the judicial side. 'Government of India' level includes all officers on deputation there and officers from one province/state temporarily working in another. 'Other' for 1919 includes ICS officers posted to Burma (123) and recruited in 1919 (101). 'Other' for 1991 includes IAS officers who were working in public enterprises (438), and those on leave, in transit, under suspension and other miscellaneous (189); 1990 probationers (106) appointed on the results of the 1989 civil service examination but not yet allotted a state cadre are not included.

Sources: The data has been collected and compiled by the author on the basis of a careful classification of all the entries in the relevant civil lists. For various reasons, the 1921 Civil List is the best source for the 1919 position: The India Office List of 1921 (London, 1921, pp. 453–796). For 1991: Government of India, Ministry of Personnel, Public Grievances and Pensions, The Indian Administrative Service Civil List, 1991 (New Delhi, 1991, pp. 1–399, 448–49). The list gives the position as on 1 January 1991.

may seem. There were actually more IAS officers per district on average in 1991 than ICS officers per district in 1919 (1,354 IAS in 466 districts, 497 ICS in 233 districts). There were, however, far more secretariats in 1991 (twenty-five plus the centre) than in 1919 (eight plus the centre), and it is this change which largely explains the changing ICS/IAS percentages between the district and provincial/state secretariats.

In the 1930s, Nehru was extremely hostile to the ICS, which he perceived as the central instrument of colonial rule.[2] He thought it 'quite essential that the ICS and similar services must disappear completely, as such, before one can start real work on a new order' (Nehru, 1962: 445). His view changed somewhat in the 1940s; in *The Discovery of India*, there is the same general hostility to the ICS as an institution distinct from the individuals who inhabit it, but he does not quite say that it should be wound up (Nehru, 1956). Although he changed his position regarding the abolition of the ICS, he was not thereby converted into an enthusiast for the ICS. It was Sardar Vallabhbhai Patel who was the enthusiast on this issue. Nehru appears, by comparison, as a figure dragged along by forces beyond his control. This is well illustrated by Nehru's muted response to a proposal brought to a cabinet meeting on 30 April 1948 by Patel to provide special protection in the new Constitution for the all-India services (including the ICS and IAS) (Shiva Rao, 1968). The draft constitution at this time made no reference to the all-India services. Such a proposal for a constitutional guarantee for an administrative elite was quite extraordinary and probably unique in the history of constitutions. Clearly it would strengthen the position of the ICS/IAS enormously within the Indian state. Nehru let it go through. He was also not present at the subsequent Constituent Assembly sessions in 1949 when the guarantees were debated and approved (Articles 308–14); nor did he attend the session where Patel made his celebrated speech defending the ICS (Government of India, 1949), a speech which was subsequently circulated in written form by the ICS (Central) Association to all ICS Indians throughout the country and received by them with delight (quoted in Das, 1973).

From then on, until 1964, Nehru appears to have maintained a distant, unenthusiastic stance regarding the ICS (and the IAS), although his position was not entirely consistent on the subject. This characterization can be gleaned from a study of the letters that Nehru wrote to the chief ministers in the states; 378 such letters written between October 1947 and December 1963 have been published in five volumes.[3] Initially Nehru set out to write at some length to the chief ministers every fortnight, but he was unable to adhere rigidly to that schedule due to pressure of work. Some of these letters are brief, touching on only one subject. A majority of them, however, are Nehru's 'fortnightly letters' in which he writes at length on the range of issues and current events, both domestic and international, that were uppermost in his mind at the time. The letters were marked 'secret', although they were apparently copied by some chief ministers and some of their contents were leaked to the press, much to Nehru's annoyance). Nehru expressed himself quite freely in these letters, and it therefore seems reasonable to suppose that they give a fairly accurate indication of his views on government and politics during the period.

It is striking that in these 378 letters bound together in five fat volumes, the administration, and more generally the services, are referred to only occasionally. Only sixty-three letters make any explicit mention of the subject; fifteen give it more than one paragraph; twenty-two up to one paragraph; the other twenty-six only one or two sentences in passing in 'fortnightly letters' each of which normally ran on for between twenty and thirty numbered paragraphs. The letters with only one or two sentences on administration need not detain us here, but the contents of the thirty-seven letters in which there is up to one paragraph or several paragraphs on the subject give the essentials of Nehru's views. Their contents can be summarized under four headings.

First, one of the main themes is the need for an overhauling of the whole administrative apparatus inherited from the British colonial rule. A basic reform of the administrative structure is required; 'superficial reforms and improvements' will not be enough (6 November, 1953). The old bureaucratic approach 'is not good enough', he says, and we must 'get out of the ruts and routines of signing papers and files' (5 August, 1961). The problems of inefficiency, lack of coordination, red tape, inaccessibility, corruption and so on cannot be resolved unless the 'archaic' administrative machinery is overhauled (5 May, 1948). The inherited administration also does not really 'fit' the needs of democracy and development (28 September, 1953). At the same time Nehru is somewhat ambivalent about that inheritance. It was 'more or less efficient' for colonial purposes and we have inherited 'good men', yet many of them are inefficient, inaccessible, slow and corrupt (16 November 1948; 28 September 1953). Another thing to notice from the dates of the letters is that Nehru wanted major administrative reform in 1948 and still wanted it fifteen years later.

Second, there are remarks in these letters suggesting that Nehru believed that the ICS tradition, in particular, was unsuitable in the changed circumstances, although he was not entirely consistent on the subject. The whole structure 'built up on the district officer . . . must necessarily change', he says, because it is unsuitable in a 'democratic set-up' (1 August 1949). Appointing ICS/IAS administrative generalists as heads of technical departments 'is not a good practice', he says, because technical officers with expertise are thereby defined as 'a lesser breed' (2 November 1957). The practice, peculiar to the all-India services like the ICS/IAS, of members serving in central government posts on deputation from provincial/ state cadres and then reverting to provincial/state cadres after some years 'is a good one', says Nehru, although he is critical of the tendency of some officers 'remaining too long at a time at the centre' (1 October 1953). The special guarantees and assurances for the ICS/IAS written into the Constitution 'petrify' the caste-like inequalities 'in our administrative system', he says, and 'hardly fit into a democratic structure' (24 May 1953; 28 September 1953). He is silent regarding what should replace the ICS/IAS, or how these 'generally good and efficient' persons might be redeployed (27 September 1950).

Third, it is noticeable that sixteen of the letters date from 1953 to 1954 only. Most of these refer to the Report on Public Administration submitted to the Government of India in early 1953 by Professor Paul Appleby. Nehru thinks the Report is of 'outstanding importance', presumably in part because Appleby proposed some alternatives to the existing administrative structures (19 April 1953). He read it 'two or three times', the Cabinet gave it 'much thought', and he also urged the chief ministers in the states to think about its implications 'in a basic way' (28 September 1953; 6 November 1953). But a year later Nehru made plaintive remarks like: 'We do not seem to get a move on' and 'What are we to do?' (1–8 January 1954). The matters seemed to defeat him. In May 1954, he informed the chief ministers that he was actually going to set aside some time for further study of Appleby's Report in full 'and in July I hope we can come to grips with it as a Government' (20 May, 1954). However, there are no references to these promises in the letters that summer. Indeed, Nehru appears to have lost interest in administrative reform altogether after nothing emerged out of his efforts in 1953–54. It is remarkable that between 15 August 1954 and 31 December 1957, he sent seventy-six letters to chief ministers, but only one had a paragraph on administration and three others had a sentence or two.

Finally, eleven of the thirty-seven letters date from 1958–59 and most of these, prompted by the report of the Balwantrai Mehta Committee (Government of India, 1957) complain about subordinate officials in rural districts. Nehru is 'alarmed at the growth of bureaucracy . . . in the lower ranks' (15 January, 1958). The agriculture departments are 'embedded in their old routines' and 'our development programmes move much more slowly than they ought to' (23/24 January 1958; 16 September 1958). The tendency of lower level bureaucrats to convert self-reliance into dependence on the state 'is thoroughly bad' and 'nothing can be more fatal than this terrible reliance on official agency to do everything' (12 November, 1958, 28 May, 1959). Some years later, in 1963, he complained that it would be 'a tragedy if the BDO [block development officer] and the village level worker even behaved like bureaucrats' (14 April, 1963).

The ICS tradition prospered during Nehru's time, yet he appears never to have been reconciled to this development. In the spring of 1964, shortly before his death, he was apparently asked at a private meeting by some friends what he considered to be his greatest failure as India's first prime minister. He reportedly replied: 'I could not change the administration, it is still a colonial administration', and went on to elaborate his belief that the continuation of the colonial administration was one of the main causes of India's inability to solve the problem of poverty (Vittachi, 1978).

From 1966 onwards, the two major Congress Prime Ministers, Indira Gandhi and Rajiv Gandhi, complained publicly from time to time about the bureaucracy along the lines that Nehru had articulated. Indira Gandhi, for example, 'had occasion to regret that her father had not seized the opportunity to overhaul our administration' (Singh, 1981). But no major reform occurred. As for the non-Congress prime ministers—Morarji Desai, Charan

Singh, V.P. Singh and Chandra Shekhar—they did not have the time or the inclination to take on the major struggle that would have been involved. During Morarji Desai's period as Prime Minister, the Shah Commission vaguely said that the whole admin- istration must be overhauled, 'for there is a long standing problem of relations between politics and administration in India . . ., yet nothing is done' (1978). However, no specific proposals were made.

There was only one major proposal which threatened the dominance of the ICS tradition between 1964 and the early 1990s. This occurred in 1969 as a result of a comprehensive examination of Indian administration by the Administrative Reform Commission (ARC). One of ARC's nineteen formal reports recommended, essentially, that specialists should become increasingly important in policy making and that 'the doors of senior management should be open to all sectors of the civil service' (1969). By opening up a road to the top for all civil servants, and thereby putting an end to IAS generalists coming on deputation from states to command automatically all (or most) of the top posts, the ARC in fact sounded the death-knell of the ICS tradition. IAS people saw the danger immediately. One said quite bluntly that the 'elitist concept is the very substance of the IAS, and any arrangement that disturbs this concept also demolishes the service', and added that the 'more honest course for the Commission would have been to suggest the abolition of the IAS' (Mohanty, 1969). This quite fundamental ARC proposal was never acted on by Indira Gandhi's government (for reasons referred to later), although many minor ARC proposals were implemented.

The basic organizing principle of the bureaucracy has remained the same through all the comings and goings of prime ministers since 1947, but there were also changes 'at the margins', so to speak, brought about largely as a consequence of the changing styles of prime ministers. One of the most noticeable changes was the increasing importance of 'political loyalty'. This change began to be noticed from 1969–70 when Indira Gandhi and other Congress Party leaders called for more 'commitment' from civil servants, agruing that 'the so-called neutral administrative machinery is a hindrance, not a help' and 'is hardly relevant to Indian conditions' (Aiyar, 1971). These remarks were hotly debated within the bureaucracy at the time. Indira Gandhi even tried to clarify what she had meant by commitment in the Lok Sabha:

It has been said that . . . I am planning to use the civil service for political purposes . . . . My remark about committed civil servants has been twisted . . . . I meant . . . that they should be loyal to the guiding principles of our Constitution and the objectives which have been adopted by Parliament . . . . I certainly do not want civil servants who are in any way servile or politically convenient because if they were so they would not be helpful to the Government or to the administration (Lok Sabha Debates, 1970).

But her actions subsequently spoke more loudly than her words. From the early 1970s onwards, it seemed that loyalty to the prime minister and the party in power in New Delhi began to become part of the IAS reward structure. This had not been true before.

The Emergency imposed by Indira Gandhi in 1975 drove home these tendencies. The evidence which appeared in the Shah Commission of Inquiry Reports after the Emergency suggested that many district officers 'obediently carried out the instructions emanating from politicians and administrative heads issued on personal or political considerations'. These men told the Shah Commission (1978: 299) that in the circumstances they had no choice—they were 'helpless' due to fear of the consequences of not obeying. In the state and central secretariats, the Shah Commission found instances of IAS officers engaged in the 'forging of records, fabrication of grounds of detention, ante-dating of detention orders, and callous disregard of the rights of detainees as regards revocation, parole, etc.' (1978: 142). There were many cases where officers 'curried favour' with politicians 'by doing what they thought the people in authority desired' (1978: 230). One journalist remarked that the Emergency represented 'the high-water mark of the politicians' victory in the long-drawn-out struggle against the service' (Vohra, 1978: 14).

This 'long-drawn-out struggle' continued for the rest of the 1970s. The elections of 1977 swept the Congress out both at the centre and, later, in many states. Some IAS administrators were rewarded at that time for the rapidity with which they had moved to assist the new non-Congress governments. Then in January 1980, Indira Gandhi swept back to power at the centre and by May, the Congress was back in most states. IAS administrators formerly loyal to the Congress were reinstated, whereas others who had done well under the Janata Party were shunted aside. Years later that experience was still being talked about as having marred the reputation of the IAS by making political loyalty an even more important value than before as one of the norms for advancement to plum jobs.

Indira Gandhi's tendency to identify and reward her bureaucratic 'favourites' unsettled the bureaucracy by enhancing factional splits and intra-bureaucratic disputes. At the same time, however, she depended greatly on the bureaucracy when imposing repressive policies. During the Emergency the IAS officers 'stood forth' as the rulers of states and districts, taking orders direct from the Prime Minister's Secretariat. The IAS mechanism was neatly positioned to coordinate the Emergency throughout the country. Likewise, imposing President's Rule on individual states would have been far more difficult without an all-India service in place at district and state levels. For example, the initial decision to impose President's Rule in Punjab in 1983 was taken by Indira Gandhi and her political colleagues, but then the detailed questions of implementation and political calculation locally were left almost entirely in the hands of senior administrators and the intelligence agencies. The three advisers sent to Punjab to coordinate the action were all IAS officers, and they were briefed before they left for Chandigarh by the home secretary and the cabinet secretary (both IAS). On arrival, they immediately got in touch with their IAS colleagues controlling the Punjab Secretariat and each of the twelve Punjab districts. More generally, as regards more normal government activity, Indira Gandhi valued 'her' top civil servants (more than Nehru did 'his') and it was noticeable in the early 1980s that she met with them at least as frequently as with her ministers.

As Prime Minister, Rajiv Gandhi continued, broadly speaking, his mother's regime vis-à-vis relations between the prime minister's office and the bureaucracy. His initial moves suggested that he was interested in relaxing the hold of the PMO over the central government, but he soon gave that up. Rajiv also had his favourite bureaucrats; his 'partisan' promotions and transfers of senior bureaucrats were the subject of regular complaints by such bureaucrats in the press and elsewhere (Buch, 1987; Deshmukh, 1991; Gujral, 1991). Such alignments deepened the factional splits within the IAS and the bureaucracy generally. Sometimes Rajiv publicly lost his cool with certain senior civil servants whom he disliked. In the winter of 1986–87, for example, he was exceptionally rude to the secretary for rural development in public, and rather arrogantly dismissed a popular foreign secretary. Nevertheless, he met senior bureaucrats frequently and depended heavily on them while complaining of bureaucratic delay, inefficiency and corruption.

He experimented impatiently with several different arrangements intended to speed up work and improve efficiency in the central government: he tried creating advisory committees on administration located within the PMO; then he tried creating a set of 'super-secretaries'—a brains trust of IAS bureaucrats who could cut through red tape and enforce interdepartmental decisions, answering directly to him. After this he attempted appointing in every ministry and department of the Government of India, a special 'adviser to the prime minister', each one to be a senior bureaucrat on the verge of retirement and given the rank of minister of state (reported in *India Today*, 15 May, 1987: 22). None of these schemes worked well. Never during his time as prime minister does he appear to have expressed interest in more fundamental bureaucratic reform or in ending the ICS tradition of administration. Even after he and his government were voted out of office in 1989, he continued to demonstrate his essentially partisan handling of senior civil servants, at formal social occasions at the Rashtrapati Bhavan (the president's residence) or elsewhere where he was invited as leader of the opposition, he was regularly observed to spend nearly all his time there talking to 'his' bureaucrats rather than engaging with other political leaders and the main dignitaries.[4]

Between 1989 and 1991, three prime ministers followed in rapid succession. Till the time of the writing of this article, none has had the time to make a major impact on the bureaucracy inherited from Indira and Rajiv, but certain developments are worth noting. V.P. Singh had identified 'his' senior civil servants, and upon becoming prime minister, a large number of 'political transfers' took place to bring them into key positions, as had happened with changes of government since the 1970s. Narasimha Rao, however, has not followed suit at the time of writing, and perhaps the overheating of the transfer bazaar that habitually attended the arrival of new prime ministers has passed its zenith. The power of the PMO was also reduced by 1991. At this time there was a noticeable trend under Narasimha Rao to loosen up the central government somewhat, in the sense that ministers and departments were beginning to be allowed more autonomy, with the Cabinet

Office coming again into the picture to some extent for purposes of coordination. Also, the days of the PMO ringing up district officers had gone, suggesting that the administrative over-centralization was being relaxed nationally. At another level, however, administrative centralization was shortly to increase due to the development of an extensive computer network, linked to a national main frame, with the actions of key IAS and other administrators at block, district, state and national levels beginning to be shaped by what the computer said was national policy.

The main organizing principle of India's bureaucracy today is still the ICS tradition of administration (Potter, 1986; 1989). Over the years, prime ministers and many other people had been critical of this tradition and the bureaucratic pathologies that it had spawned. But it survived. Why? How does one explain this bureaucratic continuity in the face of prime ministerial hostility? The subject is vast, of course, and cannot be gone into thoroughly in a chapter of this length. Vital ingredients of an explanation, however, can be indicated by considering two historical 'moments' when the ICS tradition was most seriously threatened and yet the prime ministers involved did not act decisively to change it. One was the period immediately following the end of British rule in 1947, the other was the early 1970s following the ARC proposal to end IAS dominance. In both cases one needs to examine the relevant party structure involved and the bureaucratic lobbying that was going on.

Nehru's changing views of the ICS in the late 1930s and the 1940s were shaped by the changing character of the Congress, which represented a disparate amalgam of interests, classes and groups. There were considerable differences on this score from province to province, but one can perhaps say that the Congress was gaining support from sections of the urban working class and from the peasantry in some provinces, and also from certain professional groups in the towns during this period. It also represented and was beholden to India's small, but increasingly important indigenous capitalist class, whose interests, to some extent, conflicted with the maintenance of British rule because of the restrictions placed on their activities for the benefit of British capital. Bigger Indian capitalists were divided and uncertain as to whether or not they should align with the Congress. However, they tended to keep aloof from provincial politics. At the lower levels of the Congress organization, merchants and traders appear to have increased their influence mainly through their control of the financial resources that the Congress required to contest elections. These relationships affected ideological struggles within the Congress, and the right wing of the Congress became increasingly alarmed at the strength of socialists like Nehru within the organization and gradually took control. By the 1940s, these more conservative elements in the Congress were in the ascendant and increasingly in a position to control the state. Unity, continuity, order and a political posture not unfriendly to capitalist enterprise became the main orientations, and were indeed paramount considerations in the decisions taken by the new Congress leadership in the interim government and the Constituent Assembly between 1946 and 1950. More precisely, Markovitz (1985) has argued that (*a*) Indian capitalists were not 'particularly attached to democratic forms of government', (*b*) they 'appreciated strong bureaucratic rule', and (*c*) they 'primarily wished to see a set of British bureaucrats replaced by a set of indigenous ones who would be more open to Indian capitalist influence'. Such thinking, translated into definite proposals by conservative Congress leaders including Sardar Patel, saved the ICS tradition.

Nehru's views were affected by these changing orientations within the Congress. As a Congress leader, he had perhaps more freedom to manoeuvre within the organization than many others, including the ability to shape thinking within the Congress itself. But conservative forces within the Congress in the 1940s were sufficiently formidable to force Nehru to modify his position on the ICS and on the nature of the bureaucratic apparatus of the state more generally. He may not have felt he was being forced; it was more a matter of accepting the 'political reality' of the structure of power that he inhabited at the time and of adjusting his political positions accordingly, while holding on to certain essential aims and principles. Whether or not the ICS survived was probably less important to Nehru at that time than other aims like achieving political independence and becoming prime minister. Dropping the demand for ICS abolition in the 1940s made sense to a man who aspired to political leadership of the Indian state using a fairly conservative Congress as the base of his political support.

The structural point is very important, but it is also important to appreciate that during the 1940s, Indian members of the ICS were not simply sitting about idly waiting for the winds of structural forces to move in their direction. The numerous memoirs of ICS Indians suggest that many were keen nationalists who welcomed independence from British rule and made themselves useful to Congress leaders as part of a quite blatant lobbying effort meant to ensure the continuation of their service in the new India. For example, a group of senior ICS Hindus at the centre lobbied Congress leaders for precisely this reason in September 1946; Nehru actually rebuffed them, but Patel and others welcomed them (Gadgil, 1986). Similar efforts were taking place in the provinces. For example, Govind Narain (ICS, Uttar Pradesh) was collector of Farukhabad when Govind Ballabh Pant (later chief minister of Uttar Pradesh) campaigned there on an election tour in the winter of 1945–46. 'I knew the local leaders', Narain divulged years later (1976) 'and had a quiet understanding with them according to which my duty did not stand in the way of Pant's getting full facilities for his campaigning in my district.' The efforts of ICS Indians during the 1940s, in their relations with Congress leaders, help to explain how the ICS survived in the 1940s despite their lack of success with Nehru. The fruit of their effort was the constitutional guarantee of 1949. After that, only a very powerful attack would be enough to dislodge them from their commanding position within the bureaucracy.

A full explanation of why Nehru changed his views on the ICS in the 1940s and why the ICS/IAS remained untouched by his expressed desire to reform them for the rest of his life would no doubt involve more than a consideration of the political and administrative structures with which he had to contend. But the crux of any explanation must surely be the changing character of the Congress in the 1930s and 1940s, the subsequent lack of enthusiasm for radical reform within it, and the power of the ICS/IAS as an institution within the state to control administrative reform throughout the period. This constellation of forces was too powerful for Nehru.

These forces were also too powerful for the eight prime ministers (nine, if Indira Gandhi is counted twice) who came after Nehru. The Congress prime ministers, who were in power for twenty-two of the next twenty-eight years, worked within a party structure in which bureaucratic reform was never a political issue of importance, and the IAS lobbied effectively to deflect any proposal that threatened their interests. Their abilities in this regard were clearly demonstrated when the ICS tradition was severely threatened in the early 1970s. When the ARC Report on Personnel Administration was formally submitted to the Prime Minister (Indira Gandhi), the Chairman of the ARC (1969) sent a covering letter to her in which he poignantly remarked:

> The reforms we have recommended are bound to raise resistance from those who are adversely affected. Resistance from within the service is a very difficult problem for the Government to deal with. The declarations made from time to time by the Prime Minister and other Cabinet Ministers have emphasized that reforms of a fundamental character are needed. Resistance based on sectional or personal interests should not be allowed to come in the way of putting them into effect.

The IAS was 'the service' referred to in this letter and it would certainly have been 'adversely affected' if the prime minister had accepted the recommendation. The IAS moved quickly to block it. When the Cabinet delegated responsibility for implementing ARC recommendations to the small Department of Administrative Reforms in the Home Ministry and a new Department of Personnel in the Cabinet Secretariat, the IAS made sure they dominated these two organizations. The small Department in the Home Ministry was already an IAS preserve; as for the new Department of Personnel, as many as twenty IAS officers poured in there very quickly, and by 1971 the secretary and seven additional and joint secretaries were all IAS. Many of the minor ARC recommendations were accepted and implemented by those two departments, but no action was taken regarding the main proposal undermining the pre-eminent position of the IAS. Their initiative, together with the broad structure of political support, which deterred the prime minister from acting decisively, ensured the survival of the ICS tradition of administration in the early 1970s.

The ICS tradition is again under serious threat in the 1990s. The threat comes partly from the increasing number of able people in other services within the bureaucracy clamouring insistently for putting an end to large pay differentials, special privileges for the IAS, extraordinary elitism in postings at national and state levels, colonial-style district administration and the rest. Political support for the IAS may also be more precarious now, as a stronger commitment to democracy continues to spread and deepen amongst India's lower classes, thereby making the 'imperial hauteur' of the ICS tradition appear increasingly anachronistic to an increasing numbers of voters. Ending the ICS tradition may then become a political issue, and a prime minister and his/her party might finally act to dismantle the colonial framework within India's post-colonial bureaucracy.

Notes

1. The 1919 district figure is as reported in the 1921 Census. For 1962, figures compiled from GOI, Ministry of Information and Broadcasting, *India, A Reference Annual, 1962* (New Delhi, 1962, pp. 390–500).
2. I have dealt with this subject previously and at greater length in my 'Jawaharlal Nehru and the Indian Civil Service', *South Asia Research* (Nov. 1989), pp. 128–44. The account here leans partly on that, but also incorporates evidence from the fifth and final volume of Nehru's *Letters to Chief Ministers*, which was not yet available when the earlier article was written.
3. J. Nehru, *Letters to Chief Ministers, 1947–1964* (general editor, G. Parthasarathi) (Delhi, 1985–89), Vol. 1: 1947–49 (1985); Vol. 2: 1950–52 (1986); Vol. 3: 1952–54 (1987); Vol. 4: 1954–57 (1988); Vol. 5: 1958–64 (1989). All 378 letters in the five volumes were examined; the index appended to each volume was useless for my purpose here. I am grateful to Professor W.H. Morris-Jones for drawing my attention to this source.
4. I am grateful for this observation, and for the content of the next paragraph to Kuldeep Mathur—conversation, New Delhi, 19 October 1991.

References

Administrative Reforms Commission 1969. *Report on Personnel Administration*, New Delhi.
Aiyar, S.P. 1971. Political Context of Indian Administration, *Indian Journal of Public Administration* (July–September).
Buch, M.N. 1987. Promotion Policies in Civil Service, *The Times of India*, 7 April.
Centre of Publications 1991. *Directory of Central Government Officials*, New Delhi.
———— 1991. *Seminar Executives of Public Sector Undertakings*, New Delhi.
Das, D. 1973. *Sardar Patel's Correspondence 1945–50*, Vol. VIII, Ahmedabad.
Deshmukh, B.G. 1991. Role of Cabinet Secretary Post must not be Politicised, *The Times of India*, 7 October.
Gadgil, I.K. 1991. PMO's Chart, *The Times of India*, 18 October.
Gadgil, N.V. 1986. *Government from Inside*, Meerut.
Government of India 1949. *Constituent Assembly Debates*, Vol. X, Ahmedabad.
———— 1957. *Report of the Team for the Study of Community Projects and National Extension Service*, Vols. I–III, New Delhi, Committee on Plan Projects.

Government of India 1970. *Lok Sabha Debates (10th Session)*, 37 (11), 4 March, 1970.

Indian Institute of Public Administration 1958. *The Organization of the Government of India*, New Delhi.

Markovitz, C. 1985. *Indian Business and Nationalist Politics, 1931–39*, Cambridge, Cambridge University Press.

Mitra, Ashok 1991. Calcutta Diary, *Economic and Political Weekly*, 19 November.

Mohanty, N. 1969. ARC on Personnel Administration: A Study of Bias, *Indian Journal of Public Administration*, October–December.

Mook, B. 1982. *The World of Indian Field Administrator*, New Delhi, Vikas.

Narain, G. 1976. 'Same Stray Thoughts', *Administrator* (1976), p. 597.

Nehru, Jawaharlal 1956a. *The Discovery of India*, London, Methuen, 4th edition.

—— 1962b. *An Autobiography*, New Delhi.

Paranjape, H.K. 1966. A Trojan Inheritance, *Seminar*, August.

Potter, D.C. 1986. *India's Political Administrators 1919–1983*, Oxford, Clarendon Press.

—— 1989. Jawaharlal Nehru and the Indian Civil Service, *South Asian Research*, November.

Ramanadham, V.V. 1964. *The Control of Public Enterprises in India*, New York, Asia Publishing House.

Shah Commission 1978. *Third and Final Report*, New Delhi.

Shiva Rao, B. (ed) 1968. *The Framing of India's Constitution: Select Documents*, 4, New Delhi.

Singh, P. 1981. A Matter of Ambiguity, *Indian Book Chronicle*, 16 March.

Vittachi, T. 1978. Bureaucrats who won't lie down, *The Guardian* (London), 10 April.

Vohra, B. 1978. Anatomy of Maladministration, *Seminar*, October.

8

Designing Poverty Alleviation Programmes: International Agencies and Indian Politics

KULDEEP MATHUR

Since the beginning of the First Five Year Plan, several strategies have been adopted to initiate rural development. Some of the programmes formulated have attempted at overall rural development, while others have aimed at a narrow segment of the rural society. The purpose of this paper is to focus attention on poverty alleviation programmes and to examine the political roots of their design.

In formulating developmental programmes, the policy makers have been open to ideas whose source lay in experiences in India or abroad. As a matter of fact, in the entire arena of economic planning, there has been a free exchange of ideas. During the fifties, the Planning Commission had become a forum where frequent interaction between the foreign and Indian experts took place. A large number of international experts worked for varying periods in the Planning Commission. The fact that many of their Indian counterparts had their education and training abroad helped in creating an ambience of free flowing ideas. Galbraith described the atmosphere of those days thus: 'At no other place in the world at the time was there such easy and intense exchange between the people of the socialist and non-socialist worlds and the rich countries and the poor' (quoted in Rosen, 1985: 59). Thus, even while India was incorporating socialist ideals into its economic policies, it continued to be open to the ideas and influence of the West.

Contrary to popular belief, this openness was even greater in the area of rural development. Several experiments that were initiated by Indians before Independence got substantial contribution from socially concerned Westerners. For example, C.F. Andrews was involved in Tagore's Surul experiment, Miss Gretchen Green, an American, looked after the clinic in Sriniketan where Leonard Elmhirst had played a key role. Dr. Spencer Hatch managed the Marthandam project of the YMCA for 18 years; the Gurgaon scheme was initiated by F.L. Brayne, who was stationed as Deputy Commissioner there; the Pilot Project at Etawah was the brain child of Albert Mayer and so on. These personal influences later expanded to form the basis of programmes proposed by international agencies.

The Ford Foundation entered India through the gates of rural development. The Etawah-type project was cited as the self-supporting village project that America could invest in. It was this project around which the Foundation evolved its activities and suggested to the Indian government that 'there is no reason why all 500,000 of India's villages could not make a similar advance' (quoted in Rosen, 1985: 11). It was this resolve that led to the unfolding of the Community Development Programme. The fact that this programme was based on Albert Mayer's Etawah experiment is adequately emphasized when Bowles, the American ambassador, calls it our 'pilot study'.

The fact that a programme was sought to be multiplied demanded an administrative structure that provided for close monitoring and control. Thus, the administrative structure that was designed for the Community Development Programme facilitated a vertical flow of power and control. At the central level, a committee headed by the prime minister was created and an administrator with the responsibility of planning, directing and coordinating community development projects throughout the country was appointed. Later in 1956, his office was converted into a regular ministry. A corresponding committee came up at the state level headed by the chief minister and a development commissioner. At the district level, the programme was administered under the leadership of the district collector with the assistance of block development officers working under him. The result was a system in which achievements were directed and deviations from a set pattern controlled. Such an administrative structure also helped the Ford Foundation in monitoring the programme as a funding agency and in overseeing the multiplication of a single experiment.

The acceptance of a foreign assisted and externally designed programme of rural development saw the convergence of American and Indian political needs. Americans saw political crises raising their heads in India in 1950–51. There was a severe food shortage and prices were going up. Political instability could not be tolerated because communism had to be contained and as part of Cold War politics, the then Soviet Union's designs had to be thwarted. For different reasons, Indian political leaders also considered inadequate rural development as a threat to political stability. They too saw in the effort at agricultural extension a possibility of increase in agricultural output which would help stabilize the food situation in the country.

In a matter of a few years, the CDP demonstrated that it could not do what it had set out to do.[1] In 1959–60, India faced a severe food crisis and the Ford Foundation proposed an alternative strategy. This was contained in the proposal to choose a few districts in the country where efforts would be made to increase food production through intensive use of technology and other inputs. Even though the government accepted what later came to be known as Intensive Agricultural District Programme, in 1959–60 it found it politically difficult to accept the proposition that scarce resources could be concentrated in a few districts alone. This hesitation was expressed by delaying the appointment of a senior administrator at the central level who would take charge of the Programme. It was the threat of resignation by the Ford Foundation representative that led to the appointment of an appropriate officer and the commencement of the Programme.

The design of the Programme too was bureaucratic and hierarchic in nature. It was headed by a deputy director of agriculture. Agricultural extension workers concentrated on a much smaller number of farm families and there was easy availability of inputs. The result was that the IADP evaluation committee accepted that the Programme established beyond doubt that once the Indian farmer is convinced through extension effort that a particular innovation is both useful and within his means, he is as prompt as farmers in any other part of the world to accept it (quoted in

Rosen, 1985: 79). This Programme laid the foundation for the wider adoption of the new agricultural strategy that ultimately led to a remarkable increase in agricultural output since the late 1960s. The Ford Foundation supported the programme for ten years.

One of the last efforts of the Ford Foundation in rural development, which had a widespread impact on Indian public thinking, was the sponsorship of a study on poverty in India by Dandekar and Rath. This study led to widespread discussions on the distribution of development gains in India and changed the orientation of perspectives towards rural development. With this study also ended the most active period of the Ford Foundation's involvement in Indian public policy making. Speculation continues on why it came to play that prominent role in India's rural development. Of course, the personal friendship that developed between Ensminger and Nehru did strongly influence the course of events. The precepts of community development fitted very well into the kind of optimistic visions of village life which Nehru articulated. Unable to put through programmes of structural change in rural society, the Programme offered by the Foundation fulfilled the need of meeting the aspirations of the rural people and, at the same time, not disturbing the pattern of ownership of landholdings and rural assets. While Chester Bowles, Ensminger and others in the 1950s were concerned with blocking the advance of communism, Nehru and others were keen on the political stability that could come through some kind of rural development. When the IADP was promoted by the Foundation, the realization that rural development required a more concerted effort at increasing agricultural production had come about. While the concerted effort did lead to results most demonstrably on the front of food production, it also brought into prominence the issue of rural poverty which again had to be tackled to meet the need of political stability. Nevertheless, by this time, the nature of instability that demanded specific strategies of rural development had changed.

The development experience of about fifteen years (1951–52 to 1966–67) brought into serious doubt the assumptions of the planners that strategies of growth and productivity would suffice to resolve the problems of rural poverty by themselves. The efforts at promulgating land ceilings and giving land to the tillers had by and large failed. Rural tensions and violence were arising in some parts of the country. The reality of the kind of problems that policies of growth unconnected with distributive justice could generate began to be realized. The All India Credit Review Committee of the Reserve Bank of India (1969) rang the alarm bell when it said: 'If the fruits of development continue to be denied to large sections of the rural community, while prosperity accrues to some, the resulting tensions, social and economic, may not only upset the orderly and peaceful change in the rural economy but even frustrate the national effort to step up agricultural production.'

A new perspective, which advocated that growth and poverty alleviation could not be seen as distinct goals, and that the latter should be built into the growth processes began to crystallize. However, strategies to correct structural imbalances that lead to poverty were not included in this new perspective. Land reforms were not given a prominent place. Around this time, the international aid-giving agencies also began expressing dissatisfaction with a purely economic approach towards distributive justice; instead, they proposed direct attempts to benefit the rural poor through administrative packages.

In a now well-known speech, the president of the World Bank, speaking at Nairobi in 1970, drew attention to the growing rural poverty in developing countries and argued that investment limited to the modern sector increases disparites in income. He suggested, therefore, that there was need for reorienting development policy towards more equitable growth by increased investments in the rural sector, especially focused on the small farmers. The World Bank began to emphasize in its policy documents that greater attention on capital formation among poorer farmers was necessary for using their available resources and labour to generate higher incomes. The ILO also began its shift from primary occupation with growth towards creation of employment opportunity and satisfaction of basic human needs. At the World Employment Conference in Geneva in 1976, the Director General of ILO proposed that development planning should include as an explicit goal, the satisfaction of an absolute level of basic needs.

These two approaches, advocated by the World Bank and the ILO, of redirecting investments towards the poor and the satisfaction of their basic needs had a strong impact on the strategies adopted to alleviate rural poverty in India from 1970 onwards.

The new perspective found wide acceptance in India due to the 'favourable' political climate that prevailed in the country during the late 1960s. Nehru had died; India had gone to war with Pakistan in 1965–66; and Nehru's successor Lal Bahadur Shastri, who also died after holding office of prime minister for less than two years, was unable to initiate the Fourth Plan due to the economic crisis. The accute food shortage resulting from drought and low productivity had taken its toll. The era of Mrs. Gandhi began with the devaluation of the rupee, which was widely perceived as an unpopular measure. At the same time, many states had gone out of the Congress's control and coalitions of land-based elites had taken over the state governments. In such a situation, the political will to implement measures like land reforms could hardly be expected. However, poverty could not be taken out of the political agenda. Accordingly, programmes that sought to bring direct benefits to the rural poor through redirection of some investment were seen not only as instruments of containing rural unrest but also a way of fulfilling the demands of social change and distributive justice. This has been described as the fundamental paradox of India's political economy: the commitment to radical social change and yet an equal determination to avoid a direct attack on the existing structures (Francine Frankel, 1978: 3–78).

Another change also began to be discerned at the central level. The occupational pattern of the members of the Lok Sabha began to shift towards the agriculturists, who began to emerge as the largest single group in the Parliament. Those who had entered national politics when India became independent were tutored into principles of social change, and were predominantly lawyers by profession. This began to change and at the time of the Fourth and/or Fifth Plans, agriculturists had become the single largest group in the Lok Sabha (see Table 8.1). This trend got strengthened in subsequent years.

These agriculturists were the richer farmers who were taking advantage of the new agricultural strategy based on improved technology and price support policies and becoming economic entrepreneurs and harbingers of food self-sufficiency. They were trying to enter the political space to direct policies towards their own benefit. As one can see from Table 8.1, when the Fourth Plan began to directly intervene to alleviate poverty and the Fifth Plan formalized specific programmes, the Lok Sabha had around one-third of its members from agricultural occupation. The state leadership was already getting more and more agriculture-based and had

Table 8.1

Distribution of Members of Lok Sabha by Profession

Year	Agriculturists	Lawyers	Pol. and Social Workers	Total Elected Members
1952–57	22.45	35.46	–	432
1957–62	29.01	30.24	–	486
1962–67	27.44	24.46	18.72	470
1967–70	30.61	17.49	22.86	503
1971–77	33.20	20.35	18.97	506
1977–80	35.93	23.42	20.00	525
1980–84	39.38	22.17	17.20	523
1984–89	38.30	19.05	16.03	530

begun making demands on the centre for a greater role in matters which directly affected them. The Panchayati Raj, which had introduced democratization at district level and below, was stagnating because no elections to these institutions were held in the 1960s. One expectation of elections is that it provides a turnover of leadership which helps in the redistribution of power among various social groups. But when elections are not held, those elected face no threat and work only to consolidate their power. In the initial elections, the Panchayati Raj had provided a secular method of elections to the land-owning classes to legitimize their hold on the village social structure. Elected leaders based their power on land and knew that land reforms would mean a drastic reduction in the power they wielded. They used their influence by forging links with the state leadership, which began to become more and more dependent on them for votes. The consolidation of 'vote banks' was also the consolidation of power of the land-owning classes. Thus, while on the one hand, they were careful to thwart any effort to implement land ceilings, they were happy to welcome special schemes to alleviate poverty, on the other.

This new perspective on rural development began the era of special schemes, displacing the comprehensive programme of rural upliftment through community development introduced in the First Five Year Plan. The latter was allowed to wither away when the Fourth Plan introduced special measures to help the marginal farmers and agricultural labourers. This marked the beginning of a period when comprehensive programmes of rural development began to give way to a segmental view of rural development. Each aspect of rural life, from agriculture to health to housing to education, began to be looked at in a fragmented fashion.

Finally, the acceptance of special schemes for marginal farmers during the Fourth Plan projected the consensus that was emerging between the techno-economic view of development and the constraints of an emerging political environment. The special schemes, which served as appendages to the national development strategy of growth, were readily accepted because they did not, in any way, interfere with the grandiose designs of development that continued to rely on the best and the strong. Those with landed interests apparently felt relieved of the pressure put on them through policies of asset redistribution.

The political and economic situation preceding the Fourth Plan has an important bearing on the way the special schemes were conceptualized. It is crucial to note that they were accepted so readily. Politically, they provided visible methods of working for the rural poor and could thus pay political dividends (a major group of Mrs. Gandhi's constituency was that of the rural poor, SCs and STs). Economically, they were acceptable because they did not hamper the pursuit of policies of growth. Though high on the political agenda, removal of poverty was not the core theme around which the development strategy was conceived. In other words, the poverty alleviation schemes threatened neither the strategy of development nor the ongoing structural relationships in the rural society. Politically, these schemes were readily accepted because of their innocuous nature and not as a result of the expectation that they would create a more equal society.

The leadership in the international agencies and among the policy makers in India used political language to assuage the increasing anxiety about poverty and projected their reformist approaches which tended to reflect radical departures from existing development policies. The Indian documents used the same language that sharply conveyed the urgency of intent to tackle poverty.

Thus, national and international rhetoric emphasizing a campaign to remove rural poverty and making the small farmer a viable entity began to converge. The Small Farmers Development

Programme, introduced in India during the Fourth Plan, found strong support in the changing perspectives on rural development now emerging in international aid-giving agencies. One feature of this new perspective was the target-group approach like concentrating on the small farmers. This approach assumed that the condition of the target groups is not affected by the interests and pressures of forces external to them. It was then possible to frame programmes that could be implemented without taking into account the economic or socio-political factors in the background of target-groups activity. In the case of failure, this assumption allowed the policy planners to blame forces not under their control. This strategy helped in wide disbursement of funds or assets to the poor but not getting unduly worried if the poor were unable to generate additional income because of this largesse. Such a strategy then favoured a technical-managerial approach because the goal was to redirect resources towards the poor in an efficient manner. This meant that detailed planning of implementation needed to be done and institutions established to carry out the programme and monitor the process to see that major deviations from the Plan did not occur.

The Integrated Rural Development Programme (IRDP) adopted in the Sixth Plan in 1980 is a direct successor of the Small Farmer Development Programme that was adopted in the Fourth Plan and was discontinued towards the end of the Fifth Plan. This programme has wide international support from the World Bank which has prepared guidelines for its planning and implementation. These guidelines are revised from time to time. A review sponsored by the U.S. Agency for International Aid in 1980 not only laid heavy emphasis on the techno-managerial aspect of the Programme but clearly laid down how the project was to be administered. The basic argument was that without skilful management, rural development programmes were likely to fall short of their potential. The document then goes on to present propensities that would improve the implemention of the Programme (Honadle et al., 1980). The IRDP had been introduced as a centrally sponsored scheme. An important implication of this arrangement is that being centrally sponsored, it carries guidelines and design principles that are not necessarily reflective of the diverse local situations prevalent in the country. There is little flexibility available to the states (Thimaiah, 1991).

The reason why the states are interested in such schemes is that they are funded by the centre. But the centre needs to control the implementation because it wants to monitor the process of implementation and to see that the basic design is being properly carried out. The international agencies demand this process because their interest is in uniformity and holding the central government responsible for effective utilization of its funds.

When the IRDP was introduced, the Government of India directed each of the SFDAs to pass a resolution to rename themselves as DRDAs. All other characteristics of the structure remained the same. Two changes, however, did occur. The Government of India was not the only source of funds; the state government shared the burden equally and transferred its share directly to the agencies. The transfer of funds was not governed by the normal rules of the financial year and the fund did not lapse with its end. In another change, the number of professional staff was also increased. Apart from the project officer and a district planning officer, there were also assistant project officers for agriculture, animal husbandry and cooperation. Little additional staff was sanctioned at the block level or below. In a very early letter in 1971, the Government of India advised the state governments that these agencies 'will only serve as catalysts activising the existing government agencies to come to the help of weaker sections of the community in a big way and the extension staff of the various development departments of the state should attend to the work of the Agency as part of their normal duties' (Government of India, 1971: 215).

This underlying philosophy of administrative arrangements continued to be emphasized when it was initially suggested that

> our idea is that IRD should not be a programme in the narrow sense of the term. It should be all comprehensive, which should bring in its fold all the existing organizations and therefore no department as such has been created. Deliberately, there is no idea or intention to have a department of IRD or a single line hierarchical command all along the line, down to the lowest level or below. That is why we were not in favour of the suggestion of having an independent cell (at the block level) because that will alienate the field functionaries—the VLW, BDO and various other functionaries (Government of India, 1980: 68).

Though a separate agency was created, it became dependent on the state administrative system for its performance. The district collector was nominated as the chairman of the DRDA, the professional staff came on deputation from regular departments and the governing council carried all the officers connected with the rural development of the district. The project staff then looks to its own parent department for career prospects and the performance in IRDP rarely enters into such considerations. If appointments in DRDA are part of routine postings and one among many, little effort is made either to create a team or imbibe expertise that comes from knowledge of the area and people. A study conducted in a Rajasthan district shows that the average tenure of the project director was 18 months (Mathur, 1985). The longest stay of a project director was that of forty-eight months but during this period, three changes in the office of the district collector, two in that of APO (Agriculture), two in that of APO (Animal Husbandry) and five in that of APO (Co-operatives) took place.

The tendency of the larger administrative system to impose its own characteristics on even those administrative institutions that are sought to be established outside it is pervasive. Targets are set by the planners of the programmes at the central level and fulfilment of the targets tends to be equated with success and effectiveness of IRDP programme. What is success? Reaching target number of beneficiaries receiving loans and subsidies? Or getting possession of actual assets? Or the actual number of beneficiaries crossing the poverty line? (See Annexure 8.1). Not only are the targets taken to mean different things, but enforcing them to monitor performance leads to many detrimental consequences. The Administrative Reforms Commission in its Report on Agricultural Administration elaborated the impact of target setting even further when it said, 'performance is geared to inspections, inspections are based on targets and targets are related to financial provisions' (1967). Another baneful effect of targetry is perceptible in the area of performance. Individual administrators can blame other agencies for not fulfilling their part of the bargain and this can allow an alibi for not fulfilling targets. Cattle yielding substandard milk cannot be distributed because cattle farms which supposedly help augment the income of beneficiaries have not provided them. But it does not matter if cattle of low yield, which cannot help generate additional income, are provided; at least the 'target' is duly fulfilled.

This is all done not only because the administrators become part of a network in which non-existing or nondescript cattle can be bought and sold, but also because the considerations and urgency of meeting targets make them do so.

The areas that do not have the necessary infrastructural facilities, but where nationally determined targets have to be implemented, suffer the most. Rath (1985) quotes a NABARD study which says that except in Punjab, Haryana, U.P. and Gujarat, the milch cattle supplied were of poor quality and yield, but had to be delivered to the beneficiaries because nationally set targets had to be fulfilled. The difficulty was that animals of better breed and quality are just not available in such large numbers.

One other area where the characteristics of the macro-system influence the implementation of IRDP is the overall framework of a centralized planning system. The concern for decentralized planning has found expression in several government reports. It has come to be recognized that the local implementation system would improve considerably if development schemes reflect the grassroot realities and felt needs of the people rather than the needs of central planners. It is a pity that the planning exercise at the local level continues to be confined to the compilation of schemes in specified sectors according to the guidelines issued from above. The implementability of a scheme is decided on the basis of administrative and/or political reasons which can enable the reporting back of achievements of financial or physical targets. Without ascribing any motivations, the local administrator is constrained because assessment of economic viability of schemes is not undertaken without planning skills. Moreover, location decisions are often taken on an ad hoc basis partly because little systematic information is available on the distribution of local facilities.

In a recent comparative study of the IRDP in West Bengal and Tamil Nadu, Swaminathan (1990) points out that 'a common factor underlying the failure of specific schemes in both regions is the absence of serious and imaginative local level planning.' The argument is that the failures derive from 'mismatches' between (a) the structure of assets (and final output) created by the Programme and the pattern of demand (macro-mismatch), (b) the nature of demand for assets generated by the Programme and the potential supply of assets, and (c) the type of assets and pre-existing resources of a beneficiary household (micro-mismatch). Thus, imbalances are created, wasteful investments are made and beneficiaries are unable to take advantage of the assets acquired through loans and subsidies.

The concern to decentralize planning and develop district plans, which would take care of the interlinkages among sectors and ensure efficient use of local resources, has been reiterated in many official documents over so many years. The Planning Commission issued guidelines for district planning as far back as 1969. It not only emphasized the need to formulate local level plans but also linked it with the need to give sufficient freedom to the states to determine their own development priorities. It went on to say that the whole approach of directing development effort in the states through centrally assisted 'approved schemes' has to be given up. It was felt that, in the past, the tying of central assistance with such schemes led not only to the distortion of the states' priorities but also to a tendency to apply these schemes every where without due regard to the variety of conditions existing within states (Government of India, 1969: 2). During the 1977–79 Janata interlude, the Planning Commission appointed a working group under the chairmanship of M.L. Dantwala to initiate the process of block level planning in the country (Government of India, 1978). The group, while emphasizing that there has been little systematic planning at the local level, suggested that the block be the unit of planning. It recommended, however, that the planning team should be located at the district headquarters to ensure integration of block plans with the district plan. A detailed exercise was further undertaken by the Planning Commission when it appointed a working group under the chairmanship of one of its members, C.H.H. Rao. This group, while making recommendations, also presented a twenty year plan wherein steps could be taken progressively to ensure that a sudden change breeding resistance could be avoided (Government of India, 1984). There have been two other committees (Government of India, 1982 and Government of India, 1985) which were specifically concerned with the implementation of poverty alleviation programmes. These committees too came to similar conclusions and emphasized the need to initiate local-level planning. The importance attached to the practice of local level planning can be gauged from the fact that the Economic Advisory Council made it a subject of its second report submitted to the prime minister in 1984. It said that:

even schemes explicitly meant to promote decentralization and an integrated approach to development at the block level such as IRDP are in practice designed at the state capital in a manner by individual departments that precludes in effect both decentralization and integrated development. What passes now for decentralized agricultural and rural development is, therefore, primarily distribution of funds through governmental agencies and financial institutions . . . . The Council not only suggested ways to decentralize at the local level but also stressed on the role of voluntary agencies and people's participation in any effort of this kind.

It is indeed ironic that field studies reporting the 1989 or 1990 situation (e.g., Dreze, 1990; Hargopal and Ramalu, 1989; Swaminathan, 1990) continued to demonstrate that little local planning existed at the time and what passed off as a district plan was not a document that identified viable schemes in the context of comprehensive view of existing resources and markets. Nor did it provide for infrastructure to support projects with potential. At best, it apportioned financial and physical targets (Sinha, 1986). In sum, the district plan continues to be a haphazard collection of schemes.

Another set of issues that are of central concern here are related to organizational design and the administrative system. The committees cited above have given their own suggestions for improving the system of implementation. A specific committee was appointed in 1985 to look into the administrative arrangements for implementing poverty alleviation programmes (Government of India, 1985). While reiterating the need for district planning, the committee recommended a model administrative set-up at the district level which attempted to incorporate people's participatory institutions. Separately, the need to strengthen the role of Panchayati Raj and that of voluntary agencies was also expressed. At the beginning of the Sixth Plan, another committee had highlighted similar concerns (Government of India, 1982).

As if unaware of all these concerns, central organizations continue to work on the mistaken assumption that uniformity and standard pre-programming contribute to programme effectiveness and administrative efficiency. The government is reluctant to decentralize planning and the administration system despite recommendations of its own numerous committees urging it to do so. These committees have consisted of members who are distinguished civil servants and professionals. The chairmen are a galaxy of eminent names in agricultural and rural development: M.S. Swaminathan, C.H.H. Rao, G.V.K. Rao, M.L. Dantwala, to mention a few. By no stretch of imagination can the honesty of their advice be disputed. The government is also reluctant to improve upon its civil service staff that is supposed to bring a revolutionary change in the countryside. The local staff has little training and incentive to perform better. Investment in administrative overheads continues unabated at the central and state capitals, but it fails to percolate down to the district and lower levels. Any one aware of the working conditions in rural areas cannot fail to be struck by the acute deprivation of facilities in the local-level administrative apparatus.

The question is why the failings have persisted when they have persistently been pointed out through official and academic writings since at least the beginning of the Fifth Plan in 1975–76. It is not as if administrative innovations have not taken place. After all, the SFDA was established as a semi-autonomous agency at the district level. Why was it allowed, in the first instance, to be absorbed into the normal administrative processes from which it was sought to be kept away? There are also improved rules, regulations, promotional opportunities and even training facilities. Why do they all tend to be confined at levels much above the local levels?

It must be noted that administrative reform activity has usually been left to the care of administrators themselves. In their perception, the administrative system has stood the test of time and accordingly, the administrators feel little enthusiasm in bringing about far reaching change in it. Change is not welcome for another reason as well. It may disrupt the spheres of power and authority that have been built up over the years. If strengthening the Panchayati Raj system poses a threat to the local administrative and political leadership, then decentralization of planning reduces the influence of the central planner. In this scenario, the local administration is merely a good whipping boy—an errant child—and a ready alibi for failures occurring elsewhere. For all one knows, an inept local administration is necessary to prop up the 'fair' image of central planners and administrators.

The nature of the federal system, however, is such that there are some redeeming features. It can, and does, allow the states to give expression to their commitment to poverty eradication. At the general level, comparing the efforts of three states, West Bengal, Karnataka, and Uttar Pradesh, in improving the lot of the poor, Kohli (1987) has rated West Bengal higher than the other two. He has suggested four features of the regime in power to explain the existence of political capacity to initiate effective action in this regard. These primarily relate to the nature, coherence and stability of the rule of the CPM in West Bengal. This political party has attempted to penetrate the local level decision making by strengthening Panchayati Raj institutions and by getting them to implement beneficiary-oriented programme, holding regular elections, and putting up candidates who belong to the deprived classes (Leiten, 1988; Roy, 1983). There is also evidence that the party's commitment to the programme of registration of sharecroppers also contributed, in considerable measure, to its success (Bandopadhyay, 1981; Kohli, 1987). In the specific context of the implementation of the IRDP in West Bengal, Dreze (1990), after pointing out that beneficiaries include more of rural poor, suggests that 'the fact that the CPM is largely in control of the allocation of IRDP loans in villages and that the disadvantaged sections of the population are the main constituency of the CPM, are the key factors in understanding the functioning of the IRDP in West Bengal'. In a comparative study of West Bengal and Tamil Nadu, Swaminathan (1990) also comes to a similar conclusion.

But this political commitment is limited to the choice of beneficiaries and the disbursements of loans and subsidies to the appropriate targets. It has not necessarily meant that it has led to the alleviation of poverty for the mismatch of schemes is as pervasive in West Bengal as in Tamil Nadu (Dreze, 1990; Swaminathan, 1990). However, Rajasthan can be cited as an example of a benevolent bureaucracy attempting to take over the effort at poverty alleviation. It was among the few states that set up a state level department (Special Schemes Organization) headed by a secretary to administer all schemes like SFDA, IRDP and DPAP. The bureaucracy also showed considerable foresight in introducing the Antyoda programme in 1979. Many of the principles of this programme were incorporated into the IRDP, which was introduced a year later. But where the bureaucracy foundered was at the local-level.

The bureaucratic system appears to work at two levels. One is the level of preparation for institutionalizing the professional administrative system. At this stage, committees with well-meaning and experienced administrators come up with model organizations and systems that are very attractive. At another level, these organizations and personnel become part of the nexus of local politics and are unable to perform as intended. The personnel are untrained and unskilled and they just plod through their assignments. The very same group, which would like to see increased professionalization sitting in other committees, does not provide adequate support for the activity proposed earlier. In this sense, policy making and implementation are truly fractured and schizophrenic. There is possibly another reason for making it so. The central government likes to project a progressive image of its bureaucracy; bureaucrats at the centre would like to be seen as effective planners of forward-looking schemes that can bring credit in the eyes of the international funding agencies or the community of intellectuals. Failures in performance can always be blamed on local-level implementation and the inability of the local bureaucrats to rise above the corrupting influence of local politics.

This unwillingness to 'dirty hands', so to say, can be traced back to the characteristics of the 'zone of acceptability' to which a reference was made earlier. Direct actions to remove poverty become only appendages to the dominant strategy of development; and as long as they are so, the implementation concerns will be what they are. In contrast, when the intensive agricultural-development programme leading to 'green revolution' was being implemented, the districts chosen were placed in charge of a senior administrator like Deputy Director, Agriculture, with innumerable technical officers placed under his direct charge (see Mathur, 1982). The farmers' demands for increased and measured supply of inputs were met and the extension network was beefed up. If the IRDP is not to be a 'delusion', political support to effect change in the implementation system has to be strong. Even in West Bengal, political support has been limited to the plugging of leakages in including beneficiaries. Indeed, this is an important first step but does not take the programme to the goals it strives for. The solution has to be sought not only in improving the bureaucratic system but in searching for alternatives to it. This can only be done when greater flexibility is provided to it at various levels of planning and implementation. Experience has shown that variation in administrative approach among states and districts is possible and that this should be encouraged. Looking for alternatives and using them can also achieve the objectives of increased participation and 'empowerment' of the poor in tasks of national development.

During the plan period, the policy makers and experts fully accepted ideas that had their source in outside experiences. It was not as if the Indian experience did not count, but the operative part of the adopted programmes did not reflect the nuances of the Indian experiences. The complementarity between the strategies and programmes followed for rural development by India, and those suggested by international aid agencies, is most visible in the Community Development Programme and the poverty alleviation programmes culminating in the Integrated Rural Development Programme. It is possible, as Rosen (1985: 50) suggests, that in the initial years, Nehru leaned towards the American advice because it helped to relegate the British, the erstwhile colonial rulers, and the bureaucracy led by the Indian Civil Service closely identified with them, to the background. But the complementarity of the poverty alleviation programmes, between those suggested by the international agencies and followed by India, was altogether for different reasons. The complementarity arose because the concerns of the political leadership began to closely reflect the global concerns as expressed by the West.

With the failure of policies of structural change in rural areas, India began to look for strategies that would satisfy the demands of redistributive justice without upsetting the existing class and caste relationships. The strategies and programmes being suggested within the changed development model by the international agencies were very attractive. The adoption of the programmes also meant more aid and a demonstrative recognition of India's concern for the rural poor. The new strategies also allowed the continuation of policies of growth and expansion in the economy. Interestingly, India even adopted the kind of language used by international agencies to emphasize the problem of poverty in forceful terms. Military terminology has often been used: rural poor are the target group and the efforts are to 'attack', 'assault', 'combat' or 'eradicate' poverty. The strong language probably seeks to hide the weak intentions to actually do so.

The complementarity has arisen, partly because the international agencies offered the incentive of aid, and party because the levels of interaction were not purely official, but also personal and intellectual. Many Indians at the top policy echelons have been educated and trained abroad and have also occupied high positions in the international agencies which continually seek to influence India's policy making. The continuous flow helps to develop the harmony of ideas, which then sometimes lose an identifiable origin. But it must be remembered that while the Third World countries have increased their representation in the international agencies in recent years, they continue to be dominated by the thinking of the more prominent Western donor-countries.

Contrary to popular belief, then, rural development strategies have been strongly influenced by outsiders and particularly the West. For reasons of nationalism and the pride of policy makers, it is only politically right that the policy makers claim Indianness to these programmes. An important impact of adopting a model or a design that is prepared elsewhere is the concern to see that its essential components are intact at the ground level too. This led to a centralized administrative structure for both community development and poverty alleviation programmes. In a more detailed analysis of the IRDP, we find that the opportunity for local innovations is hard to come by. Local planning, or integration of other activities with this main thrust, is usually very thin. Indian initiatives can take root if indigenized thinking is encouraged and diversity is permitted. Until then our dependence on foreign ideas will continue.

Note

1. In a review sponsored by USAID, Holdcroft (1978) investigates the origin of Community Development Programme and suggests that it had great appeal for leaders of developing nations and external donor officials because it provided a non-revolutionary approach to the development of agrarian societies. But as the later developments unfolded themselves, these decision makers proved naive.

Annexure 8.1

Measures of Success of IRDP

Major States	% Eligible Beneficiaries	% Investment Intact	% Intact & no Credit Overdone	% Eligible and Crossed Poverty Line
1	2	3	4	5
Andhra Pradesh	68	76	34	9
Arunachal Pradesh	73	61	38	4
Assam	27	70	6	10
Bihar	76	85	18	3
Gujarat	78	88	43	4
Haryana	71	46	15	0
Himachal Pradesh	87	85	45	29
Jammu and Kashmir	97	80	50	19
Karnataka	85	64	26	4
Kerala	89	74	19	5
Madhya Pradesh	81	73	27	6
Maharashtra	83	69	30	10
Orissa	83	68	19	7
Punjab	30	77	57	18
Rajasthan	72	48	15	9
Tamil Nadu	83	63	28	3
Uttar Pradesh	54	79	41	5
West Bengal	46	97	23	8
Average	70	73	29	7

Source: National Concurrent Evaluation of IRDP, Ministry of Rural Development as quoted in Kakwani and Subbarao, 1990.

References

Bandopadhyay, Nripen 1981. Operation Barga and land Reforms perspective in West Bengal: A discussive view, *Economic and Political Weekly*, Review of Agriculture.

Dreze, Jean 1990. Poverty in India: The IRDP Delusion, *Economic and Political Weekly*, Review of Agriculture, 29 September.

Economic Advisory Council 1984. *Second Report on Decentralization of Development Planning and Implementation Systems in the States*, as reported in Mainstream, January 21.

Frankel, Francine 1978. *India's Political Economy 1947–77*, Princeton, N.J., Princeton University Press.

Govt of India 1969. *Report of the All India Rural Credit Review Committee*, Bombay, Reserve Bank of India.

——— 1969. *Guidelines for the Formulation of District Plan*, New Delhi, Planning Commission.

——— 1978. *Report of the Working Group on Block-level Planning*, New Delhi, Planning Commission.

——— 1980. *Integrated Rural Programme and Allied Programmes: A Manual*, New Delhi, Ministry of Agriculture.

——— 1982. *Report of the Expert Group on Programmes of Alleviation of Poverty*, New Delhi, Planning Commission.

——— 1984. *Report of the Working Group on District Planning*, New Delhi, Planning Commission.

——— 1985. *Report of the Committee to Review the Existing Administrative Arrangements for Rural Development and Poverty Alleviation Programmes*, New Delhi, Ministry of Agriculture.

——— 1988. *Report on Centre-State Relations* (Chairman: Justice R.S. Sarkaria), New Delhi, Ministry of Home Affairs, Vols. I and II.

Hargopal, G. and **C.H.B. Ramalu** 1989. Poverty Alleviation Programme IRDP in an Andhra Pradesh District, *Economic and Political Weekly*, September 2–9.

Holdcraft, Lane E. 1978. *The Rise and Fall of Community Development in Developing Countries, 1950–65*, East Lansing: Michigan State University, MSU Rural Development Paper No. 2.

Honadle, George et al., 1980. *Integrated Rural Development: Making It Work*, Washington, Development Alternatives Inc.

Kakwani, N. and **Subbarao, K.** 1990. Rural Poverty and Its Alleviation in India, *Economic and Political Weekly*, March 31.

Kohli, Atul 1987. *State and Poverty in India: The Politics of Reform*, New Delhi, Orient Longman.

Leiten, G.K. 1988. Panchayat Leaders in a West Bengal District, *Economic and Political Weekly*, October 1.

Mathur, Kuldeep 1985. Small Farmers Development Agency in India: An Experiment in Controlled Decentralization, in G. Shabbir Cheema (ed.) *Rural Development in Asia—Case Studies in Programme Implementation*, New Delhi, Sterling Publishers.

——— 1982. *Bureaucracy and the New Agricultural Strategy*, New Delhi, Concept.

Raj, K.N. 1985. *Administrative Arrangements for Rural Development: A Perspective*, Proceedings of the National Workshop, July 9–11, Hyderabad, National Institute of Rural Development.

Rath, N. 1985. Garibi-Hatao: Can IRDP Do it? *Economic and Political Weekly*, February 9.

Rosen, George 1985. *Western Economists and Eastern Societies*, New Delhi, Oxford University Press.

Ray, Amal 1987. New Panchayat System in Karnataka: Elections and After, *Economic and Political Weekly*, February 14.

Roy, Ajit 1983. West Bengal Panchayat Elections: Class Mobilization without Class Struggle, *Economic and Political Weekly*, 18 (xxvi).

Sinha, S. 1986. Poverty Alleviation: Anything Goes, *Economic and Political Weekly*, May 10.

Swaminathan, M. 1990. Village Level Implementation of IRDP: Comparison of West Bengal and Tamil Nadu, *Economic and Political Weekly*, Review of Agriculture, March 31.

Thimmaiah, G. 1991. Centrally Sponsored Schemes: Some Issues, *The Economic Times*, November 27, 28.

9

Panchayati Raj in India

GEORGE MATHEW

It is widely recognized that self-governing village communities characterized by agrarian economies have existed in India from the earliest times. Not only are they mentioned in the *Rig Veda*, which dates from approximately 1200 BC, there is also definite evidence available of the existence of village 'sabhas' (councils or assemblies) and 'gramins' (senior persons of the village) until about 600 BC. These village bodies were the lines of contact with higher authorities on matters affecting the village.

Precolonial Period

In course of time, these village bodies took the form of panchayats (the term 'panchayat' referring to an assembly of five persons) which looked after the affairs of the village. They had both police and judicial powers. Custom and religion elevated them to a sacred position of authority. Besides the village panchayats, there were also caste panchayats to ensure that persons belonging to a particular caste adhered to its code of social conduct and ethics. If this was a general pattern in the Indo-Gangetic plains, in the south, village panchayats generally had a village assembly whose executive body consisted of representatives of various groups and castes. It will not be widely off the mark if we say that these village

bodies, both in north and south India, were the pivot of administration, the centre of social life, and, above all, a focus of social
solidarity. Even during the medieval and Mughal periods, this
characteristic of the village panchayats remained unchanged.
Although under the Mughals their judicial powers were curtailed,
local affairs remained unregulated from above and village officers
and servants were answerable primarily to the panchayats.

Sir Charles Metcalfe, the provisional Governor-General of India
(1835–36), had called the Indian village communities 'the little
republics'. This does not mean that these democratic 'republics'
were ideal institutions working with the participation of all the
people. Given the caste-ridden feudal structure of the village
society of those days, they left much to be desired. B.R. Ambedkar
did not think highly of these village communities, and, in fact, his
own experience had given him a negative view of the caste-ridden
villages and their panchayats. He had remarked in the Constituent
Assembly on 4 November, 1948:

> I hold that these village republics have been the ruination of
> India. I am, therefore, surprised that those who condemn pro-
> vincialism and communalism should come forward as champions
> of the village. What is the village but a sink of localism, a den of
> ignorance, narrow-mindedness and communalism? I am glad
> that the Draft Constitution has discarded the village and adopted
> the individual as its unit (quoted in Malviya, 1956: 258).

Ambedkar may have summarized the condition of the village
communities too sharply. What is significant here is to guard
against a romantic view of the ancient village system, especially in
relation to the values of equality and democracy. Jayaprakash
Narayan had once perceptively commented that nothing of the old
village communities had survived except their physical aspect.
They were no longer living communities acting jointly for the
solution of individual or communal problems and for the development of their moral and material life.

British Colonial Period

With the advent of the British, the self-contained village communities and their panchayats ceased to get sustenance. In course of

time, they were replaced by formally constituted institutions of village administration. It is a historical fact that local self-government in India, in the sense of an accountable representative institution, was the creation of the British.

It may be emphasized here that village panchayats were not the first priority of the British rulers. Concentrated as they were mainly around the trading centres, their interest in the beginning was limited to the creation of local bodies of nominated members in the major towns. It was thus that as early as 1687 a municipal corporation came to be formed in Madras. Set up along the British model of a town council, this body was empowered to levy taxes for building a guild hall and schools. With the passage of time, the sphere of activities of this corporation and similar bodies set up in other major towns, and also their taxation powers, widened. Although symbolizing local government of a sort, the bodies continued to comprise nominated members with no elective element whatsoever.

It was in 1870 that the Viceroy, Lord Mayo, got a resolution passed by his council for decentralization of power to bring about administrative efficiency in meeting the demands of the people and to add to the finances of the 'existing imperial resources which will not suffice for the growing needs of the country' (Venkatarangaiya and Pattabhiram, 1969). As Samuel Laing, Member (Finance) of the Viceroy's Council, had put it, the revolt of 1857 had put imperial finances under considerable strain and it was found necessary to finance local services out of local taxation. It was therefore out of a fiscal compulsion that Lord Mayo's resolution on local self-government came to be adopted. Still, it was a landmark in the evolution of the British regime's policy in this sphere. It was in the wake of this resolution that the first significant step to revive the traditional village panchayat system in Bengal was taken in 1870 through the Bengal Chowkidari Act. This Act empowered district magistrates to set up panchayats of nominated members in the villages. These nominated panchayats could levy and collect taxes to pay for the chowkidars or watchmen engaged by them. The Famine Commission of 1880 had pointed to the absence of local bodies as a major impediment in reaching relief supplies to the famine-stricken people and had underlined the need to expand self-government to the villages also.

It was against this backdrop that the appearance on the scene of a liberal like Lord Ripon as the viceroy proved to be a watershed in the structural evolution of local government in the country. The Government Resolution of 18 May, 1882 during his viceroyalty, providing for local boards consisting of a large majority of elected non-official members and presided over by a non-official chairperson, is considered to be the Magna Carta of local democracy in India. The role of local administration was elevated by the introduction of this resolution. Designed to make use of that intelligent class of public-spirited men whom it is not only bad policy but sheer waste of power to fail to utilize, the resolution proposed the establishment of local rural boards, two-thirds of whose membership was composed of elected representatives.

Although the progress of local self-government along the lines of the Ripon Resolution of 1882 was tardy, with only some half-hearted steps taken towards setting up municipal bodies and boards at the district level, the term 'self-government' had begun to gain currency. In 1906, the Congress, under the presidentship of Dadabhai Naoroji, accepted 'self-government' as the political goal for the country. In 1907, the government constituted a Royal Commission on Decentralization, which, in its report released in 1909, elaborated further the principles enunciated in the Ripon Resolution. Although this Commission comprised five Englishmen and only one Indian, Ramesh Chandra Dutta, it recognized the importance of panchayats in the Indian context. The Commission recommended that 'it is most desirable, alike in the interests of decentralisation and in order to associate the people with the local tasks of administration, that an attempt should be made to constitute and develop village Panchayats for the administration of local village affairs' (Malviya, 1956: 221). Although the Commission visualized certain difficulties in the way of the success of such an effort, like 'caste and religious disputes', or the influence of the landlord with large estates which 'may prevent free action by the tenantry', it agreed that these difficulties were 'far from insurmountable'.

In the same year (1909) the twenty-fourth session of the Congress at Lahore adopted a resolution urging the government to take early steps 'to make all local bodies from village panchayats upwards elective with elected non-official chairmen' and 'to support them with adequate financial aid' (Malviya 1956: 215–16).

However, like the Ripon Resolution, the recommendations made by the Royal Commission on Decentralization also remained largely on paper, a fact underlined by the Congress in a resolution adopted at its twenty-eighth session in December 1913 in Karachi. Dr. Annie Besant, in her presidential address at the Congress session in Calcutta in 1917, blamed the 'inefficient bureaucracy' for not doing even the little that was suggested in the Report of the Royal Commission on Decentralization.

It was against this background that the Montague–Chelmsford Reforms of 1919, under the proposed scheme of diarchy, made local self-government a 'transferred subject'. This meant that local self-government was brought under the domain of Indian ministers in the provinces. It was a promising move and an advance in this sphere. To make local self-government both fully representative and responsible, the reforms had suggested that 'there should be, as far as possible, complete popular control in local bodies and the largest possible independence for them of outside control' (Khanna, 1972). Notwithstanding this professed objective of the Montague–Chelmsford scheme, it did not make the panchayat institutions truly democratic and vibrant instruments of self-government at the level of the villages due to various constraints, both organizational and fiscal. Still, in almost all provinces and a number of native states, acts were passed for the establishment of village panchayats.

By 1925, eight provinces in British India had passed such acts. These provinces were Madras (Panchayat Act of 1920), Bombay (Village Panchayat Act of 1920), Bengal (Self-government Act of 1919), Bihar (Self-government Act of 1920), Central Provinces and Berar (Panchayat Act of 1920), Uttar Pradesh (Village Panchayat Act of 1920), Punjab (Panchayat Act of 1922), and Assam (Self-government Act of 1925).

By 1926, six native states had also adopted village panchayat laws. These states were Cochin (Panchayat Regulations Act, 1919), Indore (Panchayat Act, 1920), Travancore (Village Panchayat Act, 1925), Baroda (Village Panchayat Act, 1926), Kolhapur (Panchayat Act, 1926) and Mysore (Village Panchayat Act, 1926). In subsequent years, similar laws were adopted by some other states. These were Bikaner (Village Panchayat Act, 1928), Karauli (Village Panchayat Act, 1939), Hyderabad (Village Panchayat Act, 1940), Mewar (Gram Panchayat Act, 1940), Jasdan (Village Panchayat Act, 1942), Bhavnagar (Village Panchayat Act, 1943), Porbandar (Village Panchayat Act, 1943), Bharatpur (Village Panchayat Act, 1944), Marwar (Gram Panchayat Act, 1945),

Wadia (Village Panchayat Act, 1946), Dharangadhra (Village Panchayat Act, 1946), Morvi (Village Panchayat Act, 1946), Sirohi (Village Panchayat Act, 1947) and Jaipur (Village Panchayat Act, 1948). However, these statutory panchayats covered only a limited number of villages and generally had a limited number of functions.

The 1935 Government of India Act and the inauguration of provincial autonomy under it marked another important stage in the evolution of panchayats in the country. With popularly elected governments in the provinces, almost all provincial administrations felt duty-bound to enact legislations for further democratization of local self-government institutions, including the village panchayats. Although the popular governments in the provinces governed by the Congress vacated office following the declaration of the Second World War in 1939, the position as regards local self-government institutions remained unchanged till August 1947, when the country attained Independence.

National Movement, Indian Constitution

As stated earlier, village panchayats were central to the ideological framework of India's national movement. Gandhiji had categorically defined his vision of village panchayats thus:

> My idea of village Swaraj is that it is a complete republic independent of its neighbours for its own vital wants and yet interdependent for many others in which dependence is a necessity . . . . The Government of the village will be conducted by the Panchayat of five persons annually elected by the adult villagers, males and females, possessing minimum prescribed qualifications. These will have all the authority and jurisdiction required. Since there will be no system of punishment in the accepted sense, the Panchayat will be the legislature, judiciary and executive combined to operate for its year of office. Any village can become such a republic today without much interference even from the present government, whose sole effective connection with the villages is the execution of the village revenue . . . . Here there is perfect democracy based upon individual freedom. The individual is the architect of his own Government (Gandhi, 1942).

It is a sad commentary on India's national commitment to democratic decentralization that despite the village panchayats having a history of being the basic unit of administration and despite the nationalist movement's commitment to panchayats and Gandhiji's unequivocal propagation of the ideal, the first draft of India's Constitution did not include a provision for panchayats. When Gandhiji learnt that the proposed Constitution did not provide for panchayats, he remarked that this was certainly an omission calling for immediate attention if India's Independence was to reflect the voice of the people.

Countering Ambedkar's arguments against panchayats in the Constituent Assembly, Madhava Rau of Mysore had said: 'It is true, some villages are chronically faction-ridden and indulge in petty tyrannies, or remain the strongholds of untouchability. A considerable number are pathetic or even moribund' (Venkata-rangaiya and Pattabhiram, 1969). However, he insisted that even if 30 per cent of the village panchayats could be classed as good, they could not be ignored. He quoted the example of the efforts being made by the then popular government in Mysore as 'encour-aging and, in some cases, quite gratifying'. The argument of those who pleaded for the inclusion of village panchayats in the Consti-tution finally prevailed, albeit in a modest measure. They managed to get a provision included in Part IV of the Constitution (in the Directive Principles of State Policy), which, however, is not justi-ciable. Article 40 reads: 'The state should take steps to organise village panchayats and endow them with such power and authority as may be necessary to enable them to function as units of self-government'.

There is another place in the Constitution where 'local govern-ment' is mentioned. Schedule Seven, List II (State List 5) reads: 'Local government, that is to say, the constitution and powers of municipal corporations, improvement trusts, district boards, mining settlement authorities and other local authorities for the purpose of local self-government or village administration'. Obviously, this is a curious way of defining local government without giving due place to panchayats.

The Gandhians considered panchayats both a means and also an end and sincerely believed in their immense potential for democratic decentralization and for devolving power to the people. Of course, Ambedkar's objection had not been to democratic decentralization or to the concept of giving power to the people, which would have been the outcome of an ideal panchayat system. He was speaking from his experience of what a caste-ridden village society in India had meant to him and to millions like him. No doubt his perception was as realistic as that of others.

The basic conviction that village panchayats could play an important role in the social transformation and implementation of development programmes could not be ignored so easily. But the pertinent question still remains unanswered. Why did panchayats not come under the legally enforceable part of the Constitution? Why was it not given the constitutional status and recognition it deserved? The answer is that the urban and rural elite, their representatives in politics (from the time of the National Freedom Movement onwards), and a bureaucracy conditioned by its class character had a disdain for panchayats and this has remained intact ever since. Whatever genuine attempts were made for the devolution of power, these interests saw to it that the attempts did not succeed. The story of panchayat institutions since Independence is precisely this.

Post-Independence Period: The Rise and Decline of Village Panchayat till 1977

India's development in the early 1950s was planned without taking cognizance of Gandhiji's idea of *gram swaraj*. It did not take long to realize the folly of this line of approach. The community development projects, inaugurated in 1952 and modelled after the experiments at Marthandam, Shantiniketan, Baroda, Etawah and Nilokheri, soon found themselves in a blind alley in the absence of effective instruments for people's participation. In order to suggest an institutional set-up to secure this participation in the Community Development and National Extension Service Programmes, the Committee on Plan Projects in 1957 constituted a team for the study of the two programmes. The study team was headed by Balwantrai Mehta, a Member of Parliament. The study team's view was that without an agency at the village level 'which could represent the entire community, assume responsibility and provide the necessary leadership for implementing development programmes', real progress in rural development could not come about at all. Its recommendation that 'public participation in community works should be organised through statutory representative bodies' gave a fillip to the prevailing nationwide sentiments (Government of India, 1959).

The recommendations of the Balwantrai Mehta study team, favouring democratic decentralization through the setting up of Panchayati Raj institutions, accelerated the pace of constituting these institutions in all the states. It may be recalled here that subsequently the National Development Council also affirmed the basic principles of democratic decentralization enunciated in the Balwantrai Mehta report and left it to the states to work out the structures suitable to each state.

During this stage, the term 'Panchayati Raj' came into vogue. Panchayati Raj is a process of governance; it refers to a system organically linking people from the *gram sabha* to the Lok Sabha. Etymologically, it is derived from Urdu. In one of his meetings with the author, S.K. Dey had disclosed that the term was coined by Jawaharlal Nehru. It is distinct from the term panchayat, which connotes a local body limited to a geographical area.

Rajasthan was the first state to inaugurate Panchayati Raj after the Balwantrai Mehta study team's recommendations. Prime Minister Jawaharlal Nehru inaugurated independent India's first Panchayati Raj on 2 October 1959 at Nagaur, about 260 km from Jaipur, the capital of Rajasthan. Nehru hailed the system as 'the most revolutionary and historical step in the context of new India' (*The Hindustan Times*, 3 October 1959). Democracy at the top would not be a success unless it was built from below, Nehru had felt. He expressed similar sentiments while inaugurating the new Panchayati Raj at Shadnagar, about 60 km from Hyderabad (Andhra Pradesh) nine days later. S.K. Dey, Minister for Community Development in Nehru's Cabinet and the architect of the Panchayati Raj after Independence, elevated the whole idea to a philosophical level and viewed it as an instrument which linked the individual with the universe. Within the sphere of national democracy he visualized an organic and intimate relationship between the *gram sabha* and the Lok Sabha.

By 1959 all the states had passed panchayat acts, and by the mid-1960s, panchayat had reached all parts of the country. More than 217,300 village panchayats, covering over 96 per cent of the 579,000 inhabited villages and 92 per cent of the rural population had been established. On an average, a panchayat covered a population of about 2,400, in two-to-three villages. There was enthusiasm in rural India and the people felt that they had a say in affairs affecting their daily lives. Those were the promising days of Panchayati Raj institutions in India.

It is worthwhile looking into some of the official reports to get a picture of the positive aspects of the system. The report of the Ministry of Community Development had stated in 1964–65 that younger and better leadership was emerging through Panchayati Raj institutions and that there was a fairly high degree of satisfaction among the people with their working. L.P. Shukla, a noted writer on Panchayati Raj, had underscored the significance of this new leadership. According to him, the establishment of Panchayati Raj institutions had given a boost to the emergence of local leadership by creating new seats of power to be filled by the competitive mechanism of democratic elections. This had enabled a large number of people to acquire leadership at the local levels, as in the earlier traditional, socio-political set-up they had no access to the political or administrative organs. Another perceptive writer, R.V. Jathar (1964: 10–12) had noted:

> If the policy of the government in giving impetus to the panchayati raj movement is implemented faithfully and fully, it will surely bring about the political, social and economic revolution which will not only strengthen the democratic character of our society, but will also prove a perennial source of energetic, honest and competent leaders with potentialities to change the entire face of the country and guide the destinies of the people most efficiently and effectively.

Jathar expressed this view in 1964 after looking closely at the working of Panchayati Raj institutions in India. In yet another comment, a study team appointed by the Association of Voluntary Agencies for Rural Development (AVARD) in 1962 to evaluate Panchayati Raj in Rajasthan had made the following observation:

> It was reported that the people felt that they had sufficient powers to enable them to mould their future . . . . They are fully conscious of the fact that such privileges and favours which were formerly under the control of the BDO are now under their

control. In this sense full advantage of democratic decentralisation has been secured.

The study team then proceeded to say that the conferring of power on people's representatives had improved the attendance of teachers in primary schools, while block administration had become more responsive, people were voicing their grievances before the *pradhans* and obtaining relief through them. Above all, petty corruption, both among the subordinate staff as well as the newly elected leaders, had declined, the former because the block staff had come under the panchayat samiti, and the latter because the public reputation of the *pradhans* was crucial for them to get re-elected. In other words, Panchayati Raj institutions fulfilled all the functions of a local government and acted as the nurseries or even the primary schools of democracy.

Due to the interest generated by Panchayati Raj institutions, several states set up committees to assess their working and to recommend measures for improvement. The states and committees were: (*a*) Andhra Pradesh—Purushottam Pai Committee, 1964; Ramachandra Reddy Committee, 1965; and Narasimhan Committee, 1972, (*b*) Karnataka—Basappa Committee, 1963, (*c*) Maharashtra—Naik Committee, 1961; and Bongiwar Committee, 1963, (*d*) Rajas-than—Mathur Committee, 1963; Sadiq Ali Committee, 1963; and G.L. Vyas Committee, 1973, and (*e*) Uttar Pradesh—Govind Sahai Committee, 1959; and Murti Committee, 1965.

Nevertheless, the Panchayati Raj system had been moving down-hill. In Abhijit Datta's (1985) view, Panchayati Raj institutions had become a 'living caricature of local government'. In an editorial comment in *Democratic World* (22 January 1978), Thomas Mathai had despaired that the village panchayat had been reduced to 'a focus of frustration. The gram sabha is something of a joke.' Of course, the *gram sabha's* resources were meagre. That could have been set right if there had been the political will. The critical problem was the domination of Panchayati Raj institutions by the economically and socially privileged classes. This was essentially a socio-political problem, which could have been tackled to a great extent by holding elections at regular intervals. The resulting political education of communities, oppressed for ages, would have certainly changed the scenario.

An example comes from the elections to the Tamil Nadu local bodies held in 1986 after a lapse of sixteen years. It is interesting to note the social consequences of this democratic exercise. For instance, in Kamudhi town panchayat in Ramanathapuram district, the Muslims and the Nadar community had been arch enemies for the past fifty-to-sixty years. For more than thirty years they had opposed each other in the elections to the local bodies, but in the 1986 elections they got together and fielded a common candidate and got him elected. This only shows that if regular elections are held, permutations and combinations change, traditional rivalries disappear and issue-oriented groupings emerge. In this process, simple mechanical solidarity gives way to more organic solidarity where individual freedom of opinion and group decisions emerge. In another case, a Muslim defied the local Muslim *Jamaath* organization, contested the poll and secured 276 out of the 400 votes in the three Muslim wards. Multiple examples of this nature can be found all over the country.

It is precisely this process that had been arrested for years by the state governments, either by postponing elections frequently or not holding them at all. The committee set up by the National Planning Commission, with G.V.K. Rao as Chairperson, had stated in its report:

> Apart from inadequate resources, elections to these bodies have not been held regularly. In fact, elections have become overdue for one or more tiers of the panchayati raj institutions in eleven States, and in eight States even elections to Gram Panchayats are overdue. Elections have been put off on one pretext or another . . . and the terms of the existing bodies have been extended or the bodies have been superseded (Government of India, 1985).

Evidence suggests that there was a deliberate plan by the bureaucracy and local vested interests and their elected representatives in the state legislatures and in the Parliament to cripple and eventually discard the Panchayati Raj because its ascendancy was feared.

The roots of this hidden agenda could be traced back to 1960, when the government launched an Intensive Agricultural District Programme (IADP), bypassing the Community Development Programmes. The Jayaprakash Narayan Committee of 1961 had detected double thinking and contradictory positions developing within the government in the creation of an independent intensive programme. The committee noted that after having accepted the

Panchayati Raj as the agency responsible for planning and execution of plans, 'there is no longer any valid reason for the continuing individual allocations subject-wise even to serve as a guide' (quoted in Jain et al., 1985). Evidently, the Community Development Ministry was uneasy with the launching of the Intensive Agricultural District Programme. But soon schemes like the Small Farmers Development Agency (SFDA), the Drought Prone Areas Programme (DPAP) or the Intensive Tribal Development Programme (ITDP) were also introduced outside the purview of the elected *zilla parishads*. Plan allocations for schemes under the latter's jurisdiction were tapered off.

In 1966–67, the Ministry of Community Development was reduced to the status of a department and brought under the Ministry of Food and Agriculture. Coupled with this, the government launched a few schemes of integrated district plans in twenty-eight districts of twelve states and abandoned two instruments for appraisal, that is, the Annual Development Conference and the Annual Programme Evaluation Organization. 'This lent support to the view that not only the C.D. ministry but the C.D. project itself had been downgraded' (Jain, 1985). In 1971, the very title 'Community Development' was dropped and replaced by 'Rural Development'. 'This was not just a cosmetic change. It marked the end of both the "community" and "panchayats" as agents of change and agencies of development', observes L.C. Jain (1985). In the words of the Asoka Mehta Committee: 'The essential idea that all developmental activities should flow only through the block-level organization lost ground, though the *panchayat samiti* as a key unit of decentralisation was, in most cases, conterminous with the block' (Government of India, 1977: 4). It may be emphasized here that all the development programmes became bureaucracy-centred, with hardly any participation of the people. Eventually, the Panchayati Raj became part of the Ministry of Rural Development at the centre and with a joint secretary appointed for looking after it. This situation continues even today.

Thus, the bureaucracy gained the upper hand in a grand alliance with the state and central level political elite. The role of the bureaucracy in bringing down the Panchayati Raj to its present plight is brought out sharply by the Asoka Mehta Committee:

[The] bureaucracy had probably its own role in dissociating the P.R.Is from the development process. Several factors seem to have conditioned their perception. The system of line hierarchy would find favour with them as an organizational principle. The officers would feel that they are primarily accountable for results and financial proprieties to the state government. The officials knew no better than to trust their own fraternity. They would, on the one hand, therefore be averse to the PRIs being entrusted with additional functions and, on the other, would not easily get adjusted to working under the supervision of elected representatives (Government of India, 1977: 5–6).

This was not just a phenomenon typical of Independent India. Even in the British period, whatever semblance of local self-government existed in India was destroyed by officialdom. For example, the report of the Village Panchayat Committee of the All-India Congress Committee (AICC), in analyzing the main reasons for the disintegration of village panchayats in the British period, had stated that, 'the inordinate greed of the East India Company caused slow but steady disintegration of these Village Panchayats . . . . The excessive centralisation of the executive and judicial powers in the hands of the Government officials deprived the village functionaries of their age long powers and influence' (AICC, 1954: 10–11).

We have noted that Lord Ripon made an earnest effort to introduce local self-government, but it failed. Why? The Indian Statutory Commission of 1929 had stated that whatever might have been the intentions of Lord Ripon, his reforms in the sphere of local self-government were not free from official control and 'no real attempt was made to inaugurate a system amenable to the will of the local inhabitants' (Shukla, 1964).

Why did the political elite play to the tune of the bureaucracy? The reason is not far to seek. After all, politicians would not like to see the erosion of their power by a breed of new, local leadership. Thus, it is legitimate to conclude that a combination of the bureaucracy, commercial interests, the professional middle class, the police and the political elite 'ganged up' against democratic decentralization. A thesis was developed and popularized that a centralized bureaucracy can benefit the rural poor better than local elected 'vested interests'. The result: 'We have ended up creating an impregnable alliance of urban officialdom and the rural rich, and have excluded the rural poor from it', says Rajni Kothari (quoted in Jain et al., 1985).

The bureaucracy, in alliance with local powers, state and central-level politicians, began to discredit the new system by highlighting its shortcomings. It saw in these local bodies the domination of the upper or dominant castes, corruption and total ineptitude. Had Nehru been around, he would have made his characteristic response: 'Let village authorities function and let them make a million mistakes'. The village panchayats became an epitome of frustration.

We can consider the Panchayati Raj of the Nehruvian era as of the first generation because in this period the Panchayati Raj institutions were conceived as local bodies meant to ensure people's participation in development.

Asoka Mehta Committee

The appointment of the Asoka Mehta Committee in 1977 marked a turning point in the concepts and practice of the Panchayati Raj. The Asoka Mehta Committee was set up to enquire into the working of Panchayati Raj institutions and to suggest measures to strengthen them so as to enable a decentralized system of planning and development to be effective. The Committee's report (1978) is a seminal document which seeks to make panchayats an organic and integral part of our democratic process. Panchayati Raj institutions which came into being in certain states after the Asoka Mehta Committee's recommendations could be considered the second generation panchayats.

The second generation of Panchayati Raj institutions can be said to have started when the West Bengal government took the initiative in 1978 to give a new life to its panchayats on the lines of the Asoka Mehta Committee's recommendations. West Bengal, Karnataka, Andhra Pradesh and Jammu and Kashmir either revised their existing panchayat acts or passed new acts, thereby accepting the Asoka Mehta Committee report in theory. These states adapted the recommendations to suit their conditions and learnt from each other's experiences in bringing forth new legislations or amendments to the prevailing acts.

The most important thrust of the second phase was that the panchayat emerged from being a development organization at the local level into a political institution. The emphasis shifted from the bureaucracy to the political elements. This was a welcome trend. The Balwantrai Mehta study team had made development central to the panchayat system, while in West Bengal, Karnataka, Andhra Pradesh, and later in Jammu and Kashmir, the attempt, following the Asoka Mehta Committee Report, had been to make panchayats into genuine political institutions. Thus, they were a microcosm of the state itself with all its ramifications.

Need for Constitutional Support

It is well established that constitutional support and legislative measures are necessary for bringing about social change, but they are not sufficient to achieve the goal. Our experience of more than forty-seven years since Independence bears witness to this fact. This is true of democratic decentralization also. Of course, one can argue that there was no constitutional support for self-government below the state level till April 1993, and therefore, we were in the state of affairs in which we find ourselves now. The other side of the same coin would be that we have constitutional guarantees and laws for many vexed problems we face in the society, but are not in a position to say that we are better off because of these safeguards. Political will and people's political awareness are crucial for bringing about democratic decentralization in the form of local self-government below the state level, and constitutional support or legislative measures can create only the necessary conditions. A three-dimensional approach—political will, people's awareness, the building of healthy conventions and traditions undergirded by constitutional and legislative measures—is a must for any far-reaching changes to be brought about in our society, and when one of these is weak the entire measure may remain merely in form without content.

It was evident that the non-functioning Panchayati Raj institutions brought disrepute to the entire concept and its practice. There was a growing realization that it was lack of constitutional support that had led to the sad state of affairs. For instance, Malcolm Adiseshiah, while commenting on Tamil Nadu not holding panchayat elections for fifteen years, raised a pertinent question (Tamil Nadu had announced elections twenty times and postponed them as many times, giving as many reasons):

I must say that this is a situation not peculiar to Tamil Nadu. It exists in most states. There are no elections to local bodies. As a result of this, corruption becomes rampant in all programmes affecting the people. I would like to ask the question: Why is it that we cannot have a constitutional amendment which will make it obligatory for local elections to be held on time? (Adiseshiah, 1986).

He felt that all the twenty reasons given to postpone the Tamil Nadu local elections could also be given for withholding elections to the Lok Sabha and the state assemblies. He continued: 'Here I add my plea that we should earnestly work for a constitutional amendment to put the panchayati raj elections on the same footing as the Lok Sabha and State Assembly elections'.

State governments, though, could not establish full-fledged Panchayati Raj without adequate constitutional safeguards. In all the states where devolution of power to the villages was attempted, the concentration of power at the centre worked as an impediment. For instance, in 1985 Abdul Nazir Sab, the minister for Panchayati Raj in Karnataka under the Janata government, had stated:

Soon we realised that within the limitations imposed by the Constitution, the ideology of a 'Four Pillar State'—village, district, state and centre—could not be implemented in toto by the state government . . . . Without a constitutional amendment guaranteeing the 'Four Pillar State', our efforts may not be as fruitful as we desire (Sab, 1986).

At a seminar organized by the Institute of Social Sciences in Delhi in 1985, Nazir Sab had pleaded with intellectuals to ponder over this question and to initiate a public debate on the necessity for a constitutional amendment.

It may be recalled here that the Asoka Mehta Committee made the first official recommendation for including Panchayati Raj in the Constitution in keeping with its approach that panchayats should be regarded as political rather than mere developmental institutions. This Committee also favoured participation of political parties in panchayat elections with their symbols.

Since the second generation panchayats gave more powers to the local bodies and as their orientation was more political than developmental, they evoked widespread enthusiasm both in their implementation as well as their working. The West Bengal pattern was considered a success story. The single major reason for the 1985 victory of the Janata Party in Karnataka was attributed to the party's commitment to implement the 'power to the people' promise. Abdul Nazir Sab, the Minister for Panchayati Raj and Rural Development had said that he had witnessed a real awakening in the people when they realized that they could share power at the lower level.

The remarkable enthusiasm among the ordinary people in West Bengal and Karnataka about the implementation of Panchayati Raj strengthened the moves to incorporate constitutional provisions for it. Four dominant views on this issue could be identified during the mid-1980s:

1. Constitutional amendment guaranteeing elections to local bodies at the expiry of their term is a sufficient condition for bringing life into the local bodies.
2. The constitutional guarantee of elections is not a sufficient, but only a necessary condition. What is really needed is a 'quantum jump' in political democracy providing for a three- or four-tier government, that is, the centre, state, district and village governments.
3. Local self-governments must be strengthened, but not through rigid and uniform constitutional provisions. Freedom at the state and regional levels for experimenting and evolving suitable systems is a must.
4. A 'marriage' of district governments and Panchayati Raj is possible. The concept of people's participation must be considered an ideological commitment and, therefore, the need is to take up legislative and structural measures to give legitimacy to people's participation.

It may be mentioned here that in the mid-1980s, the idea of district government came into vogue. This was mainly because of the writings of Nirmal Mukarji (1986) on the subject during this period. In fact, it was Nirmal Mukarji who introduced for the first time the concept of 'district government'. The relative success of *zilla parishads* in West Bengal and Karnataka also gave the much needed boost to the district government approach.

Constitutional Amendment

By the end of 1988, a subcommittee of the consultative committee of the Parliament under the chairmanship of P.K. Thungon made recommendations for strengthening the Panchayati Raj system. One of its important recommendations was that Panchayati Raj bodies should be constitutionally recognized.

It was against this backdrop that on 15 May, 1989, that the Constitution (64th Amendment) Bill was drafted and introduced in Parliament. By and large, it was modelled on the bill (drafted by L.M. Singhvi) appended to the Asoka Mehta Committee Report. Although the 1989 Bill in itself was a welcome step, there was serious opposition to it due to its political overtones and on two basic grounds: (a) the bill overlooked the states and was seen as an instrument of the centre to deal directly with Panchayati Raj institutions; and (b) it was imposing a uniform pattern throughout the country instead of permitting individual states to legislate the details, keeping in mind the local circumstances. There was an outcry against this bill not only from the political parties but also from the intellectuals and concerned citizens. In response to this widespread criticism of the measure, the combined opposition under the National Front appointed a committee headed by S.R. Bommai to prepare an alternative legislation. The report of this committee, which was released on 10 July 1989, gave the much needed focus to the issues and generated an intense debate. Its findings were reflected in the subsequent bills on panchayats introduced in the Parliament (Janata Dal, 1989).

Although the Constitution (Sixty-Fourth Amendment) Bill got a two-thirds majority in the Lok Sabha, in the Rajya Sabha on 15 October 1989, it failed to meet the mandatory requirement by two votes. The National Front government introduced the 74th Amendment Bill (a combined bill on panchayats and municipalities) on 7 September 1990 during its short tenure in office, but it was never taken up for discussion. In September 1991, the Congress government under Narasimha Rao introduced the 72nd (Panchayats) and 73rd (Nagarpalikas) constitutional amendment bills. They were referred to a Joint Select Committee of the Parliament. The Lok Sabha passed the bill on 22 December 1992, while the Rajya Sabha passed it the following day. Following its ratification by more than half the state assemblies, the president gave his assent on 20 April 1993, and the Act was brought into force by a government notification on 24th April 1993 as the 1992 Constitution (Seventy-Third Amendment) Act.

The main features of the Constitution (Seventy-Third Amendment) Act are:

1. Panchayats will be institutions of self-government.
2. There will be a *gram sabha* for each village or group of villages comprising all the adult members registered as voters in the panchayat area.
3. There shall be a three-tier system of panchayats at village, intermediate block/*taluk*, and district levels. Smaller states with population below 20 lakhs will have the option not to have an intermediate level panchayat.
4. Seats in panchayats at all the three levels shall be filled by direct election. In addition, chairpersons of village panchayats can be made members of the panchayats at intermediate level and chairpersons of panchayats at intermediate level can be members of panchayats at the district level.
5. MPs, MLAs and MLCs could also be members of panchayats at the intermediate or the district level.
6. In all the panchayats, seats would be reserved for SCs and STs in proportion to their population. Offices of the chairpersons of the panchayats at all levels shall be reserved in favour of SCs and STs in proportion to their population in the state.
7. One-third of the total number of seats will be reserved for women. One-third of the seats reserved for SCs and STs will also be reserved for women. One-third of the offices of chairpersons of panchayats at all levels shall also be reserved for women.
8. State legislatures have the liberty to provide reservation of seats and offices of chairpersons in panchayats in favour of backward classes.
9. Every panchayat shall have a uniform five year term and elections to constitute new bodies shall be completed before the expiry of the term. In the event of dissolution, elections will be compulsorily held within six months. The reconstituted panchayat will serve for the remaining period of the five-year term.

10. It will not be possible to dissolve the existing panchayats by amending any act before the expiry of its duration.
11. A person who is disqualified under any law for election to the legislature of the state or under any law of the state will not be entitled to become a member of panchayat.
12. An independent Election Commission will be established in the state for superintendence, direction and control of the electoral process and preparation of electoral rolls.
13. Specific responsibilities will be entrusted to the panchayats to prepare plans for economic development and social justice with respect to twenty-nine subjects listed in the Eleventh Schedule. The Seventy-Fourth Amendment provides for a District Planning Committee to consolidate the plans prepared by the panchayats and municipalities.
14. The panchayats will receive adequate funds for carrying out their functions. Grants from state governments will constitute an important source of funding but state governments are also expected to assign the revenue of certain taxes to the panchayat. In some cases, the panchayat will also be permitted to collect and retain the revenue it raises.
15. In each state a finance commission will be established to determine the principles on the basis of which adequate financial resources would be ensured for panchayats.

Thus the journey from the 'local self-government' idea of Lord Ripon to the 'institutions of self-government' concept in the 73rd constitutional amendment took more than a century. This evolution in the federal polity of the country must be especially underlined.

For the Panchayati Raj institutions to function as institutions of self-government, the essential prerequisites are: (*a*) clearly demarcated areas of jurisdiction; (*b*) adequate power and authority commensurate with responsibilities; (*c*) necessary human and financial resources to manage their affairs; and (*d*) functional autonomy within the federal structure. Since the constitutional amendment opens possibilities for filling these conditions, the new Panchayati Raj must be seen as the 'third tier of governance'.

Critical Issues Ahead

There are some who express serious doubts about the wisdom of a constitutional amendment for making Panchayati Raj institutions functional and effective. For instance, Nirmal Mukarji had asked: (*a*) Can a constitutional provision by itself be an adequate substitute for political will? (*b*) Given the harsh realities of the states, would these statutes be implemented in letter and in spirit or would they remain laws on paper only? (*c*) Is implementing decentralization below the state level through the most centralizing of all conceivable instruments—a constitutional amendment—desirable? Moreover, Mukarji was of the view that a constitutional amendment could well mean thrusting a uniform prescription on states which are widely disparate in administrative culture, in historical background and in demographic size.

Although the arguments are valid, there is no doubt that the constitutional amendment was a must for creating vibrant Panchayati Raj institutions in the country. But some issues raised by the amendment need to be highlighted here.

The major flaw of the new Act of December 1992, as suggested by Nirmal Mukarji, is that it has adopted a uniform three-tier system below the state level. Even in bigger states like Karnataka, Tamil Nadu and Assam, which had three tiers, there were structural differences in the system of panchayats. Haryana, Manipur, Kerala, Sikkim and the union territory of Lakshadweep had only two tiers. Goa, Jammu and Kashmir, Tripura and several other union territories had only one tier. It would have been better to leave the states to decide the number of tiers irrespective of a state's history and tradition. The only concession given was that at the intermediate level, panchayats need not be constituted in states with a population of less than twenty lakhs (2,000,000).

The Constitution Amendment Bill, when introduced, had provided for direct elections to the post of chairperson at the village and intermediary levels. At the district level, it was left to the legislatures to decide. The Joint Committee of Parliament went into this question, but advocated direct elections only at the village level. The Marxist members of the joint committee had objected to direct elections at any level. But in order to achieve a consensus, the Marxists had suggested that the issue of the election of the chairperson at the village level may be left to the state legislatures.

In the end, the stand of the Left prevailed. Without arguing about the pluses and minuses of indirect or direct elections, it may be said that direct elections to the post of chairpersons are more in consonance with the presidential form of government, whereas indirect elections are in conformity with the cabinet system of government, the latter being the one adopted in India.

A major lacuna in the Act is the contradictory and inconsistent approach to the idea that panchayats are institutions of self-government. The Bill had rightly defined the panchayat as an institution of self-government, but later, in defining the functions of this institution, had narrowed them down to developmental functions, as in article 243 G (a) and (b). Without policing (law and order) as a function at each level, no institution of self-government is worth the name. When the 1983 Act of Karnataka was discussed at a meeting of the Institute of Social Sciences, Swami Agnivesh (the noted social activist) had asked Nazir Sab, the prime mover of that historic bill: 'Who will wield the lathi in villages? Whose orders will the police take to use force?'. Nazir Sab's answer was: 'It is our intention that the police should come under the control of the zilla parishads. But we cannot do all these things simultaneously. We will do it step-by-step when the district government is constituted' (Sab, 1986).

Now that the 'district government' or the 'third tier of governance' idea has come into vogue, this crucial point is sadly missing. In the words of Nirmal Mukarji, this dilution of the concept of institutions of self-government is 'flawed thinking and drafting'.

Wherever panchayats have not taken root or have been uprooted after brief spells of success, it has been observed that the MPs and MLAs have been not too friendly to these institutions. Not only have these persons been indifferent to local governments, but at times they have also been hostile to these bodies. No one likes to see another centre of power emerging as a challenge, nor does one like to see one's existing powers being diluted. In an attempt to assuage their feelings and to pre-empt any mischief from them, the MPs and MLAs have been given membership and voting rights in the panchayats in the statutes now passed. This will undermine the panchayats which we are now aiming to strengthen. E.M.S. Namboodiripad's observations, incorporated in the Asoka Mehta Committee report, are worth recalling here. Namboodiripad was in favour of purely elected bodies at all levels of the Panchayati

Raj. Having co-opted members, he believed, was a hangover of the idea that Panchayati Raj institutions are concerned with development alone and are not the elected organs of administration at the appropriate level.

A crucial question not yet confronted realistically is: With the states being asked to give more powers and departments to panchayats, when will the centre devolve more powers to the states? This question will have to be confronted and answered, if not today, then in the near future.

Reservation of one-third of seats and offices for women will lead to a silent revolution. It is this author's firm belief that a social transformation aimed at women could be achieved by Panchayati Raj institutions. But the initial task is beset with enormous difficulties for women.

There is no substitute for healthy conventions and traditions in democratic politics and we must recognize them as the backbone of our society and polity. We have to build healthy and desirable conventions, and if that happens it will be extremely difficult for any one, singly or collectively, to subvert them. The country and city local government institutions below the state level in the USA have had a satisfactory existence for so many decades and one of the reasons cited for their success is the tradition of democracy that they have preserved with extreme care. In India, however, from Independence onwards, violations of conventions have been of a very high magnitude. In such a context, what is the sanctity of constitutional amendments or legislations alone?

All the states passed their acts before 24 April 1994 in conformity with the 73rd Amendment. They have also appointed state election commissions and finance commissions. However, experts feel that in many cases the states have not lived up to the expectations of the people in giving powers to the three tiers of panchayats. In other words, they have tried to follow the letter of the amendment and not its spirit. Maybe as years go by, regular elections will take place and about 30 lakh elected members all over the country, both in panchayats and municipalities, will attend to their work as expected; state laws will also be amended. The country will then witness a full-fledged grassroots-level democracy and a genuine federal structure.

References

Adiseshiah, M.S. 1986. The Need for Constitutional Safeguards, in George Mathew (ed.), *Panchayati Raj in Karnataka Today*, New Delhi, Concept.

All India Congress Committee (AICC) 1954. *Report of the Congress Village Panchayat Committee*, New Delhi, AICC.

Association of Voluntary Agencies for Rural Development (AVARD) 1962. *Report of a Study Team on Panchayati Raj in Rajasthan*, New Delhi, AVARD.

Datta, Abhijit 1985. Decentralization and Local Government Reform in India, *Indian Journal of Public Administration*, 31 (2).

Gandhi, M.K. 1942. My Idea of Village Swaraj, *Harijan*, 26 July.

Government of India 1959. *Report of the Team for the Study of Community Projects and National Extension Service (Chairman, Balwantrai Mehta Committee)*, New Delhi, Planning Commission.

——— 1977. *Report of the Committee on Panchayati Raj Institutions*, New Delhi, Department of Rural Development.

——— 1985. *Committee to Review the Existing Administrative Arrangements for Rural Development and Poverty Alleviation Programmes*, New Delhi, Department of Rural Development.

Jain, L.C. 1985. *Grass without Roots*, New Delhi, Sage.

Janata Dal 1989. *The Basics of Democratic Decentralisation Report on Panchayats and Self-Government*, New Delhi, Janata Dal Publications.

Jathar, R.V. 1964. *Evolution of Panchayati Raj in India*, Dharwar, Institute of Economic Research.

Khanna, R.L. 1972. *Panchayati Raj in India*, Ambala Cantt, English Book Depot.

Malviya, H.D. 1956. *Village Panchayats in India*, Political Research Department, New Delhi, All India Congress Committee.

Mathew, George 1986 (ed.) *Panchayati Raj in Karnataka Today: Its National Dimensions*, New Delhi, Concept.

Mukarji, Nirmal 1986. The Alternative District Government, in M.L. Dantwala et al. (eds), *Rural Development: The Indian Experience*, New Delhi, Oxford IBH.

Sab, Abdul Nazir 1986. *Towards a Four Pillar State, in Mathew*.

Shukla, L.P. 1964. *A History of Village Panchayats in India*, Dharwar, Institute of Economic Research.

Venkatarangaiya, M. and M. Pattabhiram (eds) 1969. *Local Government in India: Select Readings*, Bombay.

10

Panchayati Raj in West Bengal: Popular Participation for the People or the Party?

Neil Webster

Introduction

The aims of political participation and decentralized local government and planning are not new to discourses on development, but what is perhaps new is the inversion of the order in which development and democracy are now seen to be achievable.

Decentralization has for some time been seen as a means by which the state can be more responsive and adaptable to regional and local needs than is the case with a concentration of administrative power and responsibility in the central state. Not least, it moves administration out from the capital to the regional cities, the rural towns and towards the villages. But decentralization of government in itself does not necessarily involve a devolution of power. Far from it, the extension of the state outwards and downwards can just as well serve the objective of consolidating the power of the central state as it can serve the objective of devolving power away from the centre. It can extend the state's control over the people just as it can aid the people's control over the state and its activities. Decentralization is very much a double-edged sword. It is this ambiguous nature of decentralization that has made discussion of the need for increased popular participation more pertinent. If decentralization is about the operation of the state, popular participation is about the location of power, and questions of responsibility and accountability in the state and its actions.

Recently there has been a noticeable shift in the priority given to democracy in the process of Third World development. In the past, development tended to be seen as preceding democracy, premised on the view that the latter was not possible before progress had been made in the former. On this basis a wide range of theorists argued the need for a strong state that could push through the development process in the face of obstacles perceived as 'traditional' or 'feudal'; theorists as ideologically far apart as Samuel Huntington on the one hand and the Soviet school advocating the non-capitalist road to development on the other. If economic development could be achieved by the actions of the state, then political democracy would follow. But development theories have undergone a significant shift in emphasis. Development is suddenly less of a precondition for democracy, but a process that needs democracy if any headway is to be made against the continuing economic and political problems of high unemployment and underemployment, bias in the distribution of resources, growing inequality in the benefits from increases achieved in production, bureaucratic mismanagement and corruption, widespread malnutrition and much more. It is because of this important shift towards participatory politics in decentralized government and other local institutions that the attempt in West Bengal over the past twelve years assumes a significance that goes beyond India's own borders.

The first part of this article consists of a brief discussion of the recent shift towards policies advocating popular participation and decentralization, followed by an examination of the West Bengal state government's implementations of Panchayati Raj for the principal changes it brought about. In the second part, case study evidence collected from fieldwork in one district in West Bengal is used to assess the programme at the lowest level of its operation. The article concludes with a political assessment of the programme and its prospects for the future.

The Indian Context of West Bengal's Panchayati Raj

In India the nature and practice of the post-colonial state has tended to negate the constitutional commitment to democracy made at the time of Independence in 1947. While it is true that the Indian electorate has been able to register its approval or disapproval in both parliamentary and state assembly elections, and has occasionally done so with quite dramatic effects—as evident in its ousting of both Indira and Rajiv Gandhi in 1977 and 1989 respectively, or in its allegiance to regional parties at the state level while sustaining another opposing party at the centre—, it has been a participation that has failed to go beyond the ballot box and to extend to a more routine involvement in institutional politics. Once elected to state or national legislatures, the politicians once again become far removed from the villages that constitute the massive base of Indian society.

Within the Indian bureaucracy, as in most bureaucracies, the hierarchical structure of command and responsibility, and other factors such as the process of promotion serve to reinforce the concentration of power at the top. This has in turn reproduced the strength and power invested in the bureaucracy, which was originally developed to serve the needs of a colonial state.

From Independence onwards, despite its federal constitution, the trend has been towards increased centralization and the concentration of power at the centre and even within the centre, with ministries and departments becoming subservient to the central secretariat under the prime minister and to individuals and bodies with no constitutional legitimacy, merely the prime minister's support.[1]

Given this political reality in India, the electoral victory in West Bengal in 1977 of a political party with a specific ideological commitment to decentralize decision making towards institutions of local government and to encourage increased political participation in their formation and functioning, represented a significant break both with the first forty years of Indian Independence and with strategies of rural development in most of the other states of the Indian Union.

The Left Front Government and the Implementation of Panchayati Raj

Prior to 1977, CPI(M) had been a member of the 1967 and 1969 United Front governments, which also included several other small Left and Marxist parties and the Bangla Congress under Ajay Mukherjee, who headed the governments. The basis of this alliance was a common opposition to the Congress and a desire to prevent a Congress government in the state. The unity of opposition did not extend to any significant agreement on policies and programmes, however. Internal differences combined with pressure from the state Congress Party and the Congress central government on the one hand, and more radical forces of the Left disillusioned by the failure of the United Front governments to implement radical programmes on the other.

The 1977 situation was very different. The winning Left Front alliance was composed of Left and Marxist parties that had failed to reach an electoral pact with the Janata Party at the state level. In the ensuing elections the CPI(M) alone won 177 of the 294 state assembly seats, thereby ensuring the establishment of a Left Front government within which the CPI(M) could assert political hegemony. However, the fact remains that the Left Front came to power only at a state level within the Indian Union, a point emphasized in discussions with the veteran CPI(M) leader and Minister for Land Reforms and Panchayats, Benoy Chowdhury: 'The Left Front does not hold state power, it merely occupies a position of temporary power within the state. It must act accordingly' (pers. comm., March 1989). The CPI(M) leadership argued for the need for a high degree of realism in policy formulation and the need to identify those areas in which its occupancy of the position of state government could most effectively be utilized. The sector in which it felt maximum change could be effected was the agrarian sector since the central government had arguably the least ability to intervene here and reforms already on the statute book could be the initial basis for its policies and programmes—most notably land reform.

The initial emphasis of the agrarian programme was on structural reform. The policies were designed to radically improve the conditions of the poorest through policies directed at the distribution of illegally held land, at imbalances of power in the relationship between landowner and tenant, and at the accompanying ties of patronage involved. These in turn were supported by policies designed to challenge some of the extra-economic structures and mechanisms used for the expropriation of surplus from the poorer sections, particularly sharecroppers, marginal land-owning farmers and agricultural labourers.[2]

The radical nature of the programme lay in its challenge to vested class interests within the rural economy. While individual measures might appear quite minor and to be based upon legislation passed prior to the arrival of the Left Front government, as in the vesting of land held above the land ceiling or in the fixing of the division of sharecroppers' production with the owner, their political implications greatly outweighed their practical nature. For example, the registration of sharecroppers to secure a legally defined division between sharecropper and landowner struck at the heart of a system of economic, social and political relations that had for many years ensured a condition of inescapable dependency for the vast majority of sharecroppers.

The implementation of this political programme required two important elements: first, the mobilization and participation of the rural poor and their supporters; and second, at least tacit support from the administration at all levels down to the local land reforms officers, block development officers and other local officials. With respect to the first, the dangers of popular radicalism had been learned by the CPI(M) leader of the mass peasant front, the *kisan sabha*, and Land Minister, Harekrishna Konar, had called for mass participation in the seizure of illegally held land and for the exposure of those hoarding rice for the black market. The combative nature of his speeches against the rich peasants and landowners and their administrative allies was swiftly answered with an upsurge in confrontation and increasing levels of violence in the countryside and the emergence of the Naxalite movement with its call for peasant-based insurrection along Maoist lines. As the CPI(M) leadership struggled to salvage the party's and the government's position in the ensuing law and order crisis, Indira Gandhi was able to remove it by imposing President's Rule from the centre.

In 1977 the CPI(M) recognized the need not only to have a more disciplined approach towards policy implementation, but also to build a strong party base capable of resisting the type of onslaught unleashed upon it in the early 1970s through internal divisions and external attacks. The Panchayati Raj programme, advocated by the central government and reintroduced onto West Bengal's State Legislative Books in a 1973 Panchayati Act by the Congress state government of the time, provided the vehicle through which the CPI(M) believed the interests of the poor could be protected and the needs of the Party could best be served.

The 1973 Act had been based upon the original panchayat acts passed in West Bengal in 1957 and 1963. These had created a four-tier system of panchayats extending downwards from the district level to the village. The two higher levels, the *zilla parishad* (district) and the *anchalik panchayat* (development block), had failed to function effectively from the outset. The lower two, the *anchal panchayat* (the old Union Board which covered approximately ten villages) and the *gram panchayat* (the village), did function but with minimal participation, few powers and responsibilities; lacking in financial support, bypassed by departmental and administrative officials, they generally served as little more than an additional institutional base from which the local rural elite could assert its dominance.

There were two principal tasks facing the Left Front government. The first was to democratize the panchayati system, which required a legislative programme that recognized the powerful vested interests existing in village politics, and their ability to utilize such institutions by incorporating them into the existing framework of village politics dominated by patron–client relations and traditional social structures and alignments.[3]

The second task was to undermine the existing 'rock departmentalism'—a term used in the 1973 Minhas Report on Panchayats when describing the nature of the departments involved in rural development.[4] Rock departmentalism was rooted in the deep elitism and conservatism that permeated much of the bureaucracy, reinforced by the hierarchical administrative structure through which state policies and programmes were channelled down through the district department to the block and ultimately the village. It was top-down planning with little sideways interaction with the local government institutions and little accountability outside the departments, and was a political problem as much as it was an administrative problem.

Direct Party-Based Elections

In a series of Acts of Amendment beginning with four in 1978, the Left Front government began to reorganize and change the whole concept and nature of panchayats in West Bengal. First, the four tiers of panchayats were reduced to three. The earlier *anchal* became the basis for the new *gram panchayat*. Where the number of villages covered by the *anchal* was felt to be too large, or the population covered was too great, the old *anchal* was divided. The new *gram panchayats* covered eight to ten villages and a population of around 12,000. The former *anchalik panchayat* now became the *panchayat samiti* and the *zilla parishad* retained its title and its position as the panchayat covering the whole district.

Previously direct elections had only been for the old *gram panchayats*. Members of the higher panchayats were elected by the panchayat members of the tier immediately below. Under the new legislation, direct elections by secret ballot are held for all three levels of panchayats every five years. All those recorded on the electoral role of the West Bengal Legislative Assembly are eligible to vote. On election day each voter casts the following votes: a single vote for a *zilla parishad* candidate for whom the block is the constituency; a single vote for a *panchayat samiti* member for whom a section of the *gram panchayat* will be the constituency (up to three *panchayat samiti* members are elected from a single *gram panchayat* depending upon its size); one or two votes for *gram panchayat* candidates from her/his local constituency within the *gram panchayat*, the area of *gram panchayat* being divided into an average of eight to ten constituencies.

Obviously the reintroduction of elections to be held on a regular basis formally reintroduced the process of democratization, but the fact that all levels of panchayats are now elected by direct elections began the process of breaking the mould of traditional politics that had shaped and determined these institutions previously. That process has then been continued by making the new elections open to party politics, whereas the panchayats had previously been non-party institutions. The belief had been that local community interests transcended party politics and that the latter should not be allowed to disrupt the panchayats. It was the panchayat as conceptualized in Gandhi's vision of Swaraj, i.e., as self-governing semi-autonomous village communities—communities once divided by the British, but reunited by common values and interests. The naivety of such a view of village politics was considerable.

The new direct party-based elections broke the parochialism of the earlier system. At the village level it had been relatively easy for vested interests to mobilize blocks of votes by invoking the dependency ties of loans, tenancy, networks of kinship and caste and the wide range of other patron–client ties that prevail. However, as the constituency size increases, extending beyond the immediate village context, the mobilization of political support becomes more complex. The electoral politics of the new panchayats require a different form of organizational basis and it is this which has made the introduction of parties into panchayat

elections since 1978 so significant. The traditional rural elite, whose
strength lay in land and caste, and who had tended to locate their
interests within the framework of the local Congress Party, now
found their original control of the first panchayats called into
question. To quote Benoy Chowdhury:

> There is a wealth of difference between then and now [1989].
> Before it was only the dominant vested interests in the villages
> who had the power. The people had no initiative, no involve-
> ment in local politics, in their development. Now the poor have
> a say, they can seize the initiative . . . . In addition, you see, we
> have instituted land reforms and this has enabled the poor to be
> independent and this, with the new panchayats, has helped to
> break the power of the rich and the powerful (pers. comm.,
> March 1989).

Thus, beginning with the 1978 panchayat elections, the voter
was offered the chance of voting for a party rather than for an
individual. The change introduced party machineries into the election campaigns. Now it was possible for a person to stand in
opposition to the traditional village leadership and to draw upon
external political resources to mobilize support for his/her stand
within the village political arena.

A typical situation in a traditionally pro-Congress village would
see a local CPI(M) supporter combine a campaign of support for a
local sharecropper prepared to register in defiance of his landowner's wishes, with the introduction of outside party activists to
establish a village *krisak samiti* (local committee of the *kisan sabha*
or peasant front). This would establish an initial basis for an
election campaign that combined local disputes with wider issues
in an area where the CPI(M) previously had little or no base.

For the CPI(M) the combination of the introduction of party
political organization with the political momentum achieved in the
1977 State Assembly elections brought a clear victory at all levels
of the panchayats in 1978, and, in the short term, secured the local
institutional base for implementing the Left Front's agrarian programme. In the longer term, the introduction of parties has politi-
cized development in the minds of the villagers. Development is
now associated with a party, its programme and policies, and
involves the voter, the local politician, the departmental officer

and the local party organization which the voter might belong to, all within a single set of institutions and relations.

The Attack on Rock Departmentalism

The second change was set in motion once these first elections had been held. The new panchayats began the formidable task of radically altering the relationship between administrative technical officers on the one hand and locally elected politicians on the other, in order to achieve a working and democratic arrangement within the new panchayats. Although the 1973 West Bengal Panchayat Act and the amending acts passed from 1978 onwards laid down the formal basis for the relationship between the two at the different levels of panchayats, in practice the officials and the predominantly CPI(M)/Left Front elected panchayat members viewed each other with deep suspicion and distrust.

Prior to 1978, the block development officer (BDO) had reigned supreme in the community block. In the village the *gram sevak* worker implemented local work and reported to the block. At the level of the district, the district magistrate (DM) was the ultimate authority, with particular responsibilities delegated to district engineers, additional district magistrates and other officers. After 1978 these officers could no longer exercise authority over their respective domains as they had been accustomed to do. Now they were required to work alongside locally elected politicians in a co-operative framework of panchayats and their committees, where decisions were passed by the vote. The BDO found him/herself an ex officio member of the *panchayat samiti* and was expected, along with other block level departmental officers, to implement the decisions passed by the panchayat. Similarly the DM and other district officers were required to work with the elected *zilla parishad* and its standing committees.

All these officials were now faced with a political climate that called for the decentralization of powers and popular participation in decision making from below emanating from a Left Front government, many of whose members and supporters distrusted the ability of the officials to accept such changes. Many CPI(M) activists elected to the panchayats saw the administration as representative of vested interests entrenched in the social order that they sought to change.

From interviews in Burdwan District, a relatively prosperous agrarian district with a long history of support for the Left and the CPI(M) and the site for this investigation into the panchayats, it was apparent that many of those elected to the new panchayats in 1978 brought with them a political animosity towards the administrative officers. This was based on a combination of bitter personal experience of their support for the rural elite in the past and an ideological commitment to reorganize local administration and undermine the power of local civil service mandarins. The previous administration of rural development, with its officials' lack of empathy with the poor in the villages was seen as the antithesis of an administration based on the principles of a people's democracy.

The tension within the new situation was not helped by the Left Front government entrusting important tasks from its agrarian programme to the new *gram panchayats*. Identifying and encouraging sharecroppers to be legally registered under 'Operation Barga'; identifying land held above the legal land ceiling and helping in organizing its redistribution; rural development under programmes such as the Intensive Rural Development Programme (IRDP), the Food for Work Programme and relief work—these were all responsibilities that would have previously belonged to departmental officials at the block level.

At the same time, the CPI(M) and other Left Front activists were using situations such as registration of sharecroppers, demand of agricultural labourers for the legal minimum wage and demand of maidservants for a higher wage, as a means to promote their party bases in the villages. CPI(M) party activists and supporters sought to mobilize poor peasants and agricultural labourers against those identified as oppressors and opposed to reform through these programmes; in so doing, they undoubtedly came into increasing conflict with many administrative officials. BDOs were frequent targets for such action at the local level. Village supporters mobilized by party activists would blockade the BDO in his/her office. Naturally such actions did little to help relations between officials and elected members in panchayat meetings and business.

The state government and the CPI(M) combined pressure and platitudes in their efforts to resolve this early conflict between political activists and administrative officials, pointing out that if civil servants and ministers could work together at the state level then it should also be possible at the lower levels in the panchayats. In some instances, administrative officials were moved when relations reached an impasse, but the most important contribution towards resolving the conflicts came from within the CPI(M) and the other Left Front parties. From the outset, their leadership argued the need to work with and not against the administrative officers. Now it tried to impress, and where necessary, to impose this upon the local membership.

The change from a conflictual to a cooperative relationship has taken time. It has been aided by a number of factors including the Left Front's shifting the emphasis of its agrarian programme towards less antagonistic issues; the panchayats increasingly assuming a developmental role in programme planning and implementation; the civil service's recognition of the electoral strength of the Left Front and the weakness of the political opposition so that a change in government is not likely in the near future. Since the Left Front won the panchayat elections in 1983 and 1988 with increased support, panchayats have become fora for compromise more than conflict.

Today, while both sides agree that tensions might occur, a working relationship has been established that permits the panchayats to function according to plan. Officials say that the elected members have learned how to manage the administration of local government with the need to prepare budgets, maintain records and accounts, construct plan proposals and the many other tasks required. For their part, those elected as CPI(M) party members as well as supporters and other party activists say that the administrative and technical officers 'have been brought down a little, but still have to be watched' (pers. comm., *panchayat samiti* members, Burdwan Block, Burdwan District, May 1989).

The improvement of the relations between administrative and elected personnel has enabled the work of the panchayats to be increased by the devolution of planning. From 1985 all state development plans have been drawn up on the basis of annual district plans, which in turn are based upon proposals from the panchayat committees below. With the introduction of these committees, the institutional structure for planning and administering development in West Bengal has assumed the form illustrated in Figure 10.1. However, rock departmentalism remains a problem that has no permanent solution. The turnover in officers that their career structure demands brings a constant flow of new officers

Figure 10.1

Structure of Planning in West Bengal

Institutions of Government	Institutions of Planning
STATE	
State Government	State Planning Board
	(Departments)
DISTRICTS	
Zilla Parishad	District Planning and
Standing Committee	Co-ordinating Council
	District Planning
	Committee
BLOCKS	
Panchayat Samiti	Block Planning Committee
Standing Committee	
VILLAGES	
Gram Panchayat	(Basic needs proposal)
Scheme Committees, etc.	
(*Krisak Samiti*, etc.)	

into contact with the elected members. For example, a BDO moves every three years or so, a district magistrate stays a little longer before moving. Younger BDOs interviewed in 1989 expressed a strong belief that greater efficiency in development administration could be achieved if they were granted wider powers and greater autonomy from the *panchayat samiti*, the panchayat with which they worked most closely serving as its ex officio executive officer. Such beliefs are mirrored by *panchayat samiti* members speaking of the need to 're-educate' their BDOs on occasion.

There is one additional factor which influences the administrative officers' perceptions of the panchayats, namely the role of the CPI(M). The CPI(M) has increasingly organized itself along strong democratic–centralist lines. As well as the main party structure there exist a number of mass front organizations whose purpose is to mobilize particular social groups to the CPI(M)'s political cause. In rural areas the *kisan sabha* (peasant association) with its village *krisak samitis* (local committees) organizes the small and medium landowning peasant cultivators, sharecroppers and, in most areas, the agricultural labourer as well; the Democratic Youth Front of India (DYFI) is designed to bring the young and not so young into political activities; the *mohila samiti* is the women's front.[5]

The party and mass front organizational structures closely parallel the panchayat structure; the party asserts a strong control over its members and its supporters in the mass front organizations, including those serving as members of the panchayats.[6] At the higher levels of the *panchayat samiti* and the *zilla parishad* all those elected as CPI(M) or other Left Front party candidates are almost certainly full party members. However, at the level of the *gram panchayats*, the number of local party members available to stand for election is usually very few. In most cases the party (assuming CPI[M] is the main Left party in the locality) will allocate one or two members to stand for each *gram panchayat*. On election these will be appointed to the positions of *pradhan* and *upa-pradhan* (chairperson and vice-chairperson) if the CPI(M)/Left Front controls a majority on the panchayat through the election of its supporters. 'Supporters' might be under consideration for party membership, but they are not members and do not attend party meetings. The *gram panchayat's* affairs are discussed by the local party members in closed meetings and the elected supporters are then advised as to how party policy should be carried out through the *gram panchayat*.

There are two views as to the impact of the party upon the affairs of the panchayats. One sees it as an undemocratic interference in the working of the panchayats, a view widely expressed by political opponents of the Left Front and central to many of their grievances and criticisms. It is a view also expressed by some administrative officials, not necessarily from a specific animosity towards the Left Front, but from a civil servant's belief in the need for neutrality in administrative affairs. The second view sees the party's role as predictable, even essential, given its commitment to implement Panchayati Raj and the need to challenge vested and entrenched interests in order to achieve that goal. For Panchayati Raj to have any real impact on local development requires an improvement in the bargaining position of the rural poor, which in turn requires the implementation of land reform, minimum wage legislation and similar policies. Likewise, if there is to be efficiency and accountability and the prevention of corruption in the work of the panchayats, the type of discipline that a committed party can impose is important. Without these the programme would be largely ineffective.

The Panchayats and Participation

At the time of its election and in the years immediately following, the CPI(M) clearly possessed the type of strong ideological commitment necessary to implement and carry through these changes. What is less certain is whether the principal reason for promoting panchayats remains that of a radical approach towards rural development with a political commitment to the poor, or it has shifted to the more instrumentalist purpose of securing the party's electoral strength in order to remain in government, with all the compromises and alliances which that might require. While the two are far from being mutually exclusive, they can result in significantly different outcomes in the longer term.

Whatever the priority has become, the introduction of direct party-based elections and the transformation of the relations between elected local politicians and the administrative service have been of central importance for both politics and development in many rural areas. The popular support for the strategy can be clearly seen in the successes of the CPI(M) and Left Front in panchayat elections, as shown in Table 10.1.

Table 10.1

West Bengal Panchayat Election Results: Percentage of Seats Won

	Gram Panchayat			Panchayat Samiti			Zilla Parishad		
	1978	1983	1988	1978	1983	1988	1978	1983	1988
CPI(M)[a]	60	53	65	66	60	72	75	68	85
Forward Bloc[a]	3	2	3	4	2	3	6	4	2
RSP[a]	4	3	3	4	3	3	4	2	3
CPI[b]	2	2	2	2	1	1	4	0	1
Congress (I)	10	32	23	7	29	19	3	23	7
Congress (R)	1			1					
Janata	0	0	0	0	0	0	0	0	0
BJP	0	0	0	0	0	0	0	0	0
Independents	20	7	4	16	5	3	8	3	2

Notes: *a* denotes principal members of the Left Front winning more than 0.5%.
   b denotes members of Left Front from 1988.
Source: Results collected from various Bengali newspapers.

But what is the view from the villages, from the lowest tier of panchayats, the *gram panchayats?* Research was carried out in two *gram panchayats*; the question of development and participation was examined on the basis of socio-economic status, caste and gender through a survey of seventy-five households in each of two *gram panchayats* in Burdwan District (renamed Kanpur II and Saldya for the purpose of this article). Socio-economic status was determined on the basis of the household's relationship to land-ownership and cultivation, along with the main source of income. The principal caste distinctions made were between general castes, Scheduled Castes and Scheduled Tribes, with Muslims as a fourth category. Women were interviewed from each household in order that the gender experience of panchayats might also be included. The following is a summary of some of the findings.[7]

Kanpur II

The two *gram panchayats* lie in the eastern half of Burdwan district on the alluvial plains of central West Bengal. Kanpur II is in a relatively prosperous agricultural area with canal irrigation and increasingly shallow tubewells providing irrigation for a second rice crop. The *gram panchayat* covers six villages, the old *anchal* of Kanpur having been divided into two in 1978 with the reorganization of panchayats. Two of the villages had long been a stronghold for Congress and then Congress (I) after the party split in 1977. The other four villages have been associated with the communist and *kisan* movements for a similar length of time. Important communist leaders such as Benoy Chowdhury, Harekrishna Konar and Heleram Chatterjee were all activists in the area during the anti-British canal tax movements of the 1930s and afterwards.

In 1977–78, political support in the *gram panchayat* was clearly polarized between the two political parties and their supporters, and the factional nature of the politics reflected in the support's demarcation along village boundaries. The traditional domination of Congress was achieved through the patronage role of the local leadership and its control over institutions such as the library committees, primary school boards and the old *anchals* and *gram panchayats*. There was no Congress Party organization as such, and it was this that perhaps allowed the CPI(M) to mobilize and organize from its own village bases into the Congress territory.

During 1977–78, a number of violent clashes between Congress and CPI(M) supporters occurred, particularly over the registration of sharecroppers. This provided the CPI(M) with an initial foothold, and support from the poorer households was then built up through strikes for higher wages for the agricultural labourers, the organization of government-funded employment on work in their neighbourhoods, usually road improvements, and by presenting a strong and dynamic profile through public activities, meetings, parades and so on. Much of this work was carried out by the *krisak samitis*.

By 1981–82 the CPI(M) was also succeeding in winning over sections of the middle peasantry, those with more adequate landholdings and often small businesses or those employed in government service such as teaching. Landowners who refused to register sharecroppers or to abide by the legal division were now persuaded rather than confronted. *Krisak samitis* began to discuss the share with landowners in advance, aiming for a mutually acceptable division—an approach reflected in the fact that in most years it has been lower for the sharecropper than the legal division established at the state level.

There has been a shift away from the highly conflictual politics of land distribution, registration of sharecroppers, and granting of ownership rights of homestead land to the occupant, towards the reformist politics of development management, the resolution of village conflicts, the 'management' of village affairs. The move has made the CPI(M) electorally secure while at the same time allowing it to firmly establish its own organizations throughout the *gram panchayat*, with an inner core of between twenty and thirty full party members—activists who have met the standards of personal and political behaviour that are laid down by the party. Around this core are a larger number of supporters working in the local *kisan* and *mohila samitis* and in the DYFI.

Congress (I) remains in the locality as a rump of long-term supporters and those who for personal or ideological reasons remain antagonistic to CPI(M) and its local members and activists. The local condition of Congress (I) is summed up in the fact that the two remaining Congress (I) members of Kanpur II *gram panchayat* failed to take the required oath to take up their seats after the 1988 election. Officially the CPI(M) has not locally pushed for their removal and new elections due to a lack of funds, but in practice their non-presence serves to reinforce the image of Congress as politically impotent and the two elected leaders as personally spiteful.

Saldya

Saldya *gram panchayat* is in a poorer agricultural area as the land is higher, sandier and possesses only limited irrigation for a second non-monsoon crop. This *gram panchayat* is larger than Kanpur II, with nineteen villages under its control, though some of these are little more than extensions of other villages. One village, Saldya, dominates in size, facilities and prosperity. The politics of the area is quite different from that of Kanpur II's in that the CPI(M) has long been the dominant party in the area, having come to the fore in the 1950s through a series of local movements organized by the then united CPI and the *kisan sabha*.

The new panchayat elections in 1978 saw the CPI(M) successfully convert its dominance into a very strong position on the *gram panchayat*. It was able to move smoothly into the efficient administration of development programmes, to fully utilize its allocated funds and to generate the information, proposals and detailed accounts required by the *panchayat samiti* above it. In many ways the *gram panchayat* could serve as an exemplary model for others. But its strength is also a cause for its political weakness.

The local CPI(M) has some forty full-party members, most of whom have been members for many years, are well educated, with quite a few serving as teachers, and come from well established family households in the village. It was the combination of party and personal reputations that saw the CPI(M) achieve its 1978 electoral success in the Saldya *gram panchayat*, not a campaign of political activism and mobilization as witnessed in Kanpur II. In particular, the agrarian programme failed to focus on the resolution of conflict and tension and this resulted in the *krisak samitis* failing to achieve the dynamism of their Kanpur II counterparts.

Since 1978, Saldya has witnessed a decline in the electoral strength of the CPI(M) for quite basic political reasons. The developmental work undertaken by the *gram panchayat* is limited by the programmes' funding and by predetermined rules for programme implementation such as a certain percentage of funds having to go to Scheduled Caste households. In the absence of a popular sense of responsibility and involvement in the decision-making processes and a general lack of awareness of the constraints and limitations involved, it is easy to see how village compares itself with village, social group with social group, village faction with village faction.

In their recent political histories, Kanpur II and Saldya *gram panchayats* reveal important elements of the problems faced by the CPI(M). The poor constitute the majority in the villages of these areas, with landless households constituting nearly 50 per cent, those owning more than two acres of land only 29 per cent, and sharecroppers 24 per cent. But can the CPI(M) politically afford to promote the interests of the poor exclusively? Such a strategy brought the party its initial success in the Congress villages of Kanpur II, but electoral strength came from diluting the demands and changing the tactics away from confrontation in order to avoid alienating the middle ground—the typical general caste household with very little land but with a small shop or a government service income. A radical strategy that supports a campaigning politics for the poor would make Panchayati Raj a vehicle of short-lived political utility as these middle peasants fell back upon traditional political structures and allegiances uniting with the political opponents of the CPI(M). Administrators would similarly disrupt and undermine the work of the panchayats.

For the CPI(M), Kanpur II must be something of a success story as it has sustained the political activism established in 1977–78, through the work of the *krisak samitis* in particular, while also winning over the middle peasantry electorally. But Saldya's electoral decline serves as a warning of the dangers of political apathy. The lack of campaigning politics and of political discourse in different forms and locations throughout the *gram panchayat* area, the over-reliance upon the party to manage and direct both local politics and local development through the efficient functioning of the *gram panchayat* can all cost Panchayati Raj the dynamism of a political movement.

The roots of the problem lie to a considerable extent with the strategy of the CPI(M) as a whole, as discussed by Kohli and others (Kohli, 1987; Westergaard, 1986). But the recurral of the problem can also be found at the micro level in the social and economic profiles of those representing the party at the local level. Here the effects of the strategy can be located and the political condition of the *gram panchayats* assessed.

Membership of Gram Panchayats

Tables 10.2 to 10.9 provide an overview of the socio-economic, caste and gender status of those elected to the two *gram panchayats* in the three elections held to date. The tables include those co-opted on to the *gram panchayats* according to the provisions that ensure adequate representation of women and the Scheduled Castes.

Table 10.2

Kanpur II *Gram Panchayat* Members by Party and Land-ownership (in acres)

	Landless	0.1–2.0	2.1–5.0	5.1–10.0	10.1+	Total
CPI(M):						
1978	3[a]	0	3	1	3	10
1983	3	2	2	0	0	7
1988	3[b]	2	4	1	2	12
Congress (I):						
1978	0	1	2	2	0	5
1983	0	0	2	2	0	4
1988	0	0	0	2	0	2

Notes: *a* denotes two co-opted members; *b* denotes one co-opted member.
Source: Fieldwork (1989).

Table 10.3

Saldya *Gram Panchayat* Members by Party and Land-ownership (in acres)

	Landless	0.1–2.0	2.1–5.0	5.1–10.0	10.1+	Total
CPI(M):						
1978	4[a]	14	0	0	0	18
1983	4	14	0	0	0	18
1988	5[b]	11	0	0	0	16
Congress (I):						
1978	1	1	0	0	0	2
1983	0	3	0	0	0	3
1988	2	5	1	0	0	8

Notes: *a* denotes two co-opted members; *b* denotes one co-opted member.
Source: Fieldwork (1989).

Table 10.4

Kanpur II *Gram Panchayat*: Members' Principal Occupation

	Teacher	Owner–Cultivator	Share-cropper	Business	Govt. Service	Labourer
CPI(M):						
1978	2	4	2[a]	1	0	1
1983	1	1	4[b]	0	0	1
1988	3	3	0	1	2	3[b]
Congress (I):						
1978	1	3	0	0	1	0
1983	1	3	0	0	0	0
1988	1	1	0	0	0	0

Notes: *a* denotes two co-opted members; *b* denotes one co-opted member.
Source: Fieldwork (1989).

Table 10.5

Saldya *Gram Panchayat*: Members' Principal Occupation

	Teacher	Owner–cultivator	Share-cropper	Business	Govt. Service	Labourer	House-wife
CPI(M):							
1978	5	9	0	2	0	0	2[b]
1983	2	10	0	4	0	0	2[a]
1988	2	7	0	4	0	1	2[a]
Congress (I):							
1978	1	1	0	0	0	0	0
1983	0	1	0	2	0	0	0
1988	3	3	0	2	0	0	0

Notes: *a* denotes two co-opted members; *b* denotes one co-opted member.
Source: Fieldwork (1989).

When analyzing the formal participation of different social categories as members of the panchayats it is important to remember the base-line from which one is operating. Before the new panchayats there was no effective participation for the poor. They relied upon philanthropy and personal appeal to those in power, be they local officials or village leaders and their power brokers.

Table 10.6

Members' Castes

	Kanpur II Gram Panchayat				Saldya Gram Panchayat			
	Scheduled Caste	Scheduled Tribe	Muslim	General Caste	Scheduled Caste	Scheduled Tribe	Muslim	General Caste
CPI(M):								
1978	4[a]	0	0	6	3	0	2	13[b]
1983	2	0	0	5	4[b]	0	2	12[b]
1988	4[a]	0	0	8	5[b]	0	2	9[b]
Congress (I):								
1978	1	0	0	4	1	0	0	1
1983	1	0	0	3	2	0	0	1
1988	1	0	0	1	2	0	1	5

Notes: *a* denotes two co-opted members; *b* denotes one co-opted member.
Source: Fieldwork (1989).

Table 10.7

Female Members

Kanpur II *Gram Panchayat*

1978	1	elected	– General caste, agricultural day labourer from a household possessing 0.4 of an acre of vested land, CPI(M) candidate
1983	0		– None elected or co-opted
1988	1	elected	– Scheduled Caste landless day labourer, CPI(M) candidate

Saldya *Gram Panchayat*

1978	1	elected	– Scheduled Caste, household work
	1	co-opted	– General Caste, household work
1983	2	co-opted	– One Scheduled Caste, beedi maker and household work
			– One general caste, household work
1988	2	co-opted	– One general caste, college student
			– One Scheduled Caste, household work

Note: All have been or are CPI(M) supporters.
Source: Fieldwork (1989).

From the tables it can be seen that there is now significant representation in the *gram panchayats* from among the poorer and more marginal social groups. In particular, landless and marginal landowners, Scheduled Castes, women and, in Saldya, Muslims all have members in the *gram panchayat*. They have a presence and involvement in local government and development that they had never previously possessed. This is a direct consequence of the CPI(M)-led implementation of Panchayati Raj in the district.

While this is a quite dramatic improvement it must also be acknowledged that significant problems remain. The lack of members from the Scheduled Tribes is partly a reflection of their small numbers in the two localities (6.8 per cent in Kanpur II, 0.2 per cent in Saldya), but it can also be seen as reflecting the continuing negative image and attitude that other villagers have towards this group. While casteism is in obvious decline in Burdwan District, the Scheduled Tribes remain a distinct and usually physically separated social group in the villages, with no voice of their own in the *gram panchayats*. In the Saldya *gram panchayat* the Muslims (approximately 4 per cent of the population) are represented, a reflection of their strong presence in the two constituencies and the economic and political standing of some of their households. In Kanpur II, Muslims are very few in number and, with no mosque, have a very low profile and live with the Scheduled Caste community.

Women have achieved only a token presence in the two *gram panchayats*, and that too more often by co-option than by election. Social structures and cultural practices mitigate very strongly against a woman standing for election, with the pressure of a woman's household being very important in this matter. At the same time, those women who have stood have been elected. This might reflect the fact that votes are given to a party and not to an individual, but it shows that a woman is not an electoral liability. In a survey of 150 households no one suggested that a woman representative would be a disadvantage: they felt that a woman was or could be as effective as a man. However, the hidden proviso appeared to be that it should not be a woman from their own household. The social pressure against women participating as members is articulated primarily through the household: it is the man's fear of the loss of status if the woman is so publicly involved in affairs outside the household. The CPI(M) appear to be acquiescent in this. Despite seeing it as a problem they seem to be doing little about it. In the absence of suitable women coming forward as candidates, they co-opt women after the election, co-option being a less public and less demanding way to the panchayat. Saldya *gram panchayat* appears to be particularly guilty of this.

While the electoral turnout is as high for women as for men in the two areas, their lack of presence on the panchayats leaves them with little possibility of expressing their needs or interests. This in turn helps to explain why they are not receiving adequate benefits from development programmes, these again tending to be allocated to households rather than individuals with men consequently the principal beneficiaries.

Certainly the position of women and Scheduled Tribes places the onus firmly upon the CPI(M) to contest at the political level the popular conceptions of development and oppression that remain and which disadvantage specific socio-cultural groups such as women and tribals. Yet this is not a priority in the party. It is difficult to pinpoint the exact reasons, but given the entrenched patriarchal and racial structures which permeate Indian politics, even within the more enlightened climate of West Bengal (as compared to the neighbouring Bihar for example), the potential electoral costs of pursuing such a strategy could be considerable; they are certainly unknown.

This leads to the question: What is the role of Panchayati Raj in challenging the structures of rural society? Dramatic in its initial implications and thrust, what of the future?

Recently the CPI(M) has been criticized by the Left for relying too much upon members and supporters whose class position is not seen as representative of the mass of poor peasants and labourers.[8] To some extent this is borne out by the evidence in Tables 10.2–10.5. Table 10.8 is taken from a survey conducted by the Government of West Bengal, Department of Panchayats and Community Development, in 1980 after the first panchayat elections.

Table 10.8

Distribution of Members by Occupation

Occupation	Number	Percentage
Owner–cultivators	743	50.7
Teachers	206	14.0
Unemployed	110	7.5
Landless labourers	70	4.8
Sharecroppers	26	1.8
Artisans	23	1.6
Shop owners	20	1.4
Technical workers	19	1.3
Doctors	16	1.1
Tailors	8	0.6
Students	8	0.6
Fishermen	6	0.4
Others	211	14.4
Total	1,466	100.0

Source: Government of West Bengal (1980).[9]

Of the 50.7 per cent who were owner–cultivators, the survey gives the following breakdown:

Acres	Percentage of Distribution
Below 2	42.9
2–5	28.2
5–8	13.0
8–10	8.1
Over 10	7.8
Total	100.0

The government report concluded that the majority of the members came from the poorer sections of the village, but if we total up the percentages of the unemployed, the landless labourers and the 42.9 per cent of the owner–cultivators with less than two acres, the percentage of total members is 35.9. It is an extremely rough measure of the poor's representation, but it shows a close similarity with the profiles of membership in the two *gram panchayats* studied. In 1988, 36 per cent of those elected in Kanpur II had less than two acres; in Saldya the figure was much higher at 96 per cent. However, remove teachers and others in government service or with businesses and the figures are 36 per cent (no change and including 17 per cent co-opted) and 46 per cent (including 9 per cent co-opted), respectively. Previous fieldwork in villages in this part of Burdwan found households with under two acres constituting 65 to 70 per cent of all village households (Webster, 1986). Therefore, not only do the poor remain under-represented, but too often their representation is on the basis of co-option and not election. But the problem goes beyond simple numbers: it is not merely a question of being elected or co-opted on to the panchayat, but also of being able to assert a presence within its meetings. Caste and prevailing norms of social behaviour with respect to elders and the educated remain serious obstacles here. The Scheduled Caste woman elected to Kanpur II *gram panchayat* in 1988 spoke of the problems she faced in meetings in overcoming both her own inhibitions and others' prejudices. Poor and Scheduled Caste members spoke of similar problems and these were physically visible in such things as the seating arrangements at meetings. In combating these problems Kanpur II appeared to have been more successful because individuals from these groups had come to the fore in the period of political activism in the late 1970s. They had become quite accomplished in addressing public meetings, and possessed greater confidence in the formal setting of panchayat meetings than their counterparts in the Saldya *gram panchayat*. Today, entry into politics in Saldya appears to be influenced more by education, by membership of families with a tradition of active political involvement and by the experience of work outside the villages.

How does the CPI(M) respond to criticisms of the class profile of its panchayat members? The main counter-argument has been that its members' and supporters' ideological stance is more important at this stage of the struggle for a people's democracy and that this is closely watched and monitored by the party. Furthermore, the party does not yet have the members or the political strength to promote a more radical process of change. The party argues that it is far better to achieve and maintain power with the support of those committed to the party and the Left Front government's programme and to have party members advise and supervise these supporters, than to fall back on the more conflictual politics of former years.

These are important arguments and they are used to justify the need for a strong disciplined party. In this way CPI(M) can win the *gram panchayats* for the Left Front and ensure that those elected follow government and party policies, thereby avoiding the dangers of personal bias and self-aggrandizement amongst those elected to positions of local influence. But it should be recognized that it does involve a broader alliance of class interests than the CPI(M) is perhaps prepared to admit, an alliance in which it is not always clear which are the dominant interests. The imposition of party diktat over its supporters in the *gram panchayat* might prevent both personal corruption and political 'waywardness', but it does not prevent a tendency towards a political ossification, a failure to extend and build on the more dynamic politics of, say, Kanpur II in the late 1970s and early 1980s.

Despite these problems, the response of the villagers towards their *gram panchayats* in both areas was overwhelmingly positive. Electoral turnout in the elections has never fallen below 80 per cent and in Kanpur II has been over 95 per cent on occasion. The aim of the CPI(M)'s strategy, however, is to go beyond the ballot box in involving people.

Attendance at the biannual public meetings in each village (i.e., a *gram sabha* meeting) is high for men, with 65 per cent attending and a further 12 per cent attending and speaking; and low for women, 17 per cent attending and a further 2 per cent attending and speaking. Of the 19 per cent of women at the meetings, only 2 per cent came from general castes, the rest were from Scheduled Castes and Tribes; for men, of the 77 per cent attending, 32 per cent were from general castes and 45 per cent from Scheduled Castes and Tribes or Muslims. Among the men attending such meetings, most of those who spoke were from the general castes, while among the women attending those who spoke were all from the Scheduled Castes.

In addition to the compulsory public meetings of the *gram sabhas*, there are other important fora for participation in the affairs of the *gram panchayats*. Informal nightly discussions in some *paras* (residential neighbourhoods) are an important means for briefing panchayat members. There are also regular public meetings on particular issues, for example planning specific work within development in programmes to decide on the division of the coming harvest between sharecropper and landowner, or to discuss the wage rate to be paid to agricultural labourers in the village.

Such meetings were more common for Kanpur II than for the Saldya *gram panchayat*. In addition, the former used the meetings to discuss a particular work project and to establish a scheme committee. This would usually be organized by the local *krisak samiti*, would be composed of local householders and would have one *gram panchayat* member on the committee responsible for administering the funds. The scheme committee was then responsible for allocating the labour days made available and ensuring the work was carried out. On completion of the work to the satisfaction of the *gram panchayat*, the scheme committee would dissolve. In Saldya, a meeting would be held in the *para* to discuss the proposed work, but its organization would be carried out by the *gram panchayat*.

When asked about such local meetings and committees, the poorer households interviewed unanimously saw them as a significant development and as part of the general process of change under the new panchayats. Most regarded them as fora where they, or at least persons they identified as having similar concerns to their own, could speak and be listened to. Most did not see them merely as platforms from which the CPI(M) could deliver party propaganda. The reverse was true among the more affluent households. They rarely attended such informal or local meetings unless they were supporters or members of the CPI(M), and they often viewed them as party-based and sectarian.

The Panchayats and Development

The overall support for the *gram panchayats* is also a reflection of their success as agencies of development. The ability of the CPI(M) to bring about a material improvement in the situation of the poor is central to the party's strategy of aiding the poor using their control of the federal state, but again it is a circumscribed ability. The evidence from the two *gram panchayats* revealed that the main programmes for which they are responsible were being implemented both efficiently and according to the purposes for which they were intended. For example, work under the employment programmes including Food for Work and subsequently the National Rural Employment Programme (NREP) and small grants under the Integrated Rural Development Programme (IRDP)— programmes for which the *gram panchayats* are entrusted with a high degree of responsibility in identifying potential recipients and in implementing—were going to the designated economic and caste groups. The amount on offer was far below the potential demand, but what was available was being handled without the degree of corruption and abuse from which equivalent programmes prior to 1978 had suffered.

There is a high degree of accountability for the *gram panchayat* members. Not only must there be the two public *gram sabha* meetings each year with the past year's accounts and proposals for future expenditures and work open to public discussion, the accounts and proposed budgets also have to be audited and passed by the *panchayat samiti* in whose constituency the *gram panchayat* lies.

There is also an internal CPI(M) accountability operating. During a one-year research visit to Kanpur II and two other *gram panchayats* in 1977–78, I was provided with many examples of overt corruption in the handling of development funds, such as bribes being demanded or deducted from grants, and road repairs completed on paper only, many of which were verifiable from documents or other sources. In 1989 there were complaints in the two *gram panchayats* studied, but they were mainly of political bias in the allocation of funds and not of the pocketing of funds by panchayat members or officials at the local level. Only one verifiable instance of misuse of funds by a panchayat member was uncovered during the fieldwork and this individual—not a party member but a local activist—was punished by the CPI(M) with removal from office, and was made to pay back the missing money.

This is not to say that corruption does not exist elsewhere, nor that there might not be some truth in the accusations of political bias made by several of those interviewed, but certainly in the localities of Kanpur II and Saldya *gram panchayats* there is a generally accepted view that these institutions and their members are not corrupt, that they do administer the programmes effectively and that a general improvement in the material condition of most villagers has ensued since 1978. Kanpur II, in particular, showed marked improvements both from the criteria of works effected and from the perception of those interviewed. Again, this reflected the activism of the CPI(M) and *krisak samitis* in their work to undermine the local base of Congress (I).

While the case study revealed a clear improvement in development work under the new *gram panchayats*, it also revealed significant problems. Financially the programmes implemented by the *gram panchayats* are under-funded and few of those in need of the benefits receive enough employment or financial support to produce a significant transformation of their economic condition. This is particularly true for landless labourers and those marginal cultivators who rely primarily upon agricultural labour. While their condition has improved—both directly through government-paid work and higher wage rates, and indirectly through infrastructural improvements—, they have no greater security and remain dependent upon central and state government's support for such policies and programmes. A political change in the state government or a reduction in funds from the central government could easily result in these improvements being lost.

Another major problem apparent from fieldwork is that while the benefits are reaching the poor, they are not reaching women in general and poor women in particular. This is a clear failing in the work of the panchayats. Although the political will to empower the poor exists in West Bengal, the poor are being identified in household units and this reinforces the invisibility of women when it comes to the allocation of benefits. As a consequence, relations of structural oppression affecting women are largely ignored in development work.

Returning to the financial status of the panchayats, an increase in financial autonomy through greater responsibility in the collection of funds might partially remove the insecurity that they, and those receiving benefits through them, currently experience. In his 1989 budget speech Ashim Das Gupta, the Minister of State for Finance, made the panchayats responsible for collecting money for a state saving scheme, with the promise that 50 per cent of funds collected above a set target would be retained by the panchayats for their own development fund. While it is a step in the right direction, the amounts involved are relatively small and it is a scheme that fails to reflect a prioritizing of the need to give greater financial autonomy to the panchayats.

Other sources of funds that could be channelled into panchayat bodies would have to be investigated, but funds raised at the district level from agricultural income tax must be one possibility, local state taxes on commodities, another.

The Party and Panchayati Raj: An Assessment

As a programme of decentralized development planning and implementation, Panchayati Raj is working in Burdwan district within the limits set for it by the state government. It is bringing about a significant material improvement in sections of the rural population, and particularly the poorer and marginal groups. At the same time, financial resources are limited and the range of responsibilities passed down to the *gram panchayats* is also restricted to involvement with specific development programmes such as IRDP, NREP and, since 1979, the broader development programme, Jawahar Rozgar Yojana.

There are other problems as well. Development is not reaching all groups equally, with women in particular remaining invisible because benefits are allocated to households. But such problems should be assessed on the basis of the previous situation where

Table 10.9

Perception of Changes under the New *Gram Panchayats* among 150 Households by Land, Caste and Gender

	Kanpur II			Saldya			Overall		
	No Benefits %	Few Benefits %	Substantial Benefits %	No Benefits %	Few Benefits %	Substantial Benefits %	No Benefits %	Few Benefits %	Substantial Benefits %
Male:									
Under 2 acres	6	9	85	15	15	70	10	12	78
Over 2 acres	20	20	60	19	14	67	20	17	63
General Caste	13	16	71	22	22	56	17	19	64
Scheduled Caste	8	11	81	9	6	85	8	8	84
Scheduled Tribe	0	0	100	0	0	0	0	0	100
Muslim	0	0	100	25	25	50	20	20	60
Female:									
Under 2 acres	40	24	46	43	11	46	41	13	46
Over 2 acres	50	25	25	62	10	28	56	17	27
General Caste	41	18	41	68	5	27	47	14	39
Scheduled Caste	43	16	41	26	15	59	36	15	49
Scheduled Tribe	40	20	40	0	0	0	40	20	40
Muslim	100	0	0	50	25	25	60	20	20

Source: Fieldwork (1989).

small amounts were distributed inequitably on the basis of political patronage and primordial loyalties. Moreover, it should be judged on the basis of the perception of the villagers themselves (Table 10.9). When asked what they think of the *gram panchayats*, the majority see them as having produced both material improvements for their villages—roads, tubewells, trees, government-paid employment in critical periods, efficient distribution of relief in time of drought and flood—and political improvements, particularly reduced conflict.

This last point includes the reduction in conflicts between land-owners and sharecroppers over registration and crop division, cultivators and agricultural labourers over wage rates and conflicts over party politics in the villages. While the late 1960s and 1970s had been characterized by tensions with sporadic clashes, the 1980s witnessed a greater peace and stability in these areas.

The *gram panchayats*, particularly those of Kanpur II, were also praised for their involvement in settling personal disputes such as those between neighbours or husbands and wives. The new pan-chayat legislation provides for *nyaya* panchayats, local village courts under *gram panchayat* jurisdiction for minor offences. To date the CPI(M) has not seen the *gram panchayats* as ready for such an extension of their powers, but the *gram panchayat* members have informally assumed the role of arbitrator in many situations, a role willingly accepted by the poorer sections of society for whom the alternatives are long and costly.

Evidence of support for the programme in Burdwan panchayats comes from interviews with officials at all levels within the District. Significantly, these interviews revealed a general acceptance of the role of the CPI(M) in the District, and the feeling that without the party's ideological commitment and the political dynamic introduced by it into the promotion and implementation of the programme, little change would have been achieved. However, the perception of success in these two localities does not necessarily mean that Panchayati Raj is successful throughout West Bengal. The Joint Director for Panchayats, Sri Prasad Roy, suggested in an interview that the Districts of Midnapore, Bankura, Birbhum, Hooghly and Burdwan are the success stories, while other districts continue to suffer from organizational weakness, economic backwardness and other problems.

Finally, in examining the role of the CPI(M) with respect to the panchayats and *gram panchayats* in particular, we must ask whether the party has encouraged or permitted the concept of Panchayati Raj to extend beyond decentralization and merely a degree of democratization to actually empower the poor. Some members of the poor have been elected or co-opted on to the new decentralized panchayats, particularly *gram panchayats*, and these individuals do have a degree of involvement in the decision-making processes of these bodies. That in itself is a radical departure from the past. But constraints upon their involvement remain, both in their ability to achieve membership for reasons of poverty (time equals lost wages, etc.), gender and ethnicity, and in the problems faced by them as a result of their low status once they are members, lack of education, gender, etc. Finally they face, as do all members, the structural limitations imposed on the *gram panchayats'* work by finance and legislation, plus the close monitoring of the local committee of the CPI(M). The combination of all these renders their involvement somewhat circumscribed.

Therefore, while it is an important step towards decentralized and democratized local government in the area of development planning, Panchayati Raj has not as yet resulted in the empowerment of the poor. That the poor are now far closer to the process of planning and development is a political phenomenon associated with the policies of different parties, rather than the patronage of particular individuals. Nor is the administrative official the source of power that s/he previously was. However, the people, i.e., the poor majority, cannot be said to be determining politics, but merely to have given their electoral support to the CPI(M)/Left Front, which for the moment has achieved and secured these changes on their behalf.

Parallel to the decentralization of the government is the opposite tendency within the CPI(M). To secure this electorally successful strategy it has imposed a strong organizational structure on its party and its mass fronts based upon democratic centralism, i.e., power emanating from the state committees downwards through the district committees and ultimately to the branch committees in the *gram panchayats*. While securing electoral strength for the party in winning panchayat elections in areas such as Burdwan, this has also required a broad alliance of rural interests at the village level including the educated, the medium-sized landowners, teachers, and small businessmen, often from the higher castes. With this broad alliance has come a reduction in the politics of confrontation. While the poor can be said to be a part of this alliance, they certainly do not lead it.

In conclusion I would emphasize that the material changes that have come about in the villages of Burdwan over the past twelve years are a powerful argument in support of Panchayati Raj and therefore the Left Front government. Without the latter, and the CPI(M) in particular, very little of this change was likely to have occurred and at any rate, would certainly not have reached the poor to the extent that it has. The future is less certain, however. The current strategy would appear to depend upon the CPI(M) continuing to be elected, and for the moment that seems to rest on their development record in the villages. The development programmes require the financial support of the central government and this presents one source of potential problems. The second source lies in the possible weakness of the party at the bottom, which can also carry an electoral cost. The lack of campaigning politics reduces the number of political activists drawn in from the poorer and marginal sections. The history of Bengal is littered with political and social movements in which the poor and the marginal have been supporters, activists and leaders. These need to be drawn into the politics of Panchayati Raj and that in turn requires greater emphasis upon political mobilization at the local level, so that the dangers of political ossification discussed earlier can be avoided.

Panchayati Raj does need a strong party, but that party needs more than just electoral support if it is to continue the movement towards a people's democracy. If it ceases to possess the dynamism of a political movement, it risks falling back into being little more than an organizational rearrangement of the state, with a democratic–centralist party at the helm. In India, to be elected in federal government is never enough. The dangers of being removed from office by the central government through manipulation or decree is always present, as the CPI(M) knows only too well.

The more the involvement of the poor and marginalized in the political process of government and development, the harder it will be for the political and economic gains achieved under Panchayati Raj to be reversed. The CPI(M) must place greater faith in the poor majority and facilitate their more active involvement—as Scheduled Castes, as tribals, as women, as marginal cultivators, etc.

Finally, we must also recognize the achievements of the policy to date and the fact that the poor who constitute the majority, having experienced Panchayati Raj, possess new expectations and new perceptions of their rights and entitlements, and how these might be secured. This new knowledge is not solely dependent upon the programme or the party. Given this, the ground for organic intellectualism within the poor and marginal groups in the Gramscian sense, and the politics this can give rise to, must be stronger because of Panchayati Raj: here lies hope for the future.

Notes

1. The many political movements in India today that possess a national or ethnic identity are themselves a reflection of the centralization of power and the political reaction to the effects of that centralization. See, for example, Kothari (1989).
2. The programme is discussed in greater detail in Webster (1990).
3. Alavi (1973, 1988) presents a clear argument for the utility of patron–client and faction as concepts in neo-Marxist analysis. For a more general discussion see Randall and Theobold (1985: Ch. 5).
4. The problem has been discussed widely, but with respect to Panchayati Raj, see, for example, Suri (1988), Naravaty (1989).
5. Agricultural workers were previously organized through the *khetmazdoors samitis*, but these have been dissolved into the *krisak samitis* in the villages. This would suggest that the political divide between agricultural labourers and share-croppers/marginal farmers that Byres (1970) and others have emphasized is not seen as significant by the CPI(M), their current interests being common ones. See Webster (1980).
6. Burdwan District, with a population of nearly five million and with a significant urban population around its industrial belt, has the following approximate membership figures for the main CPI(M) organizations: Party 10,000; *kisan sabha* (Peasant Front) 1,300,000; CITU (Trade Union Front) 80,000; AIGMS (Women's Front) 220,000; DYFI (Youth Front) 270,000. Information on local membership and the functioning of the party at the local level is regarded as highly confidential by CPI(M), reflecting the centralist internal politics of the party and the 'siege' mentality it tends to induce.
7. A detailed study of the Panchayati Raj programme and its implementation in Burdwan District can be found in Webster (1992).
8. This is discussed in 'Classification of the Panchayat' in CPI(M) (1988)—a collection of CPI(M) articles from its Bengali paper between 1980 and 1988.
9. These figures were supplied to me personally by the Director of the Department of Panchayats and Community Development in 1989.

References

Alavi, H. 1973. Peasant Classes and Primordial Loyalties, *Journal of Peasant Studies* 1(1): 43–59.

——— 1988. Village Factions, in T. Shanin (ed.) *Peasants and Peasant Societies*, London, Penguin, pp. 346–56.

Byres, T. 1977. Agrarian Transition and the Agrarian Question, *Journal of Peasant Studies*, 4(3): 258–74.

CPI(M) 1988. *West Bengal and Planning*, Calcutta, CPI(M).

Kohli, A. 1987. *The State and Poverty in India: The Politics of Reform*, Cambridge, Cambridge University Press.

Kothari, R. 1989. The Problem, *Seminar*, 357: 12–14.

Naravaty, M.C. 1989. 'Panchayati Raj: A Far Cry', *Mainstream*, XXVI(48), 10 September: 15–19.

Randall, V. and R. Theobold 1985. *Political Change and Underdevelopment*, London, Macmillan.

Suri, P.C. 1988. Panchayati Raj: Facts and Fiction, *Mainstream*, XXVI(48), 10 September: 15–19.

Webster, N. 1986. Agrarian Change in India: A Case Study of Burdwan District, West Bengal, unpublished Ph.D thesis, Manchester University.

——— 1990. Agrarian Relations in Burdwan District: From the Economics of Green Revolution to the Politics of Panchayati Raj, *Journal of Contemporary Asia*, 20(2): 117–211.

——— 1992. *Panchayati Raj and the Decentralization of Development Planning in West Bengal: A Case Study*, Calcutta, K.P. Bagchi.

Westergaard, K. 1986. People's Participation, Local Government and Rural Development, *CDR Report* 8, Copenhagen, Centre for Development Research.

11

Decentralization below the State Level: Need for a New System of Governance

NIRMAL MUKARJI

Background

British India was ruled by a governor-general under whom governors (or lieutenant-governors) ruled the provinces, and district officers, variously called collectors, district magistrates or deputy commissioners, ruled the districts. Some provinces had an intermediate layer of divisional commissioners. And all provinces had to accommodate the limited democracy extended by the Reform Acts of 1919 and 1935. But the pyramid of rulers at the centre, the provinces and the districts remained the essence of the British system. Knit together by the common purpose of preserving the Raj, these rulers ran a unitary form of government. A unitary system is often accompanied by a high degree of centralization, but the opposite was the case here. Governors and district magistrates were allowed a great deal of latitude to 'do their own thing' in many matters. It was an example of even a unitary system needing to centralize only selectively, leaving local problems to be managed through decentralized power in the provinces and districts. Thus, within the unitary pyramid, there was a nice balance between centralization and decentralization.

Independence did not bring about a revolutionary change in the system of governance. But even so, major changes did take place in at least three respects. First, the territories comprising the British provinces and the princely states were reshaped into states, of which there are now twenty-five. The political map of India bears hardly any resemblance to what the British left behind. Second, at the district level too, boundaries were drawn and redrawn, due to which the administrative map of the country is vastly different from what it was before. Third, and most significantly, the governor-general and governors were replaced by democratically elected governments at the centre and in the states. The union and state governments were accorded constitutional recognition, and a federal relationship between the two came into existence as against the command structure of earlier times. The districts continued to be administered as before, which meant that for the first time the received command structure had to operate between governments at the state level and 'ruler model' bureaucrats in the districts.

As expected, this last aspect led to friction. Neither the political leadership at the state level nor local leaders of the ruling party found it possible to accept without demur, the considerable discretionary powers left with district officers under British dispensation. The former officially took away many of these powers, ranging from such petty matters as the power to transfer primary school teachers, to more weighty items like the power to withdraw prosecutions. Both state and local level politicians exerted unofficial pressure to see that the remaining powers were exercised in line with political preferences. This virtual take-over of bureaucratic powers by the political elite was, in a way, an extension of the struggle for self-government led by the same elite. A bureaucratically decentralized system thus gave way to a politically centralized one. British provinces were unitary, but decentralized. The states, like the British provinces before them, were conceived as unitary but contrastingly started becoming centralized.

Simultaneously, there was a centralizing process on at the national level also. Having witnessed the partition of the country, a fearful constituent assembly opted for a strong centre. In pursuit of this, political and legislative provinces were enacted, thus giving the union overriding powers. Financial provisions of crucial importance, under which the union could, and did, wield enormous clout vis-á-vis the states, were made. Supplementing these constitutional provisions, planning was adopted as the corner-stone of development, and the planning regime that came into being acted as a powerful centralising force. Over time, chiefly because central planning was backed by central financing, union ministries entrusted with state subjects became overloaded with functions and staff. The union began doing much of the states' work, and the states, in turn, did the same with respect to the districts. In this way, centralization at the national level reinforced centralization in the states (for a review of major trends see Mukarji and Arora, forthcoming). Thus, paradoxically, India's federal democracy became more centralized than British India's unitary bureaucracy ever was.

It is now beginning to be realized that the upward shift of functions from the districts to the states and from the states to the union has not in the least contributed either to the strengthening of the centre or to making planning more effective. Indeed, it has had the opposite effect on both counts. The machinery of government has become excessively flabby at the centre as well as in the states. Planning has become so out of touch with the ground reality that it is in danger of losing credibility. These developments have made political parties and scholars think in terms of reversing the upward trend, which, unambiguously put, means decentralizing functions from the union to the states and from the states to the districts. Political leaders who in the early years set out to conquer the bureaucracy no longer fear decentralization on the ground that this might put power back in the hands of bureaucrats, since the bureaucracy was successfully subordinated to political control long ago. Their fears have more to do with an aversion to sharing power with anyone.

It is also beginning to be realized that at the level of the people, things are not the same as they were when the Constitution was written. Universal adult suffrage coupled with frequent and regular elections have made a previously quiescent people politically conscious. The successful overthrow of entrenched regimes in several states, and even at the centre, has made the people aware that they count. The progress of politicization is uneven, which is not surprising given the diversity of the country. There are still pockets where elite politics holds sway. But everywhere the leaven of democracy has started a process towards mass politics. People are beginning to demand a say in the running of their own affairs. It is this, more than the creeping decay of centralized governance, that has impelled political parties to turn their attention to decentralization. If their statements of intent are to be taken seriously, the task is not whether to resolve the paradox of a high degree of centralization in a federal democracy, but how to do so.

To sum up, so far, in the centralization–decentralization continuum, the system inherited from the colonial times was in many respects more decentralized than centralized. With the arrival of democratically elected governments at the centre and in the states, the balance was heavily tilted towards centralization. Four decades of experience yielded the lesson that centralized governance and central planning had not worked particularly well. Meanwhile mass politicization began to make its presence felt and generated a demand for participation. It is now both necessary as well as possible to reverse the tilt away from centralization towards more decentralized governance, including more decentralized planning.

The States

In the descending cascade of decentralization, from the union to the states and from the states to sub-state levels, the states would figure at two stages, as recipients of powers and functions at the first, and as shedders of these at the second. If the cascade stops at the first stage, the states would be choked with powers and functions, and people's participation would remain a far cry. If, on the other hand, the cascade only starts at the second stage, the states are unlikely to part with enough powers and functions to make sub-state levels viable due to the fear that this may reduce their own importance too much. All the past experiments to decentralize below the state level, especially variants of the Panchayati Raj, have suffered on this account. Therefore, the states must receive as well as give. Decentralization confined to the states-downward stage neither makes sense nor is practical. The cascade must start at the union level and go all the way down, stage by stage.

Since the states occupy a cardinal position in union–states relations on the one hand, and in downward relations on the other, it may be useful to have a close look at them. The concept of partially self-governing states has its roots in pre-Independence thinking. The Constitution gives it place of pride in the very first article, declaring that India shall be a union of states. It is not necessary to trace in detail how the present configuration of states has evolved. It is sufficient to recall the major phases of that evolution. There was, first, the incorporation of the princely states, which occasioned the division of the country into parts A, B, C and D states. Next, there was the demand triggered by Andhra for recognition of the linguistic principle, which led to a comprehensive and largely durable reorganization of state boundaries. Third, the grant of full statehood to a relatively small territory like Nagaland initiated a course in which, on tribal or other grounds, several other small states came into being. It cannot be said that the number of states will stay twenty-five at the present.

These twenty-five states vary greatly in many ways. Variation in size is particularly relevant to the present analysis. The elements which go into size are population, area, the nature of terrain and the state of communications. For ease of comprehension, the states could be ranked according to population alone and the other elements kept in mind when looking at the picture that emerges.

Table 11.1 shows that the states fall into two broad categories. The first fifteen having populations of above 15 million each could be regarded as major states, which makes the remaining ten with populations under 10 million each minor states. The major states account for 96.20 per cent of the country's population and the minor states for 2.67 per cent. Interestingly, the Gadgil formula for distribution of plan funds makes almost the same categorization. The formula as much applies only to the major states, leaving aside Assam. All the minor states and Assam fall outside the scope of the formula and are given special assistance. Allowing for the Assam factor, in 1980–81, the fourteen major 'formula' states, accounting for 93.30 per cent of the population, received Rs. 6,200 crore as plan assistance, while Assam and the then minor states, with only around 5 per cent population, got as much as Rs. 1,800 crore. The proportion of grants to loans for the former was 30:70, while for the latter it was a generous 90:10. All states are dependent on the union, but the extent of dependence of the minor states is so overwhelming that it puts a question mark on their viability.

The other feature that Table 11.1 brings out is that the major and minor states can each be further divided into two subcategories. The major group has seven large states each with a population well above 50 million, ranging from Tamil Nadu with a whopping fifty-eight million up to Uttar Pradesh with an almost unthinkable 133 million. These states could be viewed as not easily governable, with or without decentralization, because of their large size. The remaining eight states in the major group are medium in size,

Table 11.1

Ranking of States by Population

No.	State	Population (1989)	Area Km²
Major			
	(Large)		
1.	Uttar Pradesh	133,034,415	294,411
2.	Bihar	83,897,681	173,877
3.	Maharashtra	75,341,005	303,690
4.	West Bengal	65,496,776	88,752
5.	Andhra Pradesh	64,259,608	275,068
6.	Madhya Pradesh	62,614,613	443,446
7.	Tamil Nadu	58,089,692	130,058
	(Medium)		
8.	Karnataka	44,562,857	191,791
9.	Rajasthan	41,114,234	342,239
10.	Gujarat	40,902,959	196,024
11.	Orissa	31,644,345	155,707
12.	Kerala	30,544,416	38,863
13.	Assam	23,876,212	78,529
14.	Punjab	20,146,698	50,362
15.	Haryana	15,507,142	44,212
Minor			
	(Small)		
16.	Jammu and Kashmir		
17.	Himachal Pradesh		
	(Tiny)		
18.	Tripura		
19.	Manipur		
20.	Meghalaya		
21.	Goa		
22.	Nagaland		
23.	Arunachal Pradesh		
24.	Mizoram		
25.	Sikkim		

Note: The country's population increased by 25 per cent between 1971 and 1981. Assuming that the rate of growth has remained the same after 1981 and applying this evenly to all the states for the sake of simplicity, the state-wise population for the year 1989 is obtained by adding 20 per cent to the 1981 census figure of each state. Admittedly, this is not very sound statistically but, it is good enough to get a general idea.

Source: Compiled from *Census of India, 1981*.

having a population range of fifteen million (Haryana) to forty-four million (Karnataka), and could be regarded as reasonably governable, given workable decentralization below the state level. The minor group has two small states, Jammu and Kashmir and Himachal Pradesh, which, because of their far-flung territories, could be classed with medium states going by the governability criterion. The remaining eight states can only be described as tiny and, because of their miniature character, are probably below governability level. There is little, barring their constitutional status, to distinguish them from union territories.

The above analysis underlines the point that while decentralization must be a combination of union to states and state downward exercises, both must of necessity be influenced by the sizes of the states. Thus, any basically new regime between the union and the major states in the crucial financial domain may not be good enough to sustain the minor states, which may continue to need special category treatment. Similarly, a pattern of decentralization below the states suited to the major states and possibly also to Jammu and Kashmir and Himachal Pradesh may not be appropriate for the tiny states. Within the major states, megastates—which are large by population as well as area—such as Uttar Pradesh, Bihar and Maharashtra, may find it useful to have some form of regional governments, especially for backward areas. Thinking in this direction is to be found in the regional development boards envisioned by Article 371 and those already in existence for the development of Chhota Nagpur in Bihar and the hill areas in Uttar Pradesh. The short point is that the states are a heterogeneous lot and this needs to be borne in mind when discussing decentralization.

Below the State Level

In terms of size, the tiny states are more akin to districts elsewhere than to the other states. Some of them have district councils under the Sixth Schedule, which, being constitutional bodies, cannot be replicated in states where the Schedule does not apply. Table 11.2 ranks the smallest districts in the country in terms of population as recorded in 1981. Of the twenty-three districts having a population of less than a lakh, nineteen are in the tiny states. Tiny states and tiny districts, it would appear, go together. Both have their own distinctive problems of governance. It would be best to leave them out of the scope of the rest of this paper.

Decentralization from the state downward may be thought of as an extension of the cascade descending from the union. There would have to be intermediate levels below the ultimate level of the village. On the first point of decentralization there are broadly three views. The Balwantrai Mehta Report favoured the block as being nearest to the people (1957). The Sukhamoy Chakravarty (Economic Advisory Council, 1984) Report on decentralization of planning considered even the district to be too small for proper area planning. The Constitution contemplates a regional approach for states like Maharashtra, Gujarat and Andhra Pradesh, and Uttar Pradesh and Bihar have, as already noted, adopted this idea for backward areas. The Asoka Mehta Report (1978) on the Panchayati Raj, however, categorically favoured the district because historically it had been the pivot of local administration for centuries and also because the requisite expertise for planning and related purposes could be mustered at this level and not lower. The Dantwala Report (1978) on block-level planning and the Hanumantha Rao Report (1984) on district planning endorsed this view in essence. In political parties too thinking has crystallized on the district as the most appropriate level for first-stage decentralization from the state level.

Excluding the tiny states, there were 361 districts in 1981 with an average population of about 1.8 million per district. The number of districts has increased since then but so has the population. The Asoka Mehta Report, in a section on smaller districts, pointed out that when districts are too large, plan formulation as well as supervision of development work are rendered difficult. Also, popular representation in *zilla parishads* based on population becomes too large. It visualized a population of a million, with local variations, to be a 'reasonable target' (Ashok Mehta Report, 1978). Going by the million-per-district yardstick, the average in 1981 was on the high side. Averages notoriously obscure worrisome aspects. Districts below the average need cause no anxiety, but those above clearly should. Table 11.3 gives a list of 39 'monster' districts with a population above 3 million each in 1981. Since then several others have crossed this mark or are on the verge of doing so. If India's population can be kept down to a billion plus in the year 2001, it is necessary to now think in terms of doubling the number of districts, which then at 700 odd would at that time provide a reasonable average of a million and a half per district.

Traditional sentiment and non-plan financial implications were mentioned by the Asoka Mehta Report as the reasons for inaction in the direction of smaller districts, even when the logic was noticed. It must be said to the credit of the states that they have been seized by the need to break up large districts into smaller, more manageable ones. The largest district in 1981 comprising 24 *parganas* in West Bengal, has, for instance, recently been split into two districts, north and south. But in 1989, each new district still had a population of over 6 million. Perhaps the states would find it easier to overcome the obstacle of traditional sentiment if the obstacle of lack of funds could be got out of the way. Since introducing decentralization of any kind and degree in districts of ungovernable size is a questionable proposition, the reorganization of large districts needs to be put on the national agenda, given priority, and allotted requisite funds from national resources.

Coming to decentralization below the district, there are two parallel hierarchies in all the states: a bureaucratic one and a democratic one. On the bureaucratic side, allowing for slight variations in the states, things have remained more or less frozen in the mould of subdivisions, *talukas* or tehsils, revenue circles and village 'mauzas'. The number of subdivisions has increased here and there but without disturbing the overall pattern. The only bold innovation has been in Andhra Pradesh where *talukas* have been broken into *mandals* headed by *mandal* revenue officers. The measure is intended to bring the administration closer to the people and with this end in view, *mandals* have been constituted with an average population of only around 35,000. *Mandal* headquarters are meant to become focal points with banks, secondary schools, police stations and other local institutions. They could, in time, become growth centres, especially because they also house developmental offices and related facilities.

On the democratic side, the Balwantrai Mehta Report visualized two levels below *zilla parishads*, namely, block samitis and village panchayats. During implementation some states preferred to have samitis at the *taluka* level instead of the block level. The Asoka Mehta Report felt that below the district level, the balance between technological requirements and possibilities for meaningful participation by the people in development could best be achieved by

Table 11.2

Ranking of Smallest Districts by Population

Sl. No.	District	State	Population (1981)
1.	North Sikkim	Sikkim	26,455
2.	Dibang Valley	Arunachal Pradesh	30,978
3.	Lahaul and Spiti	Himachal Pradesh	32,100
4.	Upper Subansri	Arunachal Pradesh	39,410
5.	East Kameng	Arunachal Pradesh	42,736
6.	Tengnonpal	Manipur	56,444
7.	Wokha	Nagaland	57,583
8.	Kinaur	Himachal Pradesh	59,547
9.	Zunheboto	Nagaland	61,161
10.	Manipur West	Manipur	62,421
11.	West Kameng	Arunachal Pradesh	63,701
12.	Kargil	Jammu and Kashmir	63,992
13.	Chhimtuipui	Mizoram	66,420
14.	Leh	Jammu and Kashmir	68,380
15.	Lohit	Arunachal Pradesh	69,498
16.	East Siang	Arunachal Pradesh	70,451
17.	Phek	Nagaland	70,618
18.	West Siang	Arunachal Pradesh	74,164
19.	West Sikkim	Sikkim	75,192
20.	South Sikkim	Sikkim	75,976
21.	Mon	Nagaland	78,938
22.	Manipur East	Manipur	82,946
23.	Lamglai	Mizoram	86,511

Source: Same as Table 11.1.

grouping a number of villages to constitute *mandal* panchayats, each such panchayat to cover a population of 15,000 to 20,000 people. Karnataka has adopted such a model (Mukarji 1986). Andhra Pradesh too has done so, except that its *mandals* are twice the size and are conterminous with its unique revenue *mandals*. West Bengal has block samitis and *gram panchayats*, but the 'gram' is related to a population of 10,000 plus and not to a single village concept. There is, thus, a variety of arrangements below the district level and it may be wise to let each state continue to have the flexibility to evolve the system it considers best suited to its historical, cultural and political circumstances.

District Government

An extreme form of decentralization is to break up, or break off pieces from, a larger entity. If that were to happen to a country it would amount to balkanization or secession, and in either eventuality would be unacceptable. Bangladesh was a freak exception, if only because the two parts of undivided Pakistan were geographically far apart. But breaking up, or breaking pieces off from subnational units does not attract similar unacceptability. Thus, for instance, Andhra Pradesh was able to break up its *talukas* into *mandals* without encountering constitutional or political hurdles. Assam experienced Nagaland, Meghalaya and Mizoram breaking off, not without political unrest and constitutional change, but with the nation's acceptance since discontent with Gauhati's yoke did not mean secession from the country. If Gorkhaland were ultimately to break off from West Bengal or, for that matter, Jharkhand from Bihar, Uttarkhand from Uttar Pradesh, Vidarbha from Maharashtra and so on, the dominant elite of the mother states in each case may feel upset but the nation would survive such a minor surgery. Surgical decentralization is, however, not the central concern of this paper.

As already noted, the Constitution makers provided for elected governments at the centre and in the states, but strangely left the inherited 'district officer' system untouched in the districts. Strangely, local self-government was on the agenda of the freedom movement long before *Purna Swaraj*, and yet it came to be overlooked. Whatever the reasons for this, the objective situation now calls for a review. On the one hand, today's district officer has far too much to do and this, taken together with other constraints, means that he is unable to do anything effectively enough. On the other, the political awakening of the people has led them to expect much more from the system than it can deliver. Instead of flogging 'district officer' rule any longer, the time is ripe to consider letting the people run their own affairs through elected district governments. Decentralization must therefore take the democratic route of devolution to these governments.[1]

If such governments are not to go the way of Panchayati Raj institutions (PRIs), they must possess characteristics, the lack of which led to the failure of the latter. First, district governments must be recognized as political entities, with political parties openly contesting elections. The past approach of keeping panchayats sanitized from politics, though well intentioned in one sense, overlooked the invigorating role of politics as an engine for change. It also deprived the polity of an entry stage for new recruits into politics and a nursery for grooming such entrants for higher responsibilities. Without the political dimension there can be no real democracy. And anything short of genuine democracy will perish just as surely as guided democracy did elsewhere, or partyless democracy in the case of the first generation PRIs. The second generation PRIs of West Bengal, Karnataka and Andhra Pradesh, having remedied matters in this respect, stand out as useful precedents.

Second, district governments must look after the totality of district governance, with the district bureaucracy coming squarely under them. The division between regulatory and developmental functions, initiated by community development and continued in PRIs, is artificial and untenable. It compels development to stay within the limits set by the present societal configuration. This is so because any attempt to change the configuration, such as through land reform, inevitably comes up against the power structure. When that happens, regulatory administration all too often sides with the power elite. If there is to be any worthwhile change this collusion must go, and that can only become possible if the two arms, regulatory and developmental, are required to work together under district governments (see Namboodripad, 1978). Ultimately what matters is who wields the lathi, and if that remains with the district officer, district governments will be just as unable to deliver genuine development as PRIs.

Third, the fate of district governments must not be left to the tender mercies of state governments. This means two things. One, elections must be held at regular intervals under the overall supervision of the Election Commission. As far as possible, the method of elections should be direct because the indirect route is easily manipulable. Two, supersessions should be barred. In the case of the states there is the controversial and much misused Article 356, under which elected state governments can be removed and President's Rule imposed in the event of failure of the constitutional machinery. Sooner or later this vestige of colonial rule will have to go. With respect to the districts there is no justification for replicating a measure which would give state governments a handle to remove inconvenient district governments.

Fourth, district governments must be nested in the federal idea, forming a third tier of the polity. The third tier would subsume self-governing units at sub-district levels right down to the *gram sabhas*. This again means two things. One, that the districts must find a place in the Constitution, not perhaps in the elaborate manner of Part VI dealing with 'the states' but equally not in the perfunctory manner of Part VIII dealing with the union territories. The intervening slot of Part VII has happily been lying vacant ever since Part B States were abolished and is available for a suitable formulation for the districts to be fitted in. Two, the introduction of a third tier must not squeeze the intermediate second tier or be seen as attempting to do so. If the aim is to strengthen and enlarge India's federal democracy, it is as important to make the states more effective as to carve out a third tier for the districts. Consequently, a reordering of centre–state relations must go hand in hand with extending the federal idea to a third tier. As of now, the union has overburdened itself with functions pertaining to state subjects. If the superfluous fat were to be shed, the union might handle what remains better, and the states would have more to share with the districts.

Fifth, in a three-tier federal system, there would have to be a new financial regime as between the union, the states and the districts. On the one hand, the union must be left with resources to meet its essential obligations. On the other, the states and the districts, not being in a position to raise adequate resources on their own, must have the oxygen of assured, untied devolution of funds from the union in sufficient measure to make purposeful self-government at these levels possible. So far the percentage shares of the states in central taxes have been determined by the finance commissions. Raja Chelliah (1984), the noted expert in public finance, once urged the need for finality in this matter. Specifically, he suggested that forty per cent of income tax and corporation tax and thirty-five per cent of union excise should go to the states and, in addition, 5 per cent of income tax and corporation tax to local bodies, and that a provision to this effect should be made in the Constitution. Finance commissions should thereafter only distribute the total share of the states among the states. On the grants side, Chelliah suggested that all block and other grants should be channelled mainly through the finance commissions (rather than the Planning Commission), which should be guided not by the gap-filling approach but well-accepted

Table 11.3

Ranking of Largest Districts by Population

Sl. No.	District	State	Population (1981)
1.	24 Parganas	West Bengal	10,759,439
2.	Medinapur	West Bengal	6,742,796
3.	Bangalore	Karnataka	4,957,610
4.	Barddhaman	West Bengal	4,835,388
5.	Cuttack	Orissa	4,628,800
6.	Madurai	Tamil Nadu	4,535,897
7.	North Arcot	Tamil Nadu	4,414,324
8.	South Arcot	Tamil Nadu	4,201,869
9.	Pune	Maharashtra	4,164,478
10.	Thanjavur	Tamil Nadu	4,063,545
11.	Ahmedabad	Gujarat	3,875,794
12.	Allahabad	Uttar Pradesh	3,797,033
13.	Gorakhpur	Uttar Pradesh	3,795,701
14.	Kanpur	Uttar Pradesh	3,742,223
15.	Santhal Pargana	Bihar	3,717,528
16.	East Godavari	Andhra Pradesh	3,701,040
17.	Varanasi	Uttar Pradesh	3,701,006
18.	Murshidabad	West Bengal	3,697,552
19.	Changalpatti	Tamil Nadu	3,616,508
20.	Tiruchirapalli	Tamil Nadu	3,612,320
21.	Purnia	Bihar	3,595,707
22.	Busti	Uttar Pradesh	3,578,069
23.	Tirunelveli	Tamil Nadu	3,573,751
24.	Azamgarh	Uttar Pradesh	3,544,130
25.	Deoria	Uttar Pradesh	3,496,564
26.	Salem	Tamil Nadu	3,441,717
27.	Guntur	Andhra Pradesh	3,434,724
28.	Jaipur	Rajasthan	3,420,514
29.	Thana	Maharashtra	3,351,562
30.	Ramanathapuram	Tamil Nadu	3,335,437
31.	Munger	Bihar	3,315,627
32.	Madras	Tamil Nadu	3,276,622
33.	Moradabad	Uttar Pradesh	3,149,406
34.	Gaya	Bihar	3,134,175
35.	Ranchi	Bihar	3,070,432
36.	Coimbatore	Tamil Nadu	3,060,184
37.	Krishna	Andhra Pradesh	3,048,463
38.	Patna	Bihar	3,019,201
39.	Kheda	Gujarat	3,015,027

Source: Same as Table 11.1.

principles of equalization. As regards loans, he wrote that 'the basis of allocation of market borrowing among the states needs to be examined and new principles have to be evolved'.

Going beyond Chelliah's refreshing approach, one is inclined to suggest (as a non-expert) that in order to introduce finality and avoid recriminatory debate, a provision may be made in the Constitution that 45 per cent of the aggregate resources of the union (leaving aside obviously unshareable items like the provident funds of central employees) should go to the states, and of these funds, 5 per cent should be earmarked for being passed on to the districts. The union's aggregate resources are of two kinds, non-loan and loan. Non-loan resources (45 per cent) should go to the states and districts as unconditional devolutions. Loan resources (45 per cent) including market borrowing, external borrowing and deficit financing, should also be devolved unconditionally except for normal loan terms. Devolution of market borrowing should be by allocating ceilings within which major states should do their own borrowing, while the union may do so on behalf of the minor states. Finance commissions would then be left with the twin tasks of determining the shareable aggregate non-loan resources of the union and distributing the shares of the states and districts among the states, eschewing the gap-filling approach and adopting equalization principles. Within the states, at least the major ones, there would have to be state finance commissions which would do a similar job with respect to the districts. The states should be required to set aside 5 per cent of their own aggregate resources (excluding devolutions from the union) for devolution to the districts. These and the earmarked union devolutions would comprise the distributable pool for the districts.

Sixth, there must also be a new planning regime. We need to find a way to federalize national planning. The Planning Commission should move out of the investment-cum-growth type of planning in which it has been locked, and move into the hitherto almost unexplored terrain of policy planning. It should think anew about issues like the reasons for persistent mass poverty and deprivation; the reasons for continued backwardness of regions, 'the roots of public unrest' of various kinds; the oppression to which the weak are subjected; the decline of institutions like the policy and judicial administration; the status of women; the proper nurturing and education of children; the full implications of population growth;

the proper management of water and land resources; the restructuring of relations with neighbouring countries; the impact of external policies; the proper balance between defence and development; the rising cost of the bureaucracy; and many others. It should seek to build national consensus on the policies which the country as a whole should adopt regarding such issues. The commission may involve itself in sectoral planning for union subjects. For the rest, planning should be decentralized to the states and districts. The states for sure, and, to the maximum extent possible, the districts too, must strengthen their planning capabilities. Vigorous state and district planning within the compass of nationally accepted policies and under a financial regime which permits local innovations would be the way to harmonize the planning idea with the federal.

It seems a stage has arrived when both the Congress and important opposition groups favour democratic decentralization backed by consistitutional sanction. But this overworked term means different things to different people. Some view it as involving only incremental improvements in the Panchayati Raj within the existing framework of governance. Others like this writer think that democratic decentralization should mean a fundamentally new system of governance through two related measures: a third tier of democratic district governments to replace bureaucratic 'district officer' rule, and a new scheme of relations between the union, the states and the districts based on optimal decentralization. Some favour a uniform model for the whole country. Others, like this writer, see advantage in identifying the essentials for incorporation into the Constitution, leaving all other matters flexible so as to permit adaptation of the underlying idea to local circumstances in the different states. Some see in the Congress leadership's new-found interest a design to bypass the states and virtually to convert districts into union territories (Jain, 1988). If this is indeed the intention, it would be a serious mistake.

Given the Congress and opposition positions in favour of democratic decentralization, attention needs to be focused on giving content to what is only a concept so far. This paper is a modest effort to do just that. Before the Constitution is amended there must be a full and open debate. It would be nothing short of tragic if, like the Defamation Bill, an amendment bill in this case were to be suddenly sprung on the nation and hastily enacted. For then, a vitally needed reform in the country's system of governance would be obscured in a cloud of controversy. If combative postures which rule out the possibility of achieving consensus cannot be avoided in the run-up to the next election, it would be wiser to defer the amending legislation till after the election.

Some Questions Answered

Should an amendment bill go as far as drawing a fourth list in the Seventh Schedule for district subjects, presumably by hiving off some items from the state list? It is for constitutional experts to say whether such a list is absolutely essential to give legitimacy to democratic decentralization. There could be a view favouring a fifth list also dividing concurrent subjects between the states and districts. As against this, there is a growing impression that even the existing lists have not served as adequate markers delineating union and states functions. There is hardly any subject of importance in the State and Concurrent Lists into which the union has not made inroads. Some of these are justifiable, such as inter-state programmes like malaria eradication, research into problems transcending individual states, and relations with international agencies like FAO, UNESCO and ILO. The study team of the Administrative Reforms Commission on centre-state relations identified, after going into the working of several union ministeries and agencies, a short list of functions that were necessary for the union to perform even in relation to state list subjects (India, 1969). Inroads into functions other than these have been made possible entirely because of the union's financial strength vis-á-vis the states (Krishnaswamy et al.) It may be stated as a proposition, at least in the Indian context, that the functions go where there is money regardless of constitutional lists. Consequently it is more important to install a new financial regime than to devise new lists.

Would a third tier at the district level, inclusive of sub-district units, enhance the oppressive power of dominant groups and correspondingly place further burdens on the oppressed weaker sections? Under the present dispensation, it is the dominant groups that hold power at the state level (excluding states ruled by Left combinations), and it is largely their writ that runs at and below the district level through the bureaucracy, especially through the coercive arm, i.e., the police. The view that high-minded civil servants functioning as district officers can act as brakes or moderators may be true here or there, but is essentially divorced from reality. Democratic decentralization to a third tier would thus not worsen matters. Since the logic of democracy favours numbers, decentralized democracy would, on the other hand, open up the possibility of the oppressed majority organizing itself and capturing power in individual districts or *mandals*. The organization of the poor tends to be regarded as a pious and unrealizable hope. So it will remain as long as the poor have to organize across an entire state before exercising power. By extending the idea of democratically elected political governments to the states and stopping there, the Constitution-makers unwittingly loaded the system against the poor and the dispossessed. Carrying the idea down to lower levels would correct this imbalance. Empirical evidence from West Bengal and Karnataka, both with second generation PRIs, suggests that this is precisely what is beginning to happen.

Would it be wise to dispense with the institution of a district officer completely, despite the awareness of the linchpin role he has performed so far? The governors of the British province performed a similar role. Their replacement by elected governments was considered logical and appropriate in India's federal democracy. The performance of most of the elected state governments leaves much to be desired, but that has not produced a yearning to go back to governors. Replacing district officers by elected governments could reasonably be expected to follow the same pattern. Besides, today's district officer would be tomorrow's chief secretary of a district government. His administrative powers would then be infused by a political content due to his proximity to those in power at the district level and this would increase rather than diminish his role as a coordinator and supervisor.

Note

1. The concept of 'District Government' was first spelt out by this author in a paper presented at the seminar on Rural Development at IIM, Ahmedabad, and subsequently published in 1986 under the title 'The Alternative: District Government?', in M.L. Dantwala, Ranjit Gupta and K.C. D'Souza (eds), *Asian Seminar on Rural Development: The Indian Experiences*, New Delhi, Oxford, IBH, pp. 235–61. It was further elaborated in 'The Future of District Governance', paper presented at the workshop organized under the auspices of the Union Ministry of Rural Development at Hyderabad.

References

Chelliah, Raja J. 1984. The Economic and Equity Aspects of the Distribution of Financial Resources between the Centre and the States in India, in Seminar on Centre–State Relations: Papers, Group Reports and Conclusions, Bangalore, Economic and Planning Council, Government of Karnataka.

Government of India 1968. *Report of the Study Team on Centre–State Relationships,* New Delhi, Administrative Reforms Commission.

India 1984. *Report of the Working Group on District Planning,* New Delhi, Planning Commission.

India, Agriculture Ministry 1978. *Report of the Committee of Panchayati Raj Institutions,* New Delhi, Department of Rural Development.

India Committee on Plan Projects 1957. *Report of the Team for the Study of Community Projects and National Extension Service,* (Chairman: Balwantrai Mehta), Planning Commission.

India Economic Advisory Council 1983. *Decentralisation of Development Planning and Implementation Systems in the States,* New Delhi, Reproduced in *Mainstream,* January 21, 1984.

Jain, L.C. 1988. District Administration: PM wants Union Territories, *The Hindustan Times,* August 11.

Krishnaswamy, K.S. et al. Economic Aspects of Federalism in India, in Mukarji and Arora (eds), *Origins and Development of Federalism in India* (forthcoming).

Mukarji, Nirmal 1986. The Karnataka Model of District Government, in George Mathew (ed.), *Panchayati Raj in Karnataka Today,* New Delhi, Concept.

Mukarji, Nirmal and **Balveer Arora** (eds). *Origins and Development of Federalism in India,* New Delhi, Vikas (forthcoming).

Namboodripad, E.M.S. 1978. Note of Dissent in Asoka Mehta Committee Report, op. cit.

12

The NGO Sector in India: Historical Context and Current Discourse

D.L. Sheth
Harsh Sethi

Historical Context

Pre-Independence Phase

While entities called NGOs may appear to be a new phenomenon in India, in the past several of their roles, activities and functions were performed by a variety of local organizations. History bears continuous testimony to non-state efforts and initiatives towards building structures of socio-economic security by the people for themselves. The state did not constitute a frame of reference for these activities; the traditional mode of organizing self-help and philanthropy was essentially societal and not etatiste in nature. It is only with the growing centrality of the modern state that terms such as 'voluntary' and 'non-governmental' sectors came into prominence to describe those few welfare and developmental activities which originate outside the state structure and within society.

A clearly identifiable shift in this mode of organizing societal activities occurred during the colonial encounter. On the one hand, the para-state organizations, mainly of the Christian churches, started intervening in the social and religious life of the indigenous population through education, health, social welfare and reform. These activities often received the protection and patronage of the colonial state.

On the other hand, as part of anti-colonial resistance, the nineteenth and the early twentieth century saw the emergence of numerous indigenous organizations devoted to social and religious reform. As part of this process, several castes adopted the new function of dispensing welfare to their members. They set up associations for the specific purpose of catering for the educational, health and other welfare needs of their members.

It was with a view to regulating and monitoring activities of such new organizations that the colonial Indian state enacted the 1860 Registration of Societies Act, initially for the Bombay Presidency. Self-help and philanthropy in India originated with the emergence of voluntary organizations during the colonial period. As they were linked with social reform activities, which in turn were associated with movements of anti-colonial resistance, they also acquired a political dimension: the colonial state became a frame of reference for defining their scope of activities and their legal identity. The idea of voluntary work began to be understood as non-state or non-governmental activities. Major religious and social reform movements directed their activities to make demands on the state for enacting new social legislation to implement the reforms they sought to propagate.

Raja Ram Mohun Roy (1772–1833) and the Brahmo Samaj opposed child marriage and the Sati system, and propagated widow marriage. Ishwar Chandra Vidyasagar (1820–91) started a campaign in favour of widow marriage and education of girls. K.C. Sen (1838–84) advocated inter-caste marriage, widow marriage and the removal of the purdah system. Swami Dayanand Saraswati, founder of the Arya Samaj, opposed child marriage, idol worship and caste discrimination. Mahatma Phule (1827–88) fought for the removal of untouchability and for the welfare of the depressed classes, known today as the Scheduled Castes. Maharishi Karve (1858–1962) devoted his entire life to the education and rehabilitation of widows. These religious and social reform movements transformed the old parallelism between the state and society into a direct interaction between the two.

The second major shift in the nineteenth-century paradigm of organizing voluntary work occurred at the turn of the century, when Gandhiji entered the Indian political scene. Gandhiji sought to recapture the constructive spirit within society which drew upon the innate resources of the people. Rather than treating the indigenous population as raw material of reform, which in essence meant at best Westernization and at worst collaborating with the colonial regime, the Gandhian movement focused on reorganizing people's own resources for goals of material and spiritual well-being, which they were enabled to set for themselves. Over a period of time, a network of organizations was formed as part of this movement, covering such diverse fields as khadi and village industries, education, health, agriculture, dairying and animal husbandry, often in opposition to state policies. Several organizations for women, Harijans and tribals, and generally for the rural poor came into existence, their activities informed by an approach which did not separate politics from social work or issues of material well-being from spiritual concerns of human beings. In the process it drew the hitherto excluded sections of society into the national movement for Independence, but more particularly into the growing voluntary sector which was now described in terms of social service and constructive work.

It was during this phase that social action acquired a pronounced political content and politics a firm base in society. This fusion of social action and politics resulted in viewing the colonial state not so much as facilitator, but as a road-block to the process of social transformation. It emphasized social and cultural regeneration of the entire society in place of the late-nineteenth century accent on issue-based reform activities. Instead of making demands on the state for extending its protection and patronage to voluntary or social reform action, it emphasized people's own empowerment through constructive work.

The third trend emerged from the new realities created by the growing hegemony of the Congress Party during the Independence movement. Its roots lie not in the world of social action but in politics, which then spilled over into the world of social action. Beginning with the ideological splits in the Independence movement, this trend got consolidated in the early decades after Independence. It owes its origin to the mobilization and organization activities of the Communist and Socialist parties. Several groups of activists working either in their front organizations, or later independently, began to take up issues ignored by the groups belonging to 'social reform' or 'the Gandhian' genre. For them the central issue was the conflict of interests and the resulting exploitation of the poor. Social and economic justice, rights of the people, land reforms, tenancy rights, minimum wages for landless labour, removal of bondage and slavery, tribal rights over forest produce and rights of slum-dwellers and destitutes became the agenda for these groups. As they proceeded to work on these issues, their distance from the parent political parties increased since many of these were not considered important political issues by the parties wedded to an electoral calculus.

The Current Phase

The early years of Independence, almost until the end of the 1960s, saw a decline of the once vibrant sector of Gandhian organizations. While the more religiously inclined bodies (both Christian and non-Christian) continued their activities, periodically winning plaudits for their educational and health activities and relief of famine and distress, the Gandhian sector lagged in this regard. Many of its leading figures moved to the more lucrative sector of Congress Party politics and governance. Their organizations moved closer and closer to the state and their reliance on government funds increased, such that gradually little difference could be seen between their work and the government programmes of social welfare. With the government launching ambitious programmes of Community Development and the Panchayati Raj, most organizations became involved in implementing official programmes and began at best to be seen as local, more community-based agencies to ensure people's involvement in planned development.

The institutional framework of representative democracy, mainly the panchayats and the development blocks paralleled these developments. Studies of these experiments tended to be laudatory and hagiographic with respect to either the personalities involved or the American-style ideology of private initiative of helping to maintain the autonomy of individuals and of communities from the government. Nevertheless, government assistance and collaboration constituted the very basis of such an idea of autonomy.

Between the late 1960s and the early 1980s, a spate of famines, inflation, devaluation, unemployment, the breakdown of the hegemony of the Congress Party, and the rise of militant movements all created not only political and social instability, but impelled fresh thinking and action on the twin grids of development and politics. From the Maoist upsurge in the late 1960s to the clamping down of the Emergency (1975–77), the period was one of intense disillusionment with the conventional institutions of planning, politics and development. It was at the same time a period of excitement over new issues and movements coming to the fore. Thousands of young people outside the framework of formal party politics and the government initiated groups and activities relating to the rural and urban poor. To the earlier concerns of poverty, inequality and removal of social injustice were now added issues of gender, environment, human rights and peace. Struggles and movements for organizing the poor, conscientization and people's empowerment became key words for social activists. Politics once again became central to social activism.

Expectedly, the commentaries and the debates of this period began to acquire political overtones, quite different from the more staid period of the 1950s and 1960s. The focus on empowerment necessitated a different framework of description and analysis. The language of governance and of welfare began to be replaced by the language of rights and struggles. The non-governmental sector now began to be assessed in terms of its efficacy in promoting new issues, helping to organize the poor and contributing towards a new framework of rights and entitlements.

Even as this new spurt of activities and writings began to make its impact, most academic research still remained confined to the study of community development and Panchayati Raj oriented organizations: the youth clubs, the *mahila mandals*, to name a couple. The conventional developmental concern for 'harnessing the energies of the young', through programmes like the National Service Scheme and the *Nehru Yuvak Kendras* continued to exercise its grip over the academic imagination.

Beginning with the Janata Phase (1977–79), the discourse on non-governmental efforts and organizations has undergone a change. At one end of the spectrum is a tendency that identifies itself with both the national movement phase and the struggles of the 1970s, culminating in the anti-Emergency struggles. Intensely political, it is articulated around issues and organization of the oppressed. Whether under the broader rubric of human rights, gender, ecology and identity or around more defined issues like child labour, minimum wages, bondage and slavery, displacement of populations by big development projects, occupational health hazards, banning of harmful drugs and processes, and bride burning, this concern is reflected in both the radicalized middle class and the subaltern organizations. At the other end of the spectrum is a tendency that reflects a revised formulation of the 1950s and 1960s, namely one of viewing non-governmental organizations as links between the government and the people in the process of planning and development. It emphasizes instrumental efficacy and professionalization of NGOs. The focus here is on cost-efficiency, greater ability to involve people in 'development projects', innovation in programme and planning processes, and strengthening delivery systems. Alongside is a relatively recent tendency of the middle-class professional-support organizations involved in serving other organizations, rather than direct communities, through documentation, research, training (both management and skills), networking and publications. Their preferred activities include 'public-interest' litigation and media-exposure concerning issues being fought by smaller organizations on the ground. This new sector of agencies is fairly independent from the traditional governmental, business, political and religious influences.

The multiple and conflicting tendencies of that period, coupled with the intermeshing of different activities and concepts, has led to a proliferation of partisan writings; not reasoned argument but polemical tracts. More importantly, as we shall trace later, it has led to serious differences in the overall appreciation of the meaning and significance of NGOs and their work.

NGOs in India: A Literature Review

For the purpose of this survey, keeping in mind the definitional complexities, we have clustered the available literature under the following categories: morphological studies; intra-organizational studies; efficacy studies; relationship studies of organizations with the government, with political parties, with donor agencies, and with client/base groups; and assessment/impact studies.

Morphological Studies

Information on such aspects of NGOs as numbers of organizations, their classification by function and activity, size, location and spatial spread of work, funding, number of personnel, and profiles of members is at best available partially. To get a comprehensive listing of even the registered organizations, one would need to look at the records of the government agencies set up for this task. And even here, one would get no idea of the numbers that have become moribund, have shifted in activity mix or location, and so on. The few directories available, other than being very partial and outdated in their coverage, only give data about names of the key persons, dates of registration, activity mix, areas of operation, and number of employees. Rarely is even a brief profile/assessment of the organization and programmes added. Probably the most comprehensive listing available today is with the Ministry of Home Affairs, charged with implementing the Foreign Contribution Regulation Act. Their data, unfortunately locked into their computers, refers to about 14,000 organizations, obviously only those that have a foreign-funding linkage.

With even this basic data unavailable, questions such as who joins these organizations, for how long they stay, working conditions, further breakdown of their numbers by activity, ideology and size, are difficult, if not impossible, to answer. Nevertheless, we have a few attempts at an overview of these phenomena (Varghese, 1977; Kothari, 1984a; Sheth, 1984; Sethi, 1984, 1986; Dhanagare, 1988). The studies suggest that while a majority of the organizations are still involved with welfare, relief, charity and developmental activities (health, education, appropriate technology, local level planning, and so on), from the mid-1970s onwards there has been a significant increase both in issue-based groups (both sectoral like women, law and ecology, and single issue such as bonded labour and child labour) and in groups involved primarily in helping the poor organize to fight for their legal rights. More recently, there has been a proliferation, if not in numbers then definitely in media coverage, of groups involved in activities supportive of other locally rooted NGOs, through activities like documentation, use of audio-visuals aids, training including management training, theatre, printing journals, and advocacy.

The studies also suggest a change in the profile of those who join NGOs. Unlike the earlier phases when those involved in relief, charity and welfare activities were mostly retired persons, now more younger people (both men and women) look towards the

NGOs as a career option. The setting up of agencies like Foundation to Aid Industrial Recovery (FAIR) and PRADAN, or of the Institute of Rural Management at Anand, is indicative of the heightened interest of middle-class professionals in NGOs. Equally significant is the banding together of young people locally under an NGO banner to attract funds for local/community advancement (Bhatt, 1988).

Macro data on funding too is difficult to obtain. For instance, while there are rough estimates of the extent to which the government supports NGOs (between Rs. 250 and 300 crores over the Seventh Plan period, with talk of scaling this up by Rs. 100–150 crores/year in the eighth Plan), and of the extent of foreign funding (averaging Rs. 250–300 crores per year during the 1980s), we have no estimates of indigenous, private philanthropy (in spite of the setting up of a Centre for Corporate Philanthropy in 1986), or the extent of support offered to NGOs from beneficiary groups or sympathizers. Even less do we have an indication, particularly with respect to foreign funding, as to which regions, activities and groups this funding is directed towards.

There is an urgent need for further studies that map out this area, otherwise not just our understanding but also our policies will continue to be formulated on inferences based on policy statements of funding agencies and political parties.

Intra-organizational Studies

Closely related to the broader morphological concerns are issues related to the internal structure and functioning of NGOs. There is a common stereotype held by many observers and policy planners that an NGO is small, convivial, participative and innovative, demonstrates a high leadership quality, is cost-conscious and austere, locally rooted and responsive, and thus a worthwhile instrument for welfare, developmental and mobilization organization programmes.

Some of these commonly held assumptions can easily be challenged. It is obvious that organizations involved with different types of activities are likely to be very different. A local development or action group, a group involved in a specialized activity either in the local area or as a support group, a network or umbrella organization, attract different types of volunteer activists and display different salary and working conditions, leadership styles and levels of organizational democracy.

Though one periodically encounters very large groups, sometimes employing nearly 1,000 people and with annual budgets of Rs. 3–5 crores, the typical NGO still remains small, financially insecure, with the salary and working conditions often more severe than in comparable academic, business or governmental jobs. This is partly due to a strong sense of idealism still surviving among several non-funded groups, and the influence of the older Gandhian or religious-base organizations which lay a great emphasis on austerity. The more modern corporate NGOs are but a recent phenomenon, and with many of them operating in an insecure financial market, their viability lies in being able to work with lower salaries and perks.

Case studies provide a much better basis for understanding these questions, though it must be admitted that the few that have been published are quite dated. Shah and Chaturvedi's study (1983) of the Valod Intensive Area Scheme (VIAS) group, on behalf of a funding agency NOVIB, points out that even for a large and complex organization, salaries are low and lifestyle austere. Decision making, though concentrated in the small groups of founders, is essentially informal and involves all *karyakartas*. Recruitment is not based on formal qualifications; in fact emphasis is laid on experience. Other such evaluative studies of SWRC Tilonia (Sethi, 1977) bear out the emphasis NGOs place on evolving participative structures (both formal and informal) of decision making, and low inequalities in salary.

An earlier study by George and Srivastava (1977) of the Bhartiya Agro Industries Foundation, a pioneer in cattle breeding and dairying programmes, reflects a different picture. It does appear that as the pendulum of activities swings more towards formal skills, the number of middle-class professionals increases, the salaries and working conditions become better, and the hierarchy becomes more formal.

Bhatt's study (1988) of small action groups in the tribal belt of Gujarat presents a radically different picture, with most groups composed totally of local people who work on a purely voluntary basis. Debates about lifestyle and decision making continue to dog the sector, caught as it is between the conflicting demands of being converted into a formal sector with increasing need for professional and managerial skills, and older, deeply internalised values of austerity and service (Sundar, 1986).

The growing number of training institutes and programmes indicates that most NGOs suffer from a lack of desired skills. While many of the groups are adept at local communication and organizational tasks, their familiarity with modern technologies and techniques is low. This absence becomes more marked in the new environment of greater formality and funding intensity, where the demands now being placed on the NGO sector are different.

More important are questions related to internal democracy, participation in decision making, and the degree of institutionalization that NGOs display. While recognizing that the operational style of many of the organizations is indeed informal and collective/participative, a degree of substitutionism continues to exist between the leaders and activists and between the activists and the people (Sethi, 1984). Many of the organizations, including the more modern and professional ones, revolve around the founding, often charismatic, personalities. Rarely are they able to transcend them, either in developing a second-tier leadership or in producing new leaders after the original set has departed. This high degree of transience has serious implications, not just for institutionalization (Gupta, 1986), but also for formulating long term programmes.

Efficacy Studies

We now turn to studies which attempt to examine the popular perception of NGOs as effective development and political instruments. The issues addressed here include NGO efficiency, cost-effectiveness, ensuring better participation of client communities, flexibility and an innovativeness to conform to, adapt, and partly mould the changing environment.

While most available studies refer to a single agency, there are a few efforts which examine a spectrum of agencies to draw more general conclusions. A recent review of NGOs supported by the Ford Foundation in the areas of rural resources and poverty, social justice and human rights, and women points out that

the different reviews validate the popular perception of NGOs playing a useful intermediary role between the state and the community. This is as true of the social action as of the development groups (Sundar, 1986).

The review also confirms the flexibility, creativity, innovativeness and commitment of the NGOs while simultaneously highlighting their weaknesses and limitations. The latter stem essentially from their small size, fragmentation and powerlessness—in short a fundamental incapacity to act institutionally over a long time (Sethi, 1984; 1986). Gupta also confirms this failing, highlighting the 'PVO lack of understanding of the process of institution building, or rather the dynamics of the process of growth of an organisation' (Gupta, 1986). He further argues that while this lack of institutional sense may not harm NGOs involved with routine maintenance functions, it can cripple organizations concerned with change on structural situations.

Similarly, Oakley and Dillon (1985) in a major study of NGOs in India, Bangladesh, Brazil and Ghana point out that while NGOs were relatively successful in fostering participation of client groups, their ability to institutionalize these processes was weak. This weakness seems most marked in groups engaged in income generation activities. Collective spirit, it appears, gets progressively eroded as the activity starts generating profits.

Subramanium (1982), in a critical review, points out that the success of individual voluntary agencies can be traced to: (*a*) the halo: a great cause favoured by the founders that binds the voluntary agency's personnel; (*b*) the hero: charismatic leadership of a social entrepreneur; and (*c*) funds: disproportionate inputs of resources due to easy access to donors. He argues that since these conditions are not easily replicable, the voluntary agencies' innovations remain 'backyard glories' with little hope of being extended to other parts of the country. The gap between the project and the programme often remains unbridgeable.

While it seems generally true that projects which are successful are so because of a fairly unique constellation of circumstances, that their cost effectiveness is often due to inputs by volunteers who put in long hours on low wages/salaries, that comparing them to large government programmes is methodologically fallacious, there are nevertheless many small lessons from these experiences which can contribute to improvement in larger programmes. The entire strategy of relying on locally trained *dais* in rural medicare programmes was evolved from the experience of Dr. Arole and his team in Jamkhed (Coombe, 1980), the lesson being that instead of trying to scale up a successful project, the strategy should be incorporating replicable lessons in larger programmes.

More than as instrumentalities to implement larger, mainly official programmes, NGOs have been far more successful in raising issues (dowry death, rape), in resisting harmful legislations (the proposed forest policy legislation of 1983), in activating the public interest litigation system, in highlighting atrocities, and in working with deprived strata and communities. To put it more sharply, greater success is achieved in non-core economic areas and in regions and with strata least enmeshed in the modern capitalist process. Thus *Chipko* (Bandopadhyaya and Shiva, 1987) and similar efforts resisting ecologically degrading policies and programmes have enjoyed greater success than efforts to curb polluting and dangerous industry after the Bhopal disaster; rural medicare efforts such as those initiated by Arole, seem to fare better that those aimed at reforming modern urban hospitals.

Does this then imply that the essential role of NGOs is to help transform society from a pre-capitalist state to a capitalist one, notwithstanding their self perception as struggling for a socialist transformation? Omvedt (1980) explores this question as does Tornquist (1984). While we will touch upon these themes in a later section, such writings, though based more on exploring theoretical/ideological presuppositions, indicate potential areas of success for NGO action.

At the end, we still remain unclear as to the reasons behind the current excitement with NGOs. In the absence of detailed empirical research, it is difficult to substantiate whether the 'favoured' status of the NGOs in the development and political discourse is more due to disappointments with the traditional organizations (bureaucracy, parties) that were expected to usher in social change or the NGO sector is inherently endowed with the needed qualities. While we have many examples of successful, even innovative and exciting work by NGOs, and in many sectors, their ability to either go to scale or to successfully transplant their lessons and experiences into larger organizations or programmes remains in doubt. For this we now turn to the relationships that NGOs have managed to establish with other organizations.

Relationship Studies

The most important relationship for the NGO sector is with the government. Since both the government and the NGOs represent a diverse and confused universe, there is no fixity to their relationship, which is marked by admiration as also suspicion and hostility. As we have tried to indicate in the background sections, this conflicting relationship has itself gone through different phases, occasioned both by shifts in the environment and in official policy and perception. It is not just the government but also the NGOs who react to any move that they perceive to be detrimental to their own interest.

In a fascinating debate around proposals to set up a National Council of Rural Voluntary Agencies (NCRVA), each of these different tendencies came to the surface. The Advisor, NGOs, in the Planning Commission, purportedly the prime mover behind this effort, argued strongly for both a code of conduct for NGOs and the establishment of a National Council akin to the Press or the Bar Council of India. He was strongly attacked and blamed for wanting to officialize the sector. His spirited reply (Roy, 1986) and the further responses (Baxi, 1986) raise serious issues, both for the sector and for independent scholars, particularly of discipline accountability and legitimacy. Though the government often complains that NGOs neither meet their targets nor submit accounts, the current trend is for this relationship to widen and deepen. Even the latest programme of National Technology Missions envisions NGOs taking a lead role in the adult education, immunization and drinking water programmes.

The NGOs, while obviously relishing their newly instituted status and importance including the increased availability of funding, are still very critical of the operationalization of this relationship. Procedures for securing government grants are extremely trying, and the levels of corruption and kickbacks disturbing. What equally galls the NGOs are efforts at external monitoring and evaluation, seen essentially as incursions into their autonomy. The limitations of the current contributions stem essentially from an assumption of two well defined sectors—government and its antonym, non-government, as also a focusing on instrumental concerns. More studies are needed to trace this relationship over time and focus more on the shifting implications of collaboration and contention.

Most NGOs are in the domains of relief, welfare, charity and development. The general assumption is that unlike political parties or groups, NGOs are local rather than national and concerned more with reform in civil society rather than its transformation through the capture and subsequent development of state power. The relationship between NGOs and politics seems functionally limited to either providing space for retired and non-active politicians or at best preparing a social consciousness base for political parties to make use of as they see best. Some would grant them the role of non-political articulators of interest groups.

However, from the *Sarvodaya* and constructive work organizations in the nationalist phase to social action groups attempting to 'conscientize', mobilize and organize the poor, (both in a framework of struggling for juridical rights—even expanding the notion of rights) the political tendency among NGOs has operated differently: it has assumed that power interpenetrates and breaks out of the confines of power concentrated exclusively in the institutions of the state. Jayaprakash Narayan's notion of *Lok Satta* (people's power) as distinguished from *Raj Satta* (state power), the notions of countervailing power and non-party political process (Kothari, 1984b) are all attempts to capture this tendency.

Political parties seem sensitive to the political possibilities encoded in the voluntary sector. Be it the sharp reaction from the Left parties (Karat, 1984) of accusing social action groups, particularly those with a foreign funding linkage, of operating on 'behest of their imperialist masters to undermine the influence of the revolutionary forces', or more favourable statements by other parties, which incorporate issues raised by NGOs into their political manifestos, it is clear that political parties view the growing importance of this sector with interest and concern.

In addition to more detailed studies of the actual relationship of different types of NGOs with parties of different persuasion in different contexts (for instance most opposition parties and NGOs collaborated against the Congress Party in the anti-Emergency struggles and in the 1977 elections), what is needed is an understanding of how grassroots issues can be made viable for electoral politics. Otherwise, the relationship is likely to be an instrumentalist one—the political parties trying to make use of the moral legitimacy and material resources base of NGOs; NGOs seek help from political parties in their conflict with the government.

The relationship with donor agencies too, is not without its complications. Here the reference is primarily to foreign donor agencies since the involvement of non-government indigenous co-financing agencies in this sector is low.

While a majority of the studies seem to hover around the operationalization of the donor–recipient relationship, the availability of funds and the degree of interference, there has been interest in the wider implications of the spread and deepening of this relationship. In a major article Karat (1984), a Central committee member of the CPI(M), charged that the growth in this phenomenon was the result of a conscious strategy of Western imperialist powers, who through funds, ideological support and recognition were fostering anti-national and anti-Left forces in the country. The debate that followed (Karat, 1985; Pattanayak, 1985; Sethi, 1985) unfortunately remained at the level of polemics, with those related to the organizations named in Karat's article reacting to clear their name.

In the absence of firm data about foreign donor agencies—their background, sources of funds, modes of selecting partners, and so on—it becomes difficult to comment upon this issue. With philanthropy becoming a big business, donor agencies scout around for markets in potential recipients. And with the quantum becoming large, as for instance in neighbouring Bangladesh, co-financing agencies can often subvert or distort national priorities and policies. The decision of the donor consortium to give aid only through NGOs in the instance of the recent cyclone in that country is a pointer in this direction.

Efforts have also been made to trace the influence of foreign donors in promoting certain issues and in highlighting only certain aspects of a country's development. While we are not aware of any study along these lines, autonomous women's groups, ecology groups, groups struggling around issues of cultural identity, anti-nuclear groups and so on are often accused of being foreign inspired.

An equally crucial issue is the impact on the NGO sector of the (relatively) easy availability of large sums of money. There are, for instance, charges commonly made that the agencies cause rifts in existing NGOs and help dissenting factions to form their own organizations in an effort to widen their market. A proliferation of easy money can also alter the operating style, the cost calculus, even the basic motivations and ideological underpinning of the sector. The phrase commonly heard, 'while government funding is ideologically preferable, foreign funding is much more convenient' is disturbing because the availability of easy money may be altering the basic relationship between the agency and the community. Sharma (1987), in an incisive analysis of social movements like *Chipko* and *Swadhyaya*, traces their strength to their internalization in the community. These efforts, unlike the normal NGOs, neither need nor seek external assistance; nor do they need to look elsewhere for validation.

On the other side, various commentators have remarked about the globalization of issues made possible through the donor agency mediation. The relationship, they argue, is not one merely of cash transfers in a framework of philanthropy, but one of globally linking up like-minded groups struggling on similar issues. Thus work in India gets enriched by experiences elsewhere and vice versa.

What is needed is not only more detailed empirical examination of foreign funding and donor agencies and their impact on the thought and working processes of different NGOs, but reflections on the larger political and ethical implications of constantly relying on grants to engage in social interventionist activity. Pattanayak (1985) and Sharma (1987) have attempted to raise questions about the basic nature of voluntarism. We feel that more such contributions are required.

The real success of an NGO lies in the relationship that it is able to forge with the base group/communities with which it is directly involved. Are the NGOs in actual operation any different from either the local bureaucracy that ordinary people have to deal with, the local political–electoral bodies, or the political parties? What is the nature of participation that they are able to engender? To what extent are people satisfied with the services offered? Have the more organizationally inclined NGOs managed to ensure the emergence of base organizations, which can then look after the task of relating to the outside world? The self-description of NGOs as catalysts, their preoccupation with becoming dispensable, and their not creating dependencies, are all reflective of these concerns.

As elsewhere, research-based studies on these questions are rare. Most evaluative studies of single NGOs focus more on the intra-organizational dimension, the relationship with base groups being difficult to assess. Broadly speaking, the relief, welfare and charity groups are seen as more efficient and less corrupt dispensers of goods and services. This partly explains why at times of calamities, donor organizations in most cases prefer to work through NGOs rather than the officialdom. Developmental groups not involved in income generation programmes such as running health and education programmes, creches and distress homes for women, are also seen as more efficient, concerned and less corrupt. Nevertheless, the relationship between the agency and the people is one of structural inequality, with NGOs operating essentially as 'middlemen', albeit without the power to tax or repress.

The real test of this relationship lies in the index of organizational development. The key questions relate not only to the quantum or extent of organizational success, but to the modes of ensuring this objective. For instance, it is now commonly recognized amongst most NGOs that economic or service programmes are not very conducive to developing organizations of the poor. Equally, it is realized that it is easier to create organizations around real and perceived grievances which can be converted into demands on the state. To help set up organizations which will garner local resources for collective development has, by and large, been a difficult objective to fulfil.

In addition to working out the organizational possibilities encoded in different activities, NGOs need to be seen as 'steadfast allies' who will stand by the people in case of trouble for a genuine organization of the poor to emerge. Studies on SEWA, the Working Women's Forum, Bhoomi Sena—all cases of relatively successful organizing—indicate that what breaks the barriers of suspicion between the NGO and the people is the ability to communicate genuine risk-sharing, rather than real or perceived success.

The more political social-action groups, while successful in their initial organizational work, continue to face problems generated by their own internal weaknesses, fragmentation and the lack of control over the political climate. Particularly in regions which have seen repeated agitations and repression, people are not keen to come under an organizational banner, since that may attract more hostile attention.

In any final instance, only if the NGO is seen as existing not for its own good can a meaningful relationship of trust and confidence develop with the people. Their fear, particularly in today's climate, as more official programmes now involve NGOs, is that a blurring would take place between local government functionaries and them. As NGOs start chasing targets and become more accountable to the government or donor agencies, their internal criteria for validation are likely to shift, converting them into just another instrumentality, which unfortunately is not accountable even in the sense that politicians or administrators are accountable.

Assessment/Impact Studies

For a sector whose basic definition and contours are so little systematically studied, the commentary on the overall impact of the phenomenon is surprisingly freely available. What may be less obvious is that these assessments are strongly influenced by the structural location of the commentators.

Most commentators today accept that the NGO phenomenon is a major one, though whether it qualifies to be a 'fifth estate' is debatable. It is also accepted that the sector incorporates within itself a wide variety of organizations and activities, each with its own working methods and ideology. This variety and complexity is growing, and consequently all attempts at assessment are at best partial.

To what extent have NGOs fulfilled the expectations or the promise that they have generated? Have they successfully contributed to a deepening of equitable development or a shift in policy, to the raising of new issues, or to an increase in public awareness and in empowering the people? What have been the implications of NGO activity for the nature of institutional democracy in the country?

As we argued, both the reality and its representation present a mixed picture. Leading voluntary activists and donor agencies expectedly present a rather positive picture (Verghese, 1977; Pant, 1986); so does the literature emanating from UN Bodies and the World Bank (Quereshi, 1988). All these studies have contributed to the image of the NGO as a locally rooted, responsive, flexible, innovative, creative and effective developmental agency. It is not that they do not recognize the limitations of size, fragmentation, localism, or transience but they find the development of the NGO sector a welcome and encouraging phenomenon.

The political parties, particularly those of the Left, view this development with apprehension. Karat (1984) is perhaps the most vocal of those who are unfavourably disposed to the phenomenon in question, which is perceived as detracting from politics wedded to transforming the basic structural parameters of the society. An increasing penetration of and reliance on foreign funding only exacerbates this apprehension. The government sector, as we have seen, has a mixed view, in which they would like to involve NGOs as mediators and as delivery mechanisms, with partial recognition of the organizational role, but would like the activities kept 'within limits' (Planning Commission, 1985). Additionally, since increasing official funding is now being made available for this sector, there is a desire through efforts like the NCRVA and a code of conduct to work out the modes of accountability.

Within the academic community the response has been mixed, with different scholars disagreeing on the importance they would give to this phenomenon. Kothari (1984a), Sheth (1984) and Sethi (1984, 1986) see in this a major grassroots political movement and a hope for a deepening and a redefinition of politics in the country. The phenomena of activist groups and grassroots formations have, in their view, contributed not only to an articulation of new issues and styles of relating and working, a heightened consciousness and organization of sections of the oppressed and exploited hitherto relatively untouched by the political parties, but also to major shifts in the consciousness and working of other sectors of society. While not arguing that the voluntary, non-party tendency can by itself take on the task of transforming the state and society, they attribute to it a major catalyzing role. Bose (1985) and Dhanagare (1988) are far more cautious in their assessments, focusing more on the fragmentation of the sector. In either case, most assessments, even though tentative, share the view that the NGO phenomenon bears close watching.

What the literature clearly lacks is empirical studies with a bearing on the larger implications for governance. Is a proliferation of groups healthy for the future of institutional democracy? Do these groups and their activities help vitalize the more mainstream structures of government and local electoral bodies? Is the future tendency likely to be similar to the one in Bangladesh, where NGOs have emerged as a major power-bloc, controlling millions of dollars and many people? What does all this do to the more ingrained societal ethos of self-help, autonomy and cooperation?

Implications for Future Research

As we have argued, the major interest in the NGO phenomenon has been displayed by practitioners of development rather than the research community. The interest of the government, development co-financing agencies, international bodies like the World Bank and the United Nations not unexpectedly generated literature on issues such as training, management skills, cost-effectiveness of NGO operations, and the ability to induce participation in target communities—what we have classified as efficacy studies. An overwhelming instrumentalist bias not only diverts attention from macrosocietal concerns but also introduces an atheoretical tendency in the various contributions. It is this distortion that needs to be corrected for a proper appreciation of the induced activity and self-activity in society sought to be captured under the NGO rubric.

This overall interventionist ethos should not be deprecated because issues of action and intervention can neither be understood nor facilitated by a detached/objective outlook. More importantly, such an approach helps bring to the surface another reality, often hidden in the policy oriented writing. In the process it not only helps us to understand the NGO phenomenon from the viewpoints of the subjects of enquiry but also facilitates an alternative reading of the conventional texts of politics and governance.

Nevertheless, the overwhelming focus on issues of practice, and that too within a framework of efficient delivery of pre-decided packages, has meant that questions ranging from basic issues of definition and classification to those tracing the implications of the growth of the NGO sector on agencies of state and society have been ignored. Does, for instance, the growing support to NGOs imply a dilution of the welfare functions of the state? Does it imply a growth of private enterprise in the country? What does a proliferation of activist groups do to political parties and the political process? Does increasing funding, both governmental and foreign, lead to a decline in self-reliance and community orientation? Is the growth of the NGO sector reflective of a decentralized mode of increasing state control over society? All such questions are crucial and need to be explored, both through more detailed and rigorous empirical studies as well as through redefining the questions such that they do not remain confined to mere practical concerns.

The NGO phenomenon is, in our view, simultaneously a reflection of organizational innovation to respond to shifting market trends and an assertion of the irreducible autonomy of individuals and communities against an increasing encroachment by the state in daily life. This contradictory impulse needs to be captured to make the concept of governance more amenable to the assertions of people's rights such that the state does not function above, but is brought within the parameters of civil society.

Note

This paper is an abbreviated version of a longer monograph prepared for the Indian Council of Social Science Research for inclusion in the 'Survey of Research in Public Administration', ICSSR, Delhi, 1991.

References

Bandopadhyaya, J. and Shiva, V. 1987. The Chipko Movement, seminar paper, February.

Baxi, U. 1986. Two Threats to Democratic Social Action, *Mainstream*, 2 August.

Bhatt, Anil 1988. *Development and Social Justice*, New Delhi, Sage Publications.

Bose, Pradeep 1984. The State and Ideology of Social Action, paper presented to Seventeenth All India Sociological Conference.

Coombe, Simon 1987. The Indigenous Voluntary Agency Sector and Rural Change in India: Towards a Definition, unpublished paper, Department of Town and Country Planning, University of Sydney.

Dhanagare, D.N. 1988. Action Groups and Social Transformation in India, *Lokayan Bulletin*, 6(5): 37–59.

George, P.K. and U.K. Srivastava 1977. *Rural Development in Action*, Bombay, Somaiya.

Gupta, Ranjit 1986. Institution Building Support to Non-Government Rural Development Organisations, Ahmedabad, IIM, August.

Karat, Prakash 1984. Action Groups/Voluntary Agencies: A Factor in Imperialist Strategy, *The Marxist*, 2(2).

——— 1985. Justification for Imperialist Financed Activities, *Economic and Political Weekly*, May 4.

Kothari, Rajni 1984. Grassroots, *Seminar*, January.

Oakley, Peter and B. Dillon 1985. Strengthening People's Participation in Rural Development, unpublished paper, University of Reading, April.

Omvedt, Gail 1980. New Strategies of the Bourgeoise, *Frontier*, 5 January.

Pant, Niranjan 1986. PVOs/NGOs: Evolution, Opportunities and Constraints, mimeo., US AID, March.

Pattanayak, K. 1985. Non-Party Groups and Their Dependence on Foreign Money, *Economic and Political Weekly*, September 28.

Planning Commission 1985. *The Seventh Five Year Plan 1985–90*, Delhi, Planning Commission.

Quereshi, Moeen A. 1988. The World Bank and NGOs: New Approaches, *Lokayan Bulletin*, 6:4.

Roy, Sanjit Bunker 1986. Discipline and Accountability, *Mainstream*, September 20.

Sethi, H. 1984. Groups in a New Politics of Transformation, *Economic and Political Weekly*, February 18.

———— 1985. The Immoral Other: Debate between Party and Non-Party Groups, *EPW*, March 2.

————. 1986. NGOs in India: A Troubled Future, Delhi, *NORAD*.

Sethi, H., P.K. Das and **O. Fernandez** 1988. UCP-2: *An Interim Evaluation*, UNNYAN/NOVIB, Den Haag.

Sethi, H., J. Sharma and **R. Rosenberg** 1989. *Evaluating SWRC Tilonia*, HIVOS, Den Haag.

Shah, A.M. 1987. Untouchability, Untouchables and Social Change in Gujarat, in Paul Hockings (ed.), *Dimensions of Experience: Essays in Honour of David G. Maudelbaum*, Berlin, Moulton.

Shah, Ghanshyam and **H.R. Chaturvedi** 1983. *Gandhian Approach to Rural Development*, Delhi, Ajanta Publications.

Sharma, Suresh 1987. Voluntary Efforts and Institutional Funding, *Lokayan Bulletin*, 5(2).

Sheth, D.L. 1984. Grassroots Initiatives in India, *Economic and Political Weekly*, February.

Subramanium, Ashok 1982. The Small Step and the Great Leap, Ahmedabad, IIM Working Paper 439.

Sundar, Pushpa 1986. *Private Voluntary Agencies in India's Development: The Ford Foundation Experience*, Delhi.

Tornquist, Olle 1984. Problems of Radical Political Strategy under the Rise of New Capitalism, AKUT 28, Stockholm.

Verghese, B.G. 1977. Voluntary Action: A New Mission for New Missionaries, *Voluntary Action*, XIX(2), January–October.

Selected Additional Readings

Agnihotri, V.K. 1995. *Participatory Development: People and Common Property Resources*, New Delhi, Sage.

Arora, Balveer and **Douglas V. Varney** (eds) 1995. *Multiple Identities in a Single State: Indian Federalism in Comparative Perspective*, Delhi, Konark.

Bava, Noorjehan 1992. *The Social Science Perspective and Method of Public Administration*, New Delhi, Uppal Publishing House.

Bhagwati, Jagdish 1993. *India in Transition*, Oxford, Clarendon Press.

Bhattacharya, M. 1986. Public Administration in India: A Discipline in Bondage, *Indian Journal of Public Administration*, April–June.

——— 1987. Crisis of Public Administration as a Discipline in India, *Economic and Political Weekly*, November 28.

Brass, Paul 1992. *The Political Economy of India since Independence*, New Delhi, Cambridge University Press.

Burra, Neera 1995. *Born to Work: Child Labour in India*, Delhi, Oxford University Press.

Byres, T. (ed) 1994. *The State and Development Planning in India*, Oxford, Oxford University Press.

Cassen, Robert and **Vijay Joshi** 1995. *India: The Future of Economic Reform*, Delhi, Oxford University Press.

Chambers, Robert, N.C. Saxena and **Tushaar Shah** 1989. *To the Hands of the Poor*, New Delhi, Oxford and IBH.

Chaturvedi, Anil 1988. *District Administration: The Dynamics of Discord*, New Delhi, Sage.

Chopra, K., G. Kodekodi and **M.N. Murty** 1990. *Participatory Development: People and Common Property Resources*, New Delhi, Sage.

Dhar, P.N. 1989. The Prime Minister's Office, in Sarkar, B. (ed.) *P.N. Haksar: Our Times and the Man*, New Delhi, Allied.

Dreze, Jean and **Amartya Sen** 1995. *Hunger and Public Action*, Delhi, Oxford University Press.

——— 1995. *India Economic Development and Social Opportunity*, Delhi, Oxford University Press.

Dwivedi, O.P. et al. 1989. Imperial Legacy, Bureaucracy and Administrative Changes: India 1947–87, *Public Administration and Development*, Vol. 9.

EPW Research Foundation 1993. Poverty Levels in India: Norms, Estimates and Trends, *Economic and Political Weekly*, August 21.

Fadia, B.L. 1991. All India Services and Sarkaria Commission, *Indian Journal of Public Administration*, xxxvii, 4, October–December.

Gadgil, M. 1989. Deforestation: Problems and Prospects, *Indian Journal of Public Administration*, July–September.

Ganpathy, R.S. et al. 1985. *Public Policy and Policy Analysis in India*, New Delhi, Sage.

Haragopal, G. and **V.S. Prasad** 1990. Social Bases of Administrative Culture in India, *Indian Journal of Public Administration*, July–September.

Harriss, B., Guhan S. and **R. Cassen** eds 1992. *Poverty and India Research and Policy*, Delhi, Oxford University Press.

India 1988. *Commission on Centre—State Relations Vol. I* (Knowna Sarkaria Commission Report), Delhi, Government of India.

Jain, R.B. and **O.P. Dwivedi** 1990. Administrative Culture and Bureaucratic Values in India, *Indian Journal of Public Administration*, July–September.

Jain, S.P. and **T.W. Hochgenang** (ed.) 1995. *Emerging Trends in Panchayati Raj* (Rural Local Self-Government) *in India*, Hyderabad, National Institute of Rural Development.

Jalan, Bimal (ed.) 1992. *The Indian Economy: Problems and Prospects*, New Delhi, Viking.

Kohli, Atul 1987. *The State and Poverty in India: The Politics of Reform*, Hyderabad, Orient Longman Ltd. in association with Cambridge University'Press.

——— 1991. *Democracy and Discontent: India's Growing Crisis of Governability*, Cambridge, Cambridge University Press.

Lieten, G.K. 1993. *Community and Change in Rural West Bengal*, London, Sage.

Mathur, Kuldeep 1988. The Academic Endeavour in Public Administration in India, *The Indian Journal of Social Science*, 1(4).

——— 1991. Bureaucracy in India: Development and Pursuit of Self-Interest, *Indian Journal of Public Administration*, October–December.

Mathur, Kuldeep and **Niraja G. Jayal** 1993. *Drought, Policy and Politics*, New Delhi, Sage.

Mathur, Kuldeep and **J.W. Bjorkman** 1995. *India's Top Policy Makers: Cabinet Ministers and their Civil Service Advisers*, New Delhi, Concept.

Mehta, Prayag 1989. *Bureaucracy, Organization Behaviour and Development*, New Delhi, Sage.

Mukarji, N.K. and **Balveer Arora** (eds) 1992. *Federalism in India: Origins and Development*, Delhi, Vikas.

Pathak, Akhileshwar 1994. *Contested Domains: The State, Peasants and Forest in Contemporary India*, New Delhi, Sage.

Raghuvulu, C.V. et al. 1991. Reform in Panchayati Raj: A Comparative Analysis of Andhra Pradesh, Karnataka and West Bengal, *Indian Journal of Public Administration*, January–March.

Rao, C.H. Hanumantha 1989. Decentralized Planning: An Overview of Experience and Prospects, *Economic and Political Weekly*, xxiv(8).

Rao, V. Bhaskara and **Arvind K. Sharma** (eds) 1996. *Public Administration Quest for Identity*, New Delhi, Vikas.

Tiwari, R.K. 1990. *Rural Employment Programmes in India: The Implementation Process*, New Delhi, Indian Institute of Public Administration.

Toye, John 1988. Political Economy and the Analysis of Indian Development, *Modern Asian Studies*, 22(1).

Vanaik, Achin 1991. *The Painful Transition Bourgeoise Democracy in India*, London, Verso.

Wade, R. 1988. *Village Republics: Economic Conditions for Collective Action in South India*, Cambridge, Cambridge University Press.

———— 1985. The Market for Public Office: Why the Indian State is Not Better at Development, *World Development*, 13(4).

Wadia, F.K. 1994. Development of Administrative Services in India, *Journal of Indian School of Political Economy*, 13(4), July–September.

Wignaraja, P. et al. 1991. *Participatory Development: Learning from South Asia*, Karachi, Oxford University Press and Tokyo, U.N. University Press.

Weiner, M. 1991. *The Child and the State in India: Child Labour and Education Policy in India*, Princeton, Princeton University Press.

Yugandhar, B.N. and **B.N. Raju** 1992. Government Delivery Systems for Rural Development Malady—Remedy Analysis, *Economic and Political Weekly*, August 29.

Notes on Contributors

James W. Bjorkman studied political science at the University of Minnesota and Yale University, and is Professor of Public Policy and Administration at the Institute of Social Studies, The Hague, as well as Professor of Public Administration at Leiden University. During 1987–90 he served as Director of the American Studies Research Centre, Hyderabad. He has published extensively, and among his recent publications are *Controlling Medical Professionals: The Comparative Politics of Health Governance* (1988) and *Top Policy Makers in India* (1994, co-authored with Kuldeep Mathur).

Ishwar Dayal completed his assignment as Founder Director of Indian Institute of Management, Lucknow, in July 1988. Prior to this he has been Dean, International Management Institute, New Delhi; Chief Technical Adviser, ILO Project in Lagos, Nigeria; Director, Indian Institute of Public Administration; and Senior Professor at Indian Institute of Management at Calcutta and later at Ahmedabad. He has published over twenty books and 200 papers in national and international journals.

George Mathew is Director, Institute of Social Sciences, New Delhi. He has a large number of papers and articles to his credit. Among his notable books are *A Day with `Paulo Friere* (1980); and *Communal Road to Secular Kerala* (1989). He has recently edited *Panchayati Raj from Legislation to Movement* (1994). He currently directs research programmes on local government systems.

Kuldeep Mathur is on the faculty of Centre for Political Studies, Jawaharlal Nehru University, and is currently Director of the National Institute of Educational Planning and Administration, New Delhi. Among his recent publications are *Drought, Policy and Politics* (1993, co-authored with Niraja G. Jayal); and *Top Policy Makers in India* (1994, co-authored with James W. Bjorkman).

Ajit Mozoomdar is currently Visiting Professor, Centre for Policy Research, New Delhi. Previously in the Indian Administrative Service, he was

Secretary, Department of Expenditure, Ministry of Finance, and Secretary, Planning Commission, in the 1970s. He has also been Director, Economic Development Institute, World Bank.

Nirmal Mukarji is former Cabinet Secretary and Governor of Punjab. He was part of the Indian Civil Service. After retirement, he was a research professor at the Centre of Policy Research, New Delhi, for some years. Among his research interests are federal issues and decentralization, on which he has written extensively.

David Potter is Professor of Political Science at the Open University, U.K. He is the author of a number of studies on India's government and politics including *Government in Rural India* (1964); and *India's Political Administrators* (1986). He is also the editor of the *Journal of Commonwealth and Comparative Politics*.

Harsh Sethi, currently a free-lance writer, has earlier been associated with the Indian Council of Social Science Research, Centre for the Study of Developing Societies and Sage Publications. He has co-authored *Participatory Development: Learning from South Asia* (1991) and co-edited *Rethinking Human Rights* (1989), *Voices from a Scarred City* (1985) and *Action Research for Development* (1984). He has contributed to journals and the popular press on issues of social movements and social policy.

Tushaar Shah was formerly Director of IRMA, and is now an independent economist and management consultant. He has previously worked at the National Dairy Development Board as a staff economist and subsequently as a member of the faculty at IRMA. Among his areas of research interest are groundwater markets, management of natural resources, and farmers' organizations. His publications include *Water Markets and Irrigation Development: Political Economy and Practical Policy*; and *Making Farmers' Co-operatives Work: Design, Governance and Management*.

D.L. Sheth is Senior Fellow and former Director, Centre for the Study of Developing Societies. Editor of *Alternatives* and member of the National Commission for Backward Classes, he helped establish *Lokayan* in the early 1980s. A political sociologist, he has made major contributions to the study of comparative politics, the politics of social issues and grassroots movements.

Neil Webster is Senior Research Fellow at the Centre for Development Research, Copenhagen, Denmark. He previously taught in the Department of Sociology and Politics, Liverpool Polytechnic. He is currently working on a research project entitled 'Development and the Rural Poor in India: A Study of the Potential for Grassroots Production Co-operatives in Rural Development'.